The Homemaker's Magazine Cookbook

THE HOMEMAKER'S MAGAZINE COOKBOOK

EDITED BY THELMA DICKMAN

A COMAC/SOMERVILLE HOUSE BOOK

McCLELLAND AND STEWART

McClelland and Stewart Limited,
The Canadian Publishers,
481 University Avenue,
Toronto, Ontario
M5G 2E9

CANADIAN CATALOGUING IN
PUBLICATION DATA
Main entry under title:
The Homemaker's magazine cookbook
Includes index.
ISBN 0-7710-4205-1
1. Cookery, Canadian.   2. Cookery
I. Dickman, Thelma
II. Homemaker's magazine
TX715.H65 1986   641.5
      C86-094269-4

Creative Director: Rod Della Vedova
Designer: Catherine Wilson,
    C.P. Wilson Graphic
    Communication
Managing Editor: Joyce M. Wilson,
    Wilson Editorial Services
Editor: Betty Corson
Copy Editor and Illustrator:
    Jane Champagne
Editorial Consultant: Barb Holland,
    Home Economist

Typesetting by
Eastern Typographers Inc.
Printed and bound in Canada by
Friesen Printers Ltd.

Produced by
Somerville House Books Ltd.
24 Dinnick Crescent,
Toronto, Canada
M4N 1L5

Contents

THE REASON WHY

*I*t is with a sense of excitement and a good deal of pride that we present the first *Homemaker's Magazine Cookbook.*

Never has the term "by popular demand" been more apropos: readers have been asking us to publish a cookbook for years. We get phone calls every week asking for copies of a favorite recipe from a past issue of *Homemaker's Magazine,* used happily for years and suddenly lost in the cleaning out of a drawer, or a move to another house. We often hear about, and have seen, cupboards stacked with back copies of *Homemaker's* magazines, preserved because of a particular recipe in this issue or that. We already know the unique place we hold in the heart of Canadian cooks (men as well as women), and know as well that this book will occupy an honored place on your kitchen shelf.

It wasn't easy choosing from more than 2000 recipes printed in *Homemaker's* over the past 20 years and we may have left out one or two of your favorites. But we believe that in using the *Homemaker's Magazine Cookbook* you'll find new favorites, as well as rediscover old ones. The recipes, of course, have all been tested, and a number of them are prizewinners from our 1985 recipe contest.

Since the first issue of *Homemaker's Magazine* came off the press 20 years ago the food and cooking of Canada and, indeed, much of the world, has changed remarkably. The forte of the Canadian cook at that time was plain, down home cooking — roasts, meat loaves, jellied salads (often made with lime gelatine), and apple pie. 1968 was the year following Expo, when Canadian chefs (albeit most of them trained abroad) first offered British Columbia salmon and Atlantic fiddleheads to the rest of the world. We had been travelling prodigiously since the end of World

1

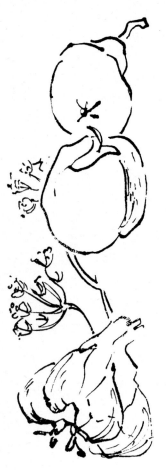

War II, absorbing the foods and flavors of other countries, and were ready to experiment in our own kitchens with new ingredients. And, with perfect timing, along came a flood of immigrants that has stopped — Germans, Italians, Portuguese, citizens of the Caribbean Islands, Greece, and, recently, China, Japan, and Korea. With them they brought a demand for their native foods, and today it's easy to buy 5-star spices, cumin, tiger shrimp, squid, arugula and guinea fowl either in local stores or by mail order. Our cooking has changed forever.

In the '70s, too, we went through a phase of raised consciousness about food that somewhat resembled the encounter groups of the feminists of the day. Canadians didn't actually become aggressive about cookery (it isn't our style), but hundreds of us flocked to cooking schools, in both North America and Europe. People collected cookbooks by the shelf, and many of them were even read. Copper pots were in, and fondue pots were out; food writers in newspapers made lists of foods that were "hot" and those that were in outer Siberia for the fashionable.

Most of that nonsense has thankfully disappeared, rather like the former rules about hemlines in fashion pages, and for rather the same reason. We have, quite simply, grown up. We've waded through nouvelle cuisine and various other fads, and have begun to arrive where most people are at their best — home. Today we can accept ourselves for what we are, a country of very good cooks, with wonderful local foods to eat and enjoy without apology, including, should we so desire, meat loaf and apple pie, and sure enough of ourselves in our kitchens to experiment with foods from other countries as well, from crème fraîche and carambolas to cherimoyas and chorizo sausages. Our local entrepreneurial cooks send antipastos, mustards, preserves, smoked fish and short-bread around the world, and we eat pasta in a dizzying variety of shapes, colors and flavors — indeed, many of us make our own.

The writers and editors through the years who watched these changes, and even helped them occur, have been among the best in Canada. Madame Jehane Benoit, who qualifies for the term "doyenne", was our first editor, and the list has included Carroll Allen, food editor for nine years, Cynthia Wine, who has since emerged as a TV personality and has had several books published. Marilyn Linton, also author of several books, now Lifestyle editor of the Toronto Sun and the current food editor, and Thelma Dickman, food editor of *Leisure Ways* Magazine and a well-known food and travel writer. Contributors to the magazine (and some are in this book) have included chefs from across the country and around the world, including the late Tony Roldan, who did so much for the renown of Canadian cooking. And then there are our readers, whose interest, enthusiasm and recipe contributions have helped make it all more worthwhile.

There's a saying "Time flies when you're having fun," and it was almost with surprise that *Homemaker's* Magazine realized it would be our 20th birthday in October, 1986. It has been a surprising, significant, whimsical, changeable, exciting, and highly satisfying 20 years for anyone remotely interested in food, and we wanted to share with our friends. We like to think this cookbook is being published for all the old friends we've known over the last 20 years — as well as for all the new ones we know we're going to make from their use of the book and some of *Homemaker's* best recipes.

We look forward to many happy returns of the day.

THE BASIC KITCHEN

Whether your kitchen is large or small, the general rule to remember about equipment is that one good saucepan or knife is worth a dozen mediocre ones. Well-made equipment will last for years (I cook my morning bacon in a cast-iron frying pan that's about 90 years old) as long as it's reasonably well cared for. A careless cook can wreak havoc with the best pans in the world — the tin lining of a copper saucepan will melt in a few minutes if left untended on a heated burner, and rapping a metal spoon on the edge of an enamelled pan will soon result in unsightly, unhealthy pitting of the surface. Hard scouring doesn't do pots and pans much good either — it's usually sufficient to soak the inside of a pan while it's still warm with hot water and dishwashing liquid; food can then be washed away without scrubbing.

Stubborn bits will generally loosen up if you add water to a pot and bring it to a boil.

The best kitchenware stores will advise against buying a set of matching pots, because no single material is good for every use. Copper is used by professional chefs because it's very sensitive to temperature — it heats up almost the moment it's placed on a stove burner, and cools off almost as fast. For food that requires careful timing, it's a winner. However, it's very expensive, requires regular polishing, and because it reacts chemically with practically everything, from salt and acids to air and moisture, it has to be lined (and eventually relined) with a nonreactive metal, usually tin. There are also copper pans on the market lined with nickel and, if you've won a lottery, silver, which shouldn't need relining. If you can only buy one copper utensil, make it a sauté pan. The wide, flat bottom

allows it to slide easily across a burner, and the straight sides prevent foods from jumping out when you shake them during the sautéing process. Food being sautéed shouldn't be crowded, so get pans that will hold enough to match the number of people you'll generally be cooking for. Incidentally, cheap copper is a very poor investment — it will be thin, and consequently will burn not only your hands but whatever you try to cook in it.

Cast iron is the opposite of copper, since it takes a very long time to heat up and retains the heat at high temperatures for a long time, which makes it horrible for hollandaise but user-friendly for almost everything else from steak to pizza. Because of the porous surface, these pans must be seasoned to prevent rust. To do this, coat the entire surface with flavorless vegetable oil, preferably peanut oil, then pour in a layer of oil ¼-inch deep. Put the pan in a 250-300°F oven for 1 hour, turn off the heat, leave it in the oven overnight before emptying it (don't re-use the oil), and wipe it dry with paper towels. Wash after each use with water and a stiff brush (never soak them, and don't use soap), dry well and coat lightly with oil. If all this seems like too much hassle, buy cast-iron equipment that's enamelled on the outside in a number of bright colors — they look wonderful on a dining room table filled with soups or stews, and have a nonstick finish inside that's virtually indestructible. The oval shape usually gets more use than does the round, since it can hold a small roast or chicken as well as items like chili.

No matter how small your kitchen,

don't try to get away with fewer than two saucepans, and three would be better, ranging in size from 1 quart to 4 quarts. In some cases — cooking green vegetables is one — stainless steel does a better job than copper. It's nontoxic, but a poor heat conductor, so make sure you buy it with a copper or aluminum core, or "sandwich," in the base for good heat conduction. The bottom should be thick, as should the sides, the lid should fit snugly and the handle should be firmly attached to the pan, preferably riveted. If you plan to use the saucepans (or any other pan) in the oven as well as on top of the stove, make sure the handles and the knobs on the covers are heatproof or can be easily taken off and replaced.

Aluminum pots are inexpensive, lightweight, durable, and a good conductor of heat. Buy the very best quality you can find, and learn what should be cooked in them. Recipes that include wine or vinegar will pit the pot and taste odd, while the metal can turn some egg dishes a nasty grey color. Aluminum pots are good for cooking large quantities of food (soups, pasta) because the pots themselves are so lightweight, but a thick bottom is still important to prevent burning. The 8-litre stockpot is good for the average kitchen: its tall, narrow shape leaves only a small surface area of simmering stock exposed, so liquid evaporates slowly as it draws out the flavors. Make sure the handgrips are sturdy; if the pot is full, it's surprisingly heavy.

You might like to include a rectangular steel pan about 10-x–14-x–2½ inches, to be used for roasting meat and fowl, making lasagna or even baking a large cake. And a double boiler should be included in any list for a basic kitchen. Buy one in glass or the newer, tougher Visions by Corning. It's the only material that allows you to see whether the water below is boiling or simmering (important to know when scrambling eggs or making a sauce in the top). The melting of chocolate is best done in a double boiler.

There are dozens of other pots, pans, and utensils peculiar to individual kitchens, depending on the ethnic background, tastes, and needs of the resident cook.

A baker will have bread pans, cookie trays, and cake pans, while a microwave owner should have a large supply of square and round pans, with and without lids for storage, made specifically for microwave ovens, to cook everything from bacon to roast chicken. Dozens of companies supply such equipment, which gets more sophisticated all the time — one of them, Anchor Hocking, offers glassware that's safe in conventional, convection, and microwave ovens. (Plastic wrap is suggested in many recipes to use as a cover while cooking — make sure the box says it's safe for use in microwave ovens.)

Families that eat a lot of fried chicken should look at a cast-iron pan specifically for this dish: its straight, high sides prevent hot fat from popping out, there's a holder on one side to help steady the pan as it's lifted, and the flat lid has a handle, so it can be turned over and used as a griddle for breakfast pancakes.

Dedicated omelet eaters should have a pan used only for this dish, usually in carbon steel, with gently rounded sides to help you shape the omelets as you slide them from the pan. The 9½-inch diameter is perfect for a four-egg omelet. Carbon steel is also used for crêpe pans, usually 8½ inches for a 6½-inch crêpe, with a widely flaring, angled side so the crêpe can be slid back and forth as it cooks, and a long handle to help tilt the pan as the batter is poured into it. If you're investigating steamed vegetables (most experts say it's the healthiest way to cook them), consider a metal steamer, or pick up an inexpensive bamboo model at a Chinese supply store. Either way, get it large enough so the steam can circulate well. A frying pan, or skillet, should be in as heavy a material as possible: copper, stainless steel, and cast iron heat quickly and evenly to seal surfaces of fried or sautéed foods. Frying pans with nonstick surfaces are good for food cooked in a small amount of fat and at moderate temperatures — always use wooden spoons or forks with such pans.

Along with cookware there's a lengthy list of utensils to be considered, beginning with knives.

They tend to be expensive, but you deserve the best you can afford. A good knife will fit well in your hand, the blade in proper proportion to the handle, which will be neither too thin nor too short. Heft the knife in your hand. It shouldn't be too light — it wouldn't be safe to use — and will undoubtedly be made of poor steel. You should consider starting your knife collection with a red-handled paring knife (less likely to wind up unnoticed in the garbage), an 8- to 10-inch chopping knife, an 8- to 10-inch slicing knife, and an 8-inch

serrated bread knife. Learn to use a sharpening steel to keep a fine edge to your knives, and after each use wash them by hand, not in the dishwasher, where the blades will get dulled from contact with other utensils. Don't toss good knives in a drawer — use a magnet board or knife block to protect them.

Kitchens can never have too many spatulas, wooden spoons, mixing bowls or measuring spoons and cups; wire whisks should be made of stainless steel and you should have a light, flexible, fairly big one for whipping cream and egg whites, as well as a heavier one for folding and blending, and a tiny one to smooth your sauces into silk. Gratin dishes will allow you to prepare anything from stuffed crêpes to scalloped potatoes; and tinned-steel tart pans with removable disks will produce foolproof tarts and quiches.

For many cooks a food processor is indispensable, and nobody can deny that they save hours of labor chopping vegetables for chili sauce, soups, and stews, grinding nuts and seeds, and making hamburger out of lean round steak for everything from fat-free burgers to steak tartare. The Robot Coupe is among the top-of-the-line, high-ticket processors, while the smaller Sunbeam Oskar is a treasure, combining lower cost with amazing speed and strength. As well, there are blenders for those cold soups that must be satin-smooth in texture, to say nothing of making fast work of frozen orange juice. Ice-cream makers have been a success story over the past few years, from the expensive but fantastic Il Gelatio, to the very reasonably priced Donvier.

As well, there's an endless supply of gadgets to make your cooking life more efficient and more fun — melon ballers to scoop little rounds of everything from watermelon to potatoes, lemon zesters to strip fragrant curls of lemon peel into apple crisp or warm-weather drinks, croissant cutters for perfect pastry triangles, spaghetti spoons so you'll get the pasta faster and won't scald your hands while doing it, the Bell cream maker from England which allows you to combine butter and milk to make thick, rich double cream at home, cherry pitters and the indispensable potato peeler. A good meat or oven thermometer is useful; so is a timer you can carry away from the kitchen.

The proper kitchen tools, carefully chosen and maintained, will help the novice cook gain confidence and creativity, and the knowledgeable cook grow to heights she never knew. Good cooking is a craft that sometimes is an art and, like all creative endeavors, it depends not only on imagination and skill but also on your equipment. If you've got both, you can be a Picasso in the pantry and a Kreighoff in the kitchen.

THE RIGHT STUFF

The word "pantry" has a comforting, rather old-fashioned ring to it, but today's generation of cooks have perhaps more need of a pantry than did their mothers, thanks to fast-track living and two working parents in many homes. Even if a homemaker doesn't have a full-time job outside her home, she often works part-time either to bolster the family income or because she feels more independent doing so — and many women are finding that volunteer work can bring a joy of its own. For whatever reasons, there's less time to cook everything from scratch except on weekends, and more need to have a good grasp of what supplies you have in the kitchen, which varieties you need most, and what to do with them once they're in your cupboard.

"Basic" to a pasta lover will mean several different varieties of this ubiquitous and justly popular food, while an entire shelf of oils and vinegars might be in the kitchen of a dedicated salad maker. We haven't attempted to cover the whole spectrum of items that might be found in a pantry, but rather have gathered together descriptions of some you will likely have on your shelves, as well as explanations of certain cooking terms that have proven to be stumbling blocks for many readers, whether they're men picking up their measuring spoons for the first time, women having trouble coping with the ever-growing supply of sophisticated cookbooks, or someone who wants to know where to find such a thing as castor sugar in Canada (it goes under the name of "superfine granulated," or you can pulverize your sugar more finely in a blender). It's an eclectic list, but it goes from A to Z.

Adjust — as in seasonings, means to taste before serving and increase seasoning if necessary.

Blanch — to precook in boiling water or steam to prepare foods for canning or freezing, or to loosen skins (e.g., tomatoes), or heighten color.

Boil — to cook in liquid kept at the temperature at which bubbles rise rapidly to the surface of the liquid and break.

Bouquet garni — a small bunch of herbs used for flavoring soups, stews, usually parsley, thyme, and bay leaf. Sometimes celery, peppercorns, or cloves are added, but if so, they'll always be mentioned. If herbs are fresh, parsley is wrapped around them and they're tied together; if they're dried, they're wrapped in cheesecloth and tied.

Butter, clarified — butter is put into a glass measuring cup and placed in a warm oven until it melts and the milky residue settles to the bottom. Skim off the clear liquid butter for cooking purposes; it's much less likely to burn than unclarified butter.

Butter, creamed — butter should always come to room temperature before creaming; don't push it by heating it up.

Butter, measuring — use the cold-water method. To measure ½ cup, for example, fill a 1-cup measure with ½ cup of cold water, then add enough butter to bring water level to 1 cup.

Butterfly — to split foods such as shrimp or a small leg of lamb through the middle, without completely separating sections, and then spread the sections open to resemble the wings of a butterfly.

Chop — to cut food into irregularly shaped pieces about the size of a pea, using a chopper, food processor, or knife.

Cream, whipping — sometimes referred to as heavy cream, it always whips better if beaters and bowl are icy cold. Don't overbeat because it will turn to butter rather suddenly.

Crème fraîche — a silky, slightly acidic heavy cream used in France to pour over fruit or apple tarts. To make a substitute, stir 4 tablespoons sour cream into 1 cup whipping cream, heat just to take off the chill and get the action going, stir, and let stand until it has thickened, 6-8 hours or overnight. Stir gently and refrigerate until ready to use.

Croutons — small cubes of bread dried out in the oven and then fried, or simply seasoned with salt, pepper, and herbs. Homemade are infinitely better than packaged.

Cube — to cut food into pieces ½ inch or larger on all sides, using a chef's knife to make lengthwise cuts and then cutting crosswise.

Deglaze — to add wine, water, alcohol, or sometimes vinegar to a pan after frying or sautéing, and cook it quickly while scraping up the browned bits from the cooked meat, fish, or fowl. The result is a concentrated, flavorful few tablespoons that will enrich a sauce or gravy.

Degrease — to skim or blot grease from a soup or sauce with a spoon or paper towel, or to chill until grease hardens and is then lifted off.

Fines herbes — minced fresh or dried parsley, tarragon, chives, chervil, sometimes basil or marjoram; very good in salads, or sprinkled over an omelet before folding and serving.

Flours — all-purpose is used for almost everything, for baking, thickening sauces, and dredging fried food. It's enriched, bleached or unbleached.

Bread flour — called hard flour in health food stores, it has a high content of protein (gluten) needed to strengthen bread. Bleached or unbleached.

Cake and pastry flour — enriched, superfine, soft flour for cakes of fine, light grain.

Self-rising — all-purpose flour, to which baking powder and salt have been added. It's handy to have in the cupboard for quick bread, rolls, etc. It must be fresh to work well.

Presifted — all-purpose, enriched flour that doesn't need sifting except for very fragile recipes.

Whole wheat — also called graham flour, is unbleached, unrefined flour still containing iron and vitamin B-rich wheat bran and wheat germ. Sifting is unnecessary. It goes rancid quickly, so store in tightly covered containers in refrigerator.

Garlic — always peel unless otherwise directed. Tap it firmly with the blade of your chef's knife (flat side down, please) and it will peel easily. Never let garlic brown when cooking in fat or it will give a bitter flavor. A clove

is one section of the bulb. Whole cloves of garlic, cooked slowly, or a whole head baked gently in a covered oven dish, will be delicate and buttery in taste, wonderful to spread on crusty bread. Garlic is now grown in Canada, and its flavor is superlative.

Giblets — the heart, liver, and gizzard of fowl and small game birds.

Julienne — food cut into small matchstick-size strips.

Lardons — strips (as of salt pork) with which meat is laced. The fat is threaded through the meat for extra juiciness and/or flavor.

Lemon juice — should be used fresh-squeezed or frozen in a pinch, but bottled lemon juice is a poor substitute.

Macerate — to soak fruits in spirits before adding to cakes, trifles.

Marinate — to soak meat, fish, or vegetables in a spicy liquid until food absorbs the flavors. The soaking medium itself is called a marinade.

Mince — to cut food into tiny, irregularly shaped pieces with a utility knife. It's a term primarily used for garlic and herbs.

Mustard — there's no longer one kind, but many dozens, from the aggressive ballpark variety to a refined Dijon mustard with tarragon. Moutarde de Meaux has mustard seeds in it, as have a few other varieties. Dried mustard remains a favorite of some who consider it a necessity on ham sandwiches — mixed to a paste with water, it has a fiery bite and should be used with care.

Oils — are a chapter in themselves, and recently oil-tastings have been conducted in some cities with the seriousness generally reserved for fine wines. Olive oils are wonderful in salads, and the highly esteemed virgin olive oil is unrefined oil from the first pressing. Further pressings produce stronger, heavier oils. Olive oil burns easily, and many people prefer corn, peanut, or vegetable oils for cooking and even for salads — the cholesterol-conscious often buy safflower oil. Walnut and hazelnut oil are light and delicious, even if somewhat expensive, and lemon juice can combine better with them than vinegars. It's best not to keep oils in the refrigerator, since they turn unpleasantly cloudy. However, if you measure what you need and allow it to come to room temperature, most of the cloudiness will clear.

Pancetta — unsmoked but cured Italian bacon found in Italian markets. It has a high fat content. Side bacon will work as a substitute, although the flavor will be different.

Paprika — a spice made from the dried pods of capsicum peppers, and the heart and soul of cooking in Hungary, whence comes the mildest and reddest paprika. Any paprika is high in vitamin C.

Pepper — *Homemaker's* advocates using whole black peppercorns and grinding them fresh for each recipe, as well as at table. It makes a terrific difference to the flavor. If whole peppercorns are needed, crush them slightly before using or the flavor will not come through. White pepper has less flavor than black, and is used in light sauces and stews so that black specks won't be seen. Cayenne pepper is fiery hot, so use it sparingly.

Green peppercorns are the berries of a special branch of the family found mainly in Madagascar. They're sold in fresh water or vinegar, and are an interesting seasoning twist.

Salt — sea salt is superior to any other for cooking, and can be found in health food stores.

Salt, kosher — originally a coarse salt made under rabbinical supervision, but today a generic term. Used largely for pickling.

Scald — to bring a liquid, usually milk or cream, to just under boiling point, until bubbles begin to gather at the edge of the pan.

Simmer — to heat a liquid slowly until bubbles begin to form, and continue to cook just so tiny bubbles break on the surface.

Soft peaks — when whipping cream or egg whites, peaks will form, but curl over at the top instead of standing up straight.

Stiff but not dry — egg whites are beaten until they stand in stiff, but still shiny, moist peaks.

Vanilla extract — should always be of the natural variety rather than artificial. It costs more but the difference in flavor, particularly in cakes, is noticeable.

Vinegar — can have many flavors. White, all-purpose vinegar is very sharp, cider vinegar is strong, red and white wine vinegars are softer, and herb vinegars are unusual and easy to make yourself (see Salads, p. 156). Balsamic vinegar is full-bodied and flavorful, as is sherry vinegar. Rice vinegar is light and refreshing.

Wine — used in cooking should always be good enough to drink. A poor wine will give poor results.

Zest — is the way you should approach cooking (as in "with zest"), but it's also the colored part of citrus peel grated and used as a flavoring.

HERBS AND SPICES

The purpose of any seasoning is to enhance natural flavors, not overwhelm the original taste of the dish. Use a gentle hand with herbs and spices. Dried herbs and spices should be stored in a dark, cool place and bought in small quantities (health food stores are often your best bet, since stock moves quickly, and you can buy as much or little as you wish, without paying for either advertising or a glass jar). Spices are sold whole or ground, and if you don't use them very often, buy a small grater and grind or grate them yourself. There's a world of difference between freshly grated and already bottled nutmeg. Sniff your herbs and spices often enough to know when their potency is beginning to subside, and replace them right away.

Fresh herbs are relatively easy to grow and take up little room in a garden or a windowbox, or even indoors in small pots on a window-ledge. Fresh basil (the red basil is not only interestingly spicy, it looks beautiful in flower arrangements for the dining room table), parsley, chives, and thyme will make your cooking more varied. In cooking with fresh herbs you'll need twice the quantity of dried herbs, and possibly even more. If you have lots of fresh herbs, preserve them by making herb butters. Chop ¼ pound of butter with 1 cup or more of fresh herbs, add a few drops of lemon juice and freeze them — startlingly good on a cold winter's day spread on crusty bread or added to hot, cooked vegetables.

Herbs and spices have changed the history of the world — kingdoms have been lost fighting over control of the spice trade, and America was discovered accidentally by Christopher Columbus searching for a sea route to the spices of the East. Gladiators in ancient Rome ate fennel to boost their courage; in Greece crowns of laurel were placed on the brows of winning athletes — and rents measured in peppercorns are still found in some places in England. Today we use spices and herbs for what they are, a magic addition to ordinary food — some of them, like basil and tomatoes, are marriages made in culinary heaven.

Generally speaking, a herb is the leaf of tender, usually fragrant annuals and biennials, while spices are the stronger roots, barks, stems, and fruits of tropical or subtropical plants. Seeds are produced by both herb and spice plants. When herbs or spices are added to cold food, such as dips, spreads, or soups, allow flavors to mature for ½ hour or more before serving.

Whenever using a new herb or spice, add with a light hand...you can always add more according to taste, but it's impossible to take it out.

APPETIZERS

There's a moment at many cocktail parties, as the silver tray with the little bits of food is passed among people who clearly want to have nothing to do with it, when one wonders whether appetizers are worth bothering about at all. The thing is, the finger foods we're used to at parties are really *hors d'oeuvre* (literal translation, "outside of work"), usually served by the French at the beginning of the meal to stimulate the appetite and establish the feeling of the food to come.

If you plan to serve hot *hors d'oeuvre*, the microwave really comes into its own. Because most appetizers are small, they can be microwaved quickly and even served in the same dish (some of the new cooking dishes are pretty spiffy). Microwave ovens can freshen up stale pretzels, crackers, and potato chips, as well as nuts, and they will reheat precooked appetizers before your guests can take off their coats.

If you choose to serve a perfect pâté, put it in a very cold crystal or silver dish, and on the plate put a silver knife for spreading hot, thinly sliced toasted triangles or rounds. Since pâté is rich, ¼ pound per person or less should be ample. Restrain yourself from the groaning board syndrome when it somes to serving appetizers, or your guests' appetites will be numbed instead of nipped.

Guacamole and Crabmeat Dip
garnished with cucumber (see recipes page 18)

PHOTO BY SKIP DEAN, FOOD STYLING BY KATE BUSH

Foie gras: Egyptians, Greeks, and Romans raised geese and so did the Britons prior to Roman occupation, although they were forbidden by their religion to eat them. The Romans enjoyed goose liver very much — it was so sought after in Rome that Pliny commented that geese were valued solely for their livers. After the fall of Rome, goose liver came back into favor in 16th-century France and has never looked back since. The blond goose livers from the Okanagan Valley of British Columbia are only now being recognized as the treasure they are.

Guacamole

Preparation time: 15 minutes
Degree of difficulty: simple
Servings: 12
Calories per serving: 72

This tangy dip could be set out beside a cheese ball as a prelude to your buffet dinner.

2 ripe avocados
2 tablespoons lemon juice
2 tomatoes, peeled, seeded, and finely chopped
1 medium onion, finely chopped
1 clove garlic, finely minced
1 jalapeño chili, seeded and chopped, or 5-6 drops Tabasco sauce
Salt and freshly ground pepper to taste

Peel avocados and mash with a wooden spoon until smooth, reserving one of the pits. Blend in lemon juice. Add remaining ingredients and mix well. If not serving immediately, bury an avocado pit in the mixture to keep it from darkening. Cover tightly and store in refrigerator. Remove pit before serving. Serve with tortilla chips or corn chips. Garnish with sour cream, chopped onions, peppers, or olives.

Crabmeat Dip

Preparation time: 5 minutes
Degree of difficulty: simple
Servings: 6-8
Calories per serving: 465 (1/6)
350 (1/8)

This is a lively and delicious dip, especially if it's made the day before. Serve with crackers, tostadas, or chunks of green pepper.

8 ounces crabmeat, canned, frozen, or fresh, carefully checked for shell fragments
8 ounces cream cheese
1 cup mayonnaise
½ cup plain yogurt
Few drops Tabasco sauce
2 large cloves garlic, minced
Salt and freshly ground pepper to taste

Soften the cream cheese and mix with the mayonnaise, yogurt, Tabasco, and garlic. Stir in the crabmeat. Add salt and pepper. Chill until ready to serve.

Chicken Liver Pear Pâté

Preparation time: 10 minutes
Cooking time: 15 minutes
Chilling time: at least 1 hour
Degree of difficulty: simple
Servings: 8-10
Calories per serving: 218 (1/8)
175(1/10)
or 49 per tablespoon

This lovely smooth pâté can be a welcome gift when packed in small crocks or individual soufflé dishes. Easily made with the help of a blender or food processor, it keeps for days in the refrigerator and is perfect with crackers and mulled wine.

1 pound chicken livers
9 tablespoons softened unsalted butter
3 tablespoons chopped shallots
1 ripe pear, pared and chopped
¼ cup Madeira
¼ cup currants
3 tablespoons whipping cream
1 teaspoon lemon juice
¼ teaspoon crumbled thyme
Salt and freshly ground pepper to taste
3-4 small bay leaves

Wash and pat dry the chicken livers. Melt 3 tablespoons of the butter in a frying pan and sauté the shallots for 4 minutes; add the pear and sauté 3 minutes more. Transfer mixture to bowl of food processor or blender. Add Madeira to currants and set aside. Melt 3 tablespoons of the butter in the same frying pan and fry chicken livers quickly over high heat until cooked through — about 4 minutes. Stir in Madeira and currants, lower heat, and simmer 2 minutes. Add the chicken liver mixture to the pear mixture; blend rapidly until smooth. Add the cream, lemon juice, and thyme and blend again until completely smooth. Salt and pepper to taste. Pack in one crock or a few individual soufflé dishes; garnish with bay leaves. Chill. Makes 2½ cups.

Brandied Chicken Liver Pâté

Preparation time: 10 minutes
Cooking time: 5 minutes
Degree of difficulty: simple
Servings: 6-8
Calories per serving: 200 (1/6)
150 (1/8)

There are lots of pâté recipes — this is one of the best.

½ pound chicken livers
½ cup butter
1 tablespoon brandy (or dry sherry)
Salt and freshly ground pepper to taste
¼ teaspoon grated nutmeg

Trim chicken livers. Melt ¼ cup butter in a saucepan; add livers, cover, and cook gently for 5 minutes. Blend livers and juices in a blender or processor. Add brandy. Cream in remaining butter together with seasonings. Spoon into a small covered dish and chill. Serve on toast or crackers.

Baked Eggplant with Yogurt

Preparation time: 5 minutes
Cooking time: 1 hour
Degree of difficulty: simple
Servings: 6
Calories per serving: 60

This simply prepared dish may be used as a dip or as an appetizer spread on crackers or pita.

2 small eggplants
2 cloves garlic, minced
1 cup yogurt
1 teaspoon lemon juice
Salt and freshly ground pepper to taste
3 green onions, minced

Preheat oven to 400°F. Pierce the eggplants several times with a fork. Bake for about 1 hour or until very soft. Cool briefly, then, using the fingers, peel off the skins and discard them. Place the eggplant pulp on a hot platter and mash. Add garlic, yogurt, lemon juice, and salt and pepper and mix thoroughly. Garnish with minced green onion.

Funghi Farciti Besciamella

Preparation time: 6 minutes
Cooking time: 25-30 minutes (total)
Degree of difficulty: simple
Servings: 6-8
Calories per serving: 165 (1/6)
125 (1/8)

Stuffed mushrooms by any other name....

6-8 large mushrooms, about 3 inches in diameter
2 shallots
2 slices cooked ham
2 tablespoons butter
½ pound fresh spinach or ½ package frozen

Remove the stems from the mushrooms. Clean mushroom caps and set aside. Fine-chop the shallots and cooked ham and stir-fry in a little butter. Add cooked spinach that has been squeezed to remove excess liquid. Make 1 cup of besciamella sauce and add to the shallots and ham combination. Or, you could use crab or shrimp, add some grated Parmesan cheese or chopped Emmenthal cheese, and omit the spinach.

BESCIAMELLA SAUCE

2 tablespoons butter
2 tablespoons all-purpose flour
½ cup milk
½ cup light cream
Salt and freshly ground pepper to taste

Preheat oven to 350°F. In a heavy saucepan, melt the butter, blend in flour, and cook over medium heat for 2-3 minutes. Beat in milk and cream off the burner and continue heating until sauce thickens. Add salt and pepper. Add the besciamella to the stir-fried ingredients and stuff the mushroom caps with the mixture. Put the mushrooms on a cookie sheet and heat in oven until the mushrooms are just cooked (about 10 minutes). Serve as an antipasto.

Cream Cheese and Smoked Oyster Spread

Preparation time: 15 minutes
Degree of difficulty: simple
Amount: makes 1 cup
Calories per tablespoon: 75

It sounds odd, but it works — better in winter than summer.

8 ounces cream cheese, softened
¼ cup whipping cream, whipped
1 tablespoon chopped onion
1 tablespoon chopped parsley
1 small can smoked oysters, drained and chopped
1 teaspoon brandy
¼ teaspoon Worcestershire sauce
Dash of Tabasco sauce
Salt and freshly ground pepper to taste

Mix the cream cheese with the whipped cream until smooth. Add the onion and parsley; mix well. Fold in the oysters and the brandy. Add the Worcestershire and Tabasco sauces, and salt and pepper. Serve with thin toasts and crackers.

Cucumber Fish Appetizer

Preparation time: 10 minutes
Standing time: 1 hour
Degree of difficulty: simple
Servings: 6-8
Calories per serving: 75(1/6)
56(1/8)

Unusual, not to say surprising.

½ pound fillet of sole
¼ cup soya sauce
2 tablespoons cider vinegar
2 tablespoons sake
2 teaspoons sugar
¼ teaspoon powdered ginger
3 cucumbers

Chop the fish very fine. Combine the soya sauce, vinegar, sake, sugar, and ginger in a bowl; stir in the fish. Let stand 1 hour. Peel the cucumbers, cut lengthwise, scoop out the seeds, and slice very thin. Pour the fish mixture over them and let stand 10 minutes. Serve in a bowl with crackers, as a dip.

Eggplant Siciliana

Preparation time: 10 minutes
Cooking time: 45 minutes (total)
Chilling time: overnight
Degree of difficulty: simple
Amount: 5 cups
Calories per cup: 110

This appetizer can be kept in the refrigerator for several days.

1 large eggplant, peeled and diced in ½-inch cubes
2-3 tablespoons olive oil
1 cup chopped onion
1 cup diced celery
1 10-ounce can tomatoes
1 tablespoon capers
¼ cup cider vinegar
2 tablespoons sugar
Salt and freshly ground pepper to taste

Sauté eggplant in oil until soft and lightly browned. Remove. Sauté onion and celery until tender. Add tomatoes and simmer, covered, for 15 minutes. Return eggplant to pan, add capers, vinegar, sugar, and salt and pepper. Cover and simmer 20 minutes more, stirring once. Cool. Refrigerate overnight. Serve in a bowl with a spoon to scoop onto firm toast rounds or crackers.

Cheese Ball

Preparation time: 10 minutes
Chilling time: at least 1 hour
Degree of difficulty: simple
Servings: 12
Calories per serving: 215

This is a breeze to make with a food processor, but a blender will do an acceptable job.

1 cup green olive pieces, drained
12 ounces Cheddar cheese, cubed
8 ounces smoke-flavored Cheddar, or processed cheese spread
1 teaspoon Worcestershire sauce
½ teaspoon dry mustard
⅓ cup chopped nuts (walnuts would be nice)

Put cheeses and olives in food processor or blender and mix until smooth. Add Worcestershire sauce and mustard and mix. Chill. Form into a ball and roll in chopped nuts. Serve with crackers or melba toast.

Butter was known in the Middle East, Egypt, and parts of northern Europe before the Greeks and Romans learned of it, though it didn't taste the way it does today. Whether it was butter or not, it must have been more liquid than ours — while we cut, knead, and spread butter, the ancient people poured it like oil. Bread, butter, and cheese were staples of the lower classes in England and northern France through the 17th century. Butter in cooking came into use later; 18th-century recipes called for large amounts of butter (green pea soup took a whole pound of it). There's a certain *je ne sais quoi* even today to butter — it just seems to make certain things taste better.

Avocados with Rum

Preparation time: 5 minutes
Degree of difficulty: simple
Servings: 4
Calories per serving: 220

The hearty flavor of rum provides an interesting contrast to the mellow richness of fresh avocado in this adventuresome recipe. Serve as a first course or as an unusual dessert.

2 large ripe avocados

Fresh lemon juice

4 teaspoons rum

4 tablespoons sifted icing sugar

Cut avocados in half lengthwise and remove pits. Rub cut surface with fresh lemon juice. Put 1 teaspoon rum in hollow of each half and sprinkle with 1 tablespoon sifted icing sugar.

PHOTO BY TIM SAUNDERS

Chicken Wings with Blue Cheese Sauce

Preparation time: 10 minutes
Cooking time: 20-30 minutes
Degree of difficulty: simple
Servings: 6
Calories per serving: 390

¼ cup sesame seeds

1 cup all-purpose flour

1 teaspoon dried oregano

2 pounds chicken wings

Vegetable oil for frying

2 tablespoons toasted sesame seeds

BLUE CHEESE DIPPING SAUCE

1 cup sour cream

¼ cup crumbled blue cheese

2 tablespoons chopped chives

1 teaspoon red wine vinegar

Combine sesame seeds, flour, and oregano in a paper or plastic bag. Add the chicken wings a few at a time and shake until well coated. Fry in hot oil until browned on all sides. Drain on paper towels and sprinkle with toasted sesame seeds. To prepare sauce, combine ingredients in a food processor or blender. Blend until smooth. Chill, then serve with wings.

PHOTO BY PETER CHOU

Cream Cheese and Cucumber Mousse

Preparation time: 20 minutes
Chilling time: 3-4 hours
Degree of difficulty: simple
Servings: 6
Calories per serving: 240

Refreshing, pretty, and light-tasting, this mousse answers every demand you can make of a summer appetizer. Serve it with biscuits or good bread.

2 envelopes or 2 tablespoons un-flavored gelatine

2½ tablespoons white wine vinegar

⅓ English cucumber, unpeeled

12 ounces cream cheese

Salt and freshly ground pepper to taste

6 egg whites

Sprinkle gelatine over vinegar in a small saucepan. Dice cucumber and liquefy in a blender or grate by hand. Soften cream cheese with a fork, add cucumber, and mix thoroughly. Place softened gelatine over low heat and stir constantly until gelatine dissolves, 3-5 minutes. Remove from heat and add to the cream cheese. Whip egg whites until fluffy and fold into mixture. Add salt and pepper. To garnish, place very thin cucumber slices in the bottom of 1 large mold or 6 individual ones; then pour in a small amount of additional dissolved gelatine and allow to set before pouring in the mixture. Chill 3-4 hours before unmolding.

Elaine McIntosh's Antipasto

Preparation time: 10 minutes
Cooking time: 10 minutes
Chilling time: 8 days
Degree of difficulty: simple
Amount: about 10 cups
Calories per serving: 35 (¼ cup)
*   140 (1 cup)*

This is one of those perfect starters — festive, easy to prepare, and best when made more than a week ahead.

3 green peppers

1 small jar pimento

¼ cup vegetable oil

1 small can tuna

1 small can whole mushrooms, drained

1 bay leaf

1 cup sweet pickle relish

12 black olives, pitted and halved

⅔ cup catsup

½ cup chili sauce

1 clove garlic, minced

⅛ teaspoon cinnamon

12 stuffed green olives, halved

½ cup white vinegar

Dice the green pepper and pimento and sauté in the oil until soft. Drain and rinse the tuna; add to the peppers and pimento together with remaining ingredients, and simmer for 10 minutes. Cool and bottle. For the best flavor, refrigerate for 8 days before using. Serve with a variety of crackers and cheeses, and either beer or white wine.

PHOTO BY SKIP DEAN

Cream Cheese and Cucumber Mousse

Recent research has shown that carefully chosen, well-timed snacks, used as part of a calorie-restricted, balanced diet, can help control the urge to overeat and increase chances of shedding excess pounds: 100-150 calories eaten a half-hour before a low-fat, high-carbohydrate meal decreased a control group's appetite enough to make a significant difference in the amount eaten at the meal. It's essential that protein and fat are given in an easily digestible food such as cottage cheese, plain yogurt, or soup.

Snails with Walnuts and Chives

Preparation time: 10 minutes
Cooking time: 10 minutes
Degree of difficulty: simple
Servings: 4-6
Calories per serving: 390 (1/4)
260 (1/6)

Centuries ago, monks, valuing snails for their lean meat, raised them in snaileries. Walnuts, brought by the Romans to England, have always been popular. The combination is a lovely alternative to traditional escargot recipes.

1 4½-ounce can snails (24 snails)
3 tablespoons white vermouth
4 tablespoons unsalted butter
½ cup chopped walnuts
¾ cup whipping cream
1 tablespoon chopped parsley
2 tablespoons chopped chives
2 tablespoons fresh lemon juice
½ teaspoon grated nutmeg
Salt and freshly ground pepper to taste

Toss snails with vermouth in a small bowl. Melt butter in medium frying pan over medium heat. Stir in walnuts, reduce heat to low and sauté about 3 minutes, taking care not to burn them. Stir in the cream. Increase heat to medium and bring to boil, stirring constantly. Add snails and vermouth; stir until mixture comes to boil again. Reduce heat. Add parsley, chives, and lemon juice; cook for 2-3 minutes more, stirring all the while. Sprinkle with nutmeg; add salt and pepper. Serve in hot ramekins.

Mushrooms Stuffed with Crabmeat

Preparation time: 10 minutes
Cooking time: 10-15 minutes
Degree of difficulty: simple
Servings: 6-8
Calories per serving: 190 (1/6)
145 (1/8)

The stuffing can be prepared a day ahead, then spooned into the mushroom caps before baking. Serve with cocktails, as an entrée at dinner or with a salad for lunch.

18-24 large mushrooms
3 tablespoons butter
1 onion, finely chopped
1 tablespoon all-purpose flour
1½ teaspoons dry mustard
¾ cup milk
Salt and freshly ground pepper to taste
8 ounces cooked crabmeat
1 teaspoon chopped parsley
1 green onion, finely chopped
Grated Parmesan cheese

Clean the mushrooms by wiping them with a damp cloth. Remove stems and chop them finely.

Sauté the chopped stems and onion in the butter for a few minutes. Sprinkle the flour and dry mustard over and stir. Remove from heat and stir in the milk. Return to heat and cook, stirring constantly, until mixture comes to a boil. Simmer for a few minutes, then add seasonings. Stir in the crabmeat and adjust seasoning. Remove from heat and stir in the parsley and chopped green onion. Cool, then chill a few minutes.

Preheat oven to 425°F. Sauté mushroom caps quickly in butter. Season lightly, then stuff with the crabmeat mixture. Sprinkle generously with Parmesan cheese and place in oven until hot and puffy.

Nibblers

Preparation time: 10 minutes
Cooking time: 10-12 minutes per cookie sheet
Degree of difficulty: simple
Amount: makes 3 dozen
Calories: 80 each

These snacks pack a good quota of protein and roughage. Use as little sugar as possible to suit your taste.

½ cup butter or margarine
¼-½ cup brown sugar
2 eggs
¾ cup all-purpose flour
¼ teaspoon nutmeg
¼ teaspoon baking soda
1½ cups rolled oats
1½ cups grated Cheddar cheese
¾ cup raisins

Preheat oven to 350°F. Cream together butter and sugar until light and fluffy. Beat in eggs. Combine flour, nutmeg, and baking soda. Add to creamed mixture. Stir in remaining ingredients. Drop by spoonfuls onto a lightly greased cookie sheet. Bake for 10-12 minutes, or until lightly browned.

Peperonata

Preparation time: 10 minutes
Cooking time: 5 minutes
Degree of difficulty: simple
Servings: 6-8
Calories per serving: 104 (1/6)
78 (1/8)

There are many versions of peperonata; this is one of the best.

½ pound mushrooms
2 green peppers
2 sweet red peppers
1 eggplant
Vegetable oil

Cut the mushrooms into pieces. Slice the peppers into strips about ½-inch wide. Slice the eggplant and sprinkle with salt (to draw out the moisture and bitterness), then dry and cube. Fry the vegetables a few at a time in about 1½ inches of oil and remove them to a hot platter. Serve the peperonata either hot or cold.

Tomato Mozzarella Toasts

Broiling time: 1-3 minutes
Degree of difficulty: simple
Servings: 6
Calories per serving: 250

So traditional they're new again.

1/2 long, thin French stick, cut in
1/2-inch-thick slices
2 tablespoons olive oil
4 medium tomatoes, peeled,
seeded, and finely chopped
1 cup shredded Mozzarella cheese
2 tablespoons fresh oregano

Preheat oven to 200°F. Dry bread rounds on cookie sheets in oven for 20 minutes. Brush with olive oil. Top each slice with some of the tomato, then some of the cheese; sprinkle with oregano. Place under broiler until cheese is bubbly and begins to brown.

Shrimp-Stuffed Tomatoes

Preparation time: 10 minutes
Standing time: 30 minutes
Cooking time: 10 minutes (for shrimp)
Degree of difficulty: simple
Servings: 6
Calories per serving: 200

The excellence of a Belgian restaurant is often judged by this dish — some use more mayonnaise than shrimp. Buy the smallest, freshest shrimp available.

6 medium, ripe but firm tomatoes
Salt to taste
1/2 pound small cooked shrimp
1/2 cup mayonnaise, preferably
homemade with lemon juice
Freshly ground black pepper
to taste
Lettuce and parsley for garnish

Cut a slice from the top of each tomato and reserve. Remove the seeds and pulp from the tomatoes, drain off most of the juice, sprinkle lightly with salt, invert and let stand 30 minutes. Mix together shrimp and mayonnaise and season with pepper to taste. Stuff tomatoes with the mixture, replace the top slice and serve on lettuce leaves, garnished with parsley.

Stuffed Vine Leaves with Yogurt Sauce

Preparation time: 50 minutes
Cooking time: 20 minutes
Degree of difficulty: simple
Servings: 8
Calories per serving: 190

Cuisine '85 Semifinalist

2 tablespoons melted butter
1 cup cooked rice
1 medium onion, finely chopped
1/2 pound lean ground beef,
browned
2 tablespoons chopped parsley
1 teaspoon crushed mint leaves,
fresh or dried
1/4 pound firm tomatoes, chopped
Salt, freshly ground pepper, ground
cumin to taste
1/2 pound jar vine leaves
2 tablespoons melted butter
Water or broth
2 tablespoons lemon juice

Mix well 2 tablespoons butter, rice, onion, ground beef, parsley, mint leaves, tomatoes, salt, pepper, and cumin to taste.

Cover bottom of pan with larger vine leaves. Handle one leaf at a time, smooth face down. Put about 1 tablespoon of the mixture in the middle of each leaf, fold sides, and wrap like a finger. Arrange in layers. Repeat until all leaves are used. Add remaining 2 tablespoons melted butter on top. Add enough water or broth to cover leaves (1 1/2 cups); bring to boil, then reduce heat until close to done, about 15 minutes. Add lemon juice. Transfer to hot plate and serve with yogurt dip.

YOGURT DIP
2 cups plain yogurt
4 cloves garlic, finely crushed
or chopped
1 teaspoon chopped fresh parsley
Salt to taste

Beat yogurt with fork until smooth; add crushed garlic, parsley and salt. Serve in bowl. Garnish with parsley.

Spanakopita

Preparation time: 20 minutes
Cooking time: 50 minutes (total)
Degree of difficulty: moderate
Servings: 6 (or more if cut small)
Calories per serving: 440

A delicious spinach and cheese pie.

1/2 pound phyllo pastry
3 tablespoons oil
3 tablespoons grated onion
1 tablespoon chopped green onion
1 package fresh spinach, washed
and drained, about 10-12 ounces
3 beaten eggs
1 cup crumbled feta cheese
2 tablespoons chopped, fresh dill
1/2 cup melted butter (enough to
coat pastry sheets)
2 tablespoons milk

In a heavy frying pan, sauté the onion in the oil until softened. Add the spinach. Stir until spinach becomes limp. Add beaten eggs, crumbled feta, and dill. Mix well, cutting through the spinach to make serving easier. Preheat oven to 325°F. Butter a baking dish (a 9-inch-square cake pan will do nicely) and add one layer of phyllo at a time, brushing each layer with melted butter, until you have 6-8 layers on the bottom. Add spinach mixture. Then one by one, add layers of phyllo on top, again brushing each layer with melted butter, and folding and tucking to maintain nice neat shape. When you have 10 layers on top, brush the last layer with butter and with milk. Score the top lightly with a knife to provide cutting lines. Bake until golden brown (about 45 minutes).

Never cut hot peppers without wearing rubber gloves. Wash the knife, the cutting surface, and your gloved hands while the gloves are still on, to minimize exposure to the irritating chemicals in the peppers. After cutting peppers, never put your hands to your eyes without first washing them.

Gravlax

Gravlax

Preparation time: 10 minutes
Marinating time: 24 hours
Degree of difficulty: simple
Servings: 6-8
Calories per serving: 268

This excellent recipe is easily adjusted for the number of servings you wish. One pound of fresh salmon fillets will serve 6 as an appetizer. The mustard sauce is a delicious plus.

Fresh salmon fillets

Sugar

Salt

White peppercorns

Fresh red or black spruce boughs (optional)

Large bunch fresh dill

SAUCE

1 tablespoon Dijon mustard

4 tablespoons oil

1 teaspoon sugar

1 tablespoon finely chopped fresh dill

Mix 3 parts sugar with 1 part each salt and pepper sufficient to cover generously both sides of the fillets. (Tablespoon measures should be enough for 1 pound of fillets.) Line a 9-x-13-inch glass container with the spruce boughs. Place half the dill on top of the boughs. Spread half the sugar mixture on one side of the fillets and arrange on the dill, putting sugared side down and spreading the remaining sugar mixture on top. Cover with more dill. Refrigerate, tightly sealed, for at least 24 hours. Mix mustard with oil, then add sugar and chopped dill. Stir until well blended. (These quantities are for 1 pound of salmon.) To serve, scrape excess sugar off fillets and slice thinly. Serve with mustard sauce.

Succulent Shrimps for Starters

Preparation time: 5 minutes
Degree of difficulty: simple
Servings: 4
Calories per serving: 305

An excellent luncheon dish or, in smaller servings, a fine starter for a dinner.

2 avocados

1 package small frozen shrimp

2 tablespoons tomato paste

3 drops Tabasco sauce

2 tablespoons Madeira

1 cup sour cream

Lettuce leaves

The avocado should be soft, firm, and green, and can be prepared in advance if dipped in lemon juice to keep it green. The shrimp should be cold.

Cut avocados in half lengthwise. Twist apart and carefully remove pit. Brush surface with lemon juice. Divide shrimp into 4 portions and fill avocados.

To make sauce, mix together the tomato paste, Tabasco sauce, and Madeira (or the heel of a bottle of sparkling red wine). Be careful not to thin the sauce too much. Heap on top of shrimp, and serve avocados on bed of lettuce.

Snow Peas Stuffed with Crab

Preparation time: 20 minutes
Chilling time: a few hours
Degree of difficulty: simple
Servings: 6
Calories per serving: 88

This inspired appetizer is from Dinah Koo of Dinah's Cupboard in Toronto. Plan on 4 to 5 snow peas per person. Serve them chilled with cold, dry white wine.

30 fresh snow peas

½ pound crabmeat, thawed, picked over for shells

2 tablespoons mayonnaise, home-made if possible

½ teaspoon dried, crushed tarragon

Squeeze fresh lemon juice

3 dashes Worcestershire sauce

Remove the strings from the snow peas, leaving the stem intact if it's not too brown. With a toothpick, carefully open the pods, spreading them to form a pocket. Combine the crabmeat with the mayonnaise, tarragon, lemon juice, and Worcestershire sauce. Fill the pockets with crabmeat mixture. Chill and serve within a few hours.

Sun-Kissed Melon

Preparation time: 10 minutes
Degree of difficulty: simple
Servings: 8
Calories per serving: 48

Japanese by intent, as well as by design.

1 honeydew melon

1 large orange

Juice of 1 orange

1 tablespoon sugar

1 tablespoon fresh grated ginger

Cut melon into 8 serving pieces. Mix orange juice with sugar and ginger, and sprinkle over melon slices. Set aside. Slice orange thinly and cut each slice into a flower shape to decorate melon slices.

Prosciutto Breadsticks

Preparation time: 10 minutes
Degree of difficulty: simple
Servings: 8-10
Calories per serving: 125 (1/8)
100 (1/10)

These easy *hors d'oeuvre* are neat, clever, and tasty. From Noodles restaurant in Toronto, the recipe is perfect for picnics.

½ cup Italian parsley leaves, washed and dried

¼ to ¾ pound prosciutto ham, sliced paper-thin

1 package long Italian breadsticks

Place one leaf of Italian parsley in the centre of a slice of prosciutto, then wrap the prosciutto around the top third of a breadstick. Repeat.

Snow Peas Stuffed with Crab (above); Prosciutto Breadsticks

Sesame, popular as a seasoning in North America in only the past 10-15 years, is one of the oldest seeds grown by man for oil. It was cultivated in the third millennium in India, and is still widely used there for cooking. Sesame was grown in ancient Greece and in Roman Italy, to be used in perfume and put on bread as decoration and seasoning. It's a rich source of protein, calcium, phosphorus, and niacin.

Stuffed Sardines Il Posto

Preparation time: 5 minutes
Cooking time: 5 minutes
Degree of difficulty: simple
Servings: 2
Calories per serving: 560

Large sardines are stuffed with spinach and cheese and quickly sautéed for this delicious appetizer from Il Posto, a luxurious classic Italian restaurant in Toronto. Smelts may be substituted.

6 fresh sardines, cleaned, fins and spines removed
2 cups finely chopped spinach
½ cup freshly grated Parmigiano Reggiano (a type of Parmesan cheese)
1 clove garlic, minced
Small bunch parsley, chopped
Dash of salt
3 eggs
Flour
1 tablespoon corn oil

Combine spinach, Parmesan, garlic, parsley, and salt. Add 2 beaten eggs. Place the sardines "tummy up" on a plate and fill with the stuffing. Dredge the sardines in flour. Beat remaining egg and dip sardines in it. Sauté in corn oil for a few minutes on both sides. When browned, place on a paper towel to absorb the excess oil.

Candace Anderson's Lemon Thyme Pasta with Grilled Baby Artichokes

Preparation time: about 1 hour
Cooking time: about 30 minutes
Degree of difficulty: challenging
Servings: 4 as a main course or 8 as an appetizer
Calories per serving: 850 (1/4)
425 (1/8)

Cuisine '85 Winner
After developing this recipe during her stint as a student at Pierre Dubrulle's well-known Vancouver cooking school, Candace Anderson graduated to become a junior chef.

SAUCE

10 baby artichokes, trimmed to inside leaves, halved and stems removed
¼ cup plus 1 tablespoon olive oil
Juice of 1 lemon
4 shallots, finely diced
1 clove garlic, minced
½ cup white wine
10 tomatoes, seeded and diced
¼ teaspoon salt
¼ teaspoon sugar
Freshly ground pepper to taste
½ cup grated Parmesan cheese
Sprigs of fresh thyme for garnish

LEMON THYME PASTA

3 cups all-purpose flour
Pinch of salt
1 tablespoon fresh thyme leaves or 1 teaspoon dried thyme
Grated peel of 1 large lemon
4 eggs
2 tablespoons olive oil

Marinate the artichokes in ¼ cup of the olive oil and the lemon juice for 1 hour. In a medium saucepan, heat the remaining tablespoon of olive oil, add the shallots and garlic, and cook until the shallots are transparent, about 5 minutes. Increase heat, add white wine, and cook until sauce is reduced by half. Add diced tomatoes, salt, and sugar; reduce heat and simmer until sauce is thick, stirring occasionally. Add ground pepper to taste; set aside and keep warm. Remove artichokes from marinade, grill or broil on a barbecue grill or in the oven, turning on all sides until artichokes are tender. Add artichokes to tomato sauce.

To prepare pasta, combine flour, salt, thyme, and grated lemon peel in the work bowl of a food processor fitted with a steel blade. Mix together the eggs and the oil and, with the machine running, slowly pour the egg mixture into the flour. Let the machine run until dough begins to form a ball. Remove dough and food processor blade and invert bowl over ball of dough; let rest 15 minutes. (Pasta may also be made without a food processor: Combine the dry ingredients in a mound on a clean, dry surface. Make a well in the centre, pour the egg mixture into the well, and gradually mix the wet ingredients into the dry using a fork; knead until smooth.) Make fettuccine or spaghetti according to the instructions with your pasta machine. Cook pasta in boiling salted water until *al dente*, about 1½ minutes. Drain and place on a heated platter. Pour sauce over pasta, sprinkle with grated Parmesan, and garnish with thyme sprigs.

Tony Roldan's Vegetable Terrine

Preparation time: 30 minutes
Cooking time: 15-20 minutes
Chilling time: 6 hours or overnight
Degree of difficulty: simple
Servings: 6
Calories per serving: 175

Colorful slices of blanched vegetables are layered in a simple aspic; fiddleheads could be substituted for one of the ingredients.

½ pound carrots, cut into thin strips lengthwise

1 stalk celery, cut into thin strips lengthwise

½ pound leeks, split in half lengthwise (green parts removed)

½ pound green beans, ends trimmed

½ red pepper, cut into thin strips lengthwise

4 whole green onions, ends removed

1 medium zucchini, cut into thin strips lengthwise

½ yellow turnip or rutabaga, cut into thin strips

4 cups chicken stock

½ pound fresh spinach, stems removed

4 tablespoons unflavored gelatine

¼ cup dry sherry

¼ cup cold water

HERB SAUCE

½ cup sour cream

½ cup homemade mayonnaise

1 teaspoon chopped dill or chervil

1 teaspoon chopped parsley

1 teaspoon Dijon mustard

Juice of ½ lemon

1 teaspoon minced chives

Salt and freshly ground pepper to taste

Blanch all vegetables separately in chicken stock except spinach, and remove with a slotted spoon. Refresh with cold water to retain color, then chill. Reserve stock. Wash spinach well, then cook in just the water on its leaves until wilted (about 4 minutes). Squeeze out water, then chill. Dissolve gelatine in sherry and water; let stand for about 10 minutes. To prepare the aspic, add gelatine mixture to the warm (but not boiling) chicken stock and season to taste. In a terrine mold or a 9-x-5-x-3-inch glass loaf pan pour a thin layer of aspic to cover the bottom of the pan. Chill. Arrange a layer of spinach on top of the base, then cover with a few spoonfuls of aspic. Arrange a layer of carrots over the spinach mixture and cover with a thin layer of aspic. Continue with a vegetable layer, followed by a layer of aspic until either the mold is full or the vegetables are used up. Finish with a layer of aspic. Chill for 6 hours or overnight. To prepare the herb sauce, combine all ingredients. To serve the terrine, dip a sharp knife into hot water and slice into ½-inch-thick pieces and serve accompanied by the sauce.

Sesame Dip

Preparation time: 15 minutes
Degree of difficulty: simple
Amount: makes 3 cups
Calories: 62 per tablespoon

Unusual, yet scrumptious, this dip from Christine Mullen of Toronto's La Cuisine caterers is a perfect accompaniment to crudités.

2 tablespoons sesame seeds, toasted to a golden brown

¼ cup soya sauce

1 egg

1½ tablespoons honey

1¼ cups vegetable (not olive) oil

2 teaspoons sesame oil (available at oriental grocers and health food stores)

½-inch cube fresh ginger root, peeled and crushed (or grated), or ½ teaspoon powdered ginger

Put sesame seeds, soya sauce, egg and honey in a food processor bowl or blender jar. Blend and slowly add oil in droplets through food processor feed tube or hole in top of blender jar. Add sesame oil and ginger. Mix well.

NOTES

BREADS AND SANDWICHES

There's nothing quite so wonderfully nostalgic as the smell of baking bread — which is one reason so many supermarkets now have their frozen baked goods cooked on the premises. It still doesn't seem to smell as good as the loaf made at home, though; nor is the taste the same.

Breads, buns, and the ubiquitous muffin are relatively new in the history of the world. Early man didn't grind grain; he bashed it with a stone on a slab, and very full of dirt, acorns, and bits of rock it was, as attested to by the worn and damaged teeth in the skulls of Stone Age man.

Flour can be temperamental to work with. When purchased, it contains a certain amount of moisture, considered acceptable by government inspectors, but if it's stored improperly, it will pick up more moisture, and this can unbalance your recipe. Flours can dry out over the winter months, and whole wheat flour can turn rancid. Bread flour, most often found in health food stores, is worth looking for because its high gluten content allows more moisture to be absorbed, and the bread will be a better texture.

More of us are baking bread these days because we don't like the preservatives in "store-bought" loaves wrapped in plastic, and bread and bakery stores are proliferating in our cities. It's a wonderful feeling to get down to kneading, shaping, and feeling the dough responding to touch, experimenting with mixing whole wheat and white flours, or sprinkling a loaf with wheat berries or oats.

Because electric ovens produce a dry heat, some bakers like to put a shallow pan of water on the bottom of the oven when baking yeast dough. Although in theory the temperature control of modern ovens is standardized, in practice it can be changeable. It's a good idea to invest in an oven thermometer if you're going to do much baking.

Employ a light hand with breads and muffins (particularly muffins); make sure your oven is preheated by a good 15 minutes before putting your bread pans inside; and remove the loaves from the pans as soon as you take them from the oven, cooling them on wire racks with lots of space around them.

And then please pass the butter.

Mary Pratt's Oatmeal Bread (see recipe page 30)

Bulgur is one of the oldest known cereal foods, and is made of wheat kernels that have been cooked, dried, and cracked. Originally it was done to preserve the wheat harvest. The method, and the name "bulgur," are of Turkish origin, from some time in the 9th century A.D. Armenians use it flavored with sugar and nuts when the arrival of a baby's first tooth is celebrated; Greeks eat it at funerals; Canadians like it both in the cold salad called tabouleh and as an accompaniment for meat or vegetable stews. Manuel Shiherian of Don Mills, Ontario, of Armenian descent, is Canada's largest bulgur manufacturer and supplier, producing 30,000 kilograms a month for distribution throughout Canada, the U.S. and countries in Southwest Africa.

Mary Pratt's Oatmeal Bread

Preparation time: 3-3½ hours (total)
Cooking time: 35 minutes
Degree of difficulty: moderate
Amount: makes 4 loaves (20 slices per loaf)
Calories per slice: 65

As well as being a formidable artist, Mary Pratt bakes marvelous bread.

3 cups warm water
1 teaspoon sugar
2 packages active dry yeast
¼ cup vegetable oil
1 tablespoon salt
½ cup honey
2 cups cooked, warm (not hot) oatmeal (use quick or rolled oats, not instant)
½ cup corn meal
¼ cup wheat germ
4-5 cups all-purpose flour
4-5 cups whole wheat flour

In the large bowl of an electric mixer, dissolve the yeast and sugar in 1 cup of the warm water. (Test the water with your wrist so that it is about body temperature. It must not be too hot.) Let stand 10 minutes. Add 2 cups warm water, the salad oil, salt, honey, cooked oatmeal, corn meal, and wheat germ. Mix with the electric beaters.

Slowly beat in some of the flour, alternating the white and whole wheat 1 cup at a time. Continue to add flour and beat until the mixture begins to form ribbons. It will take about 3 cups of flour to this point. Continue to beat for 5 minutes. Then, with beaters on slow speed, continue to add white and whole wheat flour alternately, 1 cup at a time, until the beaters no longer move easily. If your machine has a dough hook, replace the beaters with it and continue to add flour, beating continuously until the dough is very stiff and moves away from the sides of the bowl in a lump. If you have no dough hook, use a wooden spoon and continue as above. It will take another 4 or 5 cups of flour to get the dough to this point. (The total amount of flour needed will depend on the amount of moisture in the cooked oatmeal.) Let the dough rest for 10 minutes, then knead on a floured surface for 10 minutes, sprinkling it with flour if it becomes sticky. (Dough is ready when it feels firm and elastic.) Place in a bowl, cover with a tea towel, and let rise for about 1 hour. Punch the dough down and turn it over in the bowl. Preheat oven to 375°F. Cut the dough into 4 and let sit for 10 minutes. Shape into loaves or put into 9-x-5-x-3-inch loaf pans and let rise in a warm place until double in bulk (about 1 hour). Bake loaves for 35 minutes or until they are brown and sound hollow when tapped.

Breakfast Gingerbread

Preparation time: 15 minutes
Cooking time: 1 hour
Degree of difficulty: simple
Amount: makes 18 1½-inch squares
Calories per square: 180

Why not? It's better than no breakfast, and with a mug of hot cocoa, very satisfying.

½ cup butter
½ cup sugar
1 egg, beaten
2½ cups sifted, all-purpose flour
1½ teaspoons soda
1 teaspoon each cinnamon and ginger
½ teaspoon salt
1 tablespoon grated orange rind
½ cup light molasses
½ cup honey
1 cup hot water

Preheat oven to 350°F. Melt butter and cool. Beat sugar and egg together. Sift flour, soda, cinnamon, ginger, and salt and toss in orange rind. Combine molasses, honey, and hot water. Add flour and liquid alternately to butter mixture and combine till well blended. Bake in a 9-inch-square greased pan for about 1 hour.

Al's Cinnamon Buns

Preparation time: about 1 hour (total)
Cooking time: 35 minutes
Degree of difficulty: moderate
Amount: makes 10-12 large buns
Calories per bun: 852 (1/10)
*   710 (1/12)*

Serve these gargantuan buns fresh and warm, with unsalted butter

2 cups skim milk, warmed
1 teaspoon sugar
1 package active dry yeast
1 cup sugar
2 teaspoons salt
1½ cups oil
2 eggs, room temperature
7 cups all-purpose flour
Cinnamon
1 cup brown sugar
3 tablespoons butter, melted
1 cup raisins (optional)

Dissolve 1 teaspoon sugar in the milk, add the yeast, let stand for 10 minutes, then stir. Add the sugar, salt, oil, and eggs. Slowly add flour, 1 cup at a time, until the mixture forms ribbons. Let stand for a few more minutes. Continue to add flour until the beaters resist. Transfer the dough to a floured board and knead in additional flour until the dough is the right texture. Continue to knead for 10 minutes. Cover with a damp towel, and let rise in a warm place until doubled in bulk. Preheat oven to 400°F. Roll out the dough to ½-inch thick on a floured surface. Sprinkle with cinnamon and brown sugar. Roll the dough as you would a jelly roll, brushing it with melted butter and sprinkling with raisins as you roll it up. Slice the roll into 2-inch lengths. Brush a cookie sheet with melted butter and sprinkle generously with brown sugar. Place the cinnamon buns on top. Let rise for ½ hour. Bake for 35 minutes.

Caraway Rye Bread

Preparation time: 3-3½ hours (total)
Cooking time: 35-50 minutes
Degree of difficulty: moderate
Amount: makes 2 loaves
(20 slices per loaf)
Calories per slice: 84

Besides making delicious sandwiches for lunches, rye bread makes the best toast ever to go with tea.

2½ cups lukewarm water

¼ cup molasses

2 packages active dry yeast

1 tablespoon salt

2 tablespoons butter
or margarine, softened

2½ cups rye flour

1½ tablespoons caraway
seeds, crushed

5½-6 cups sifted, all-purpose flour

Small amount of corn meal

Stir 1 teaspoon of the molasses into 1 cup of the lukewarm water. Sprinkle yeast over and let stand 10 minutes, then stir. Combine remaining water, molasses, salt and softened butter or margarine with yeast mixture. Add rye flour and caraway seeds and enough all-purpose flour to make a soft dough. Beat smooth with a wooden spoon and continue adding flour until dough leaves sides of bowl. Turn out onto a floured board and knead until smooth and elastic, using enough of the remaining flour to keep dough from sticking. Place in a large buttered bowl, turning to butter all surfaces. Cover with a tea towel and let rise in a warm place, away from drafts, until double in bulk (1-1½ hours).

Butter a large cookie sheet and sprinkle lightly with corn meal. Punch dough down, turn onto a lightly floured board, and knead a few times. Invert bowl over dough and let rest 10 minutes. Divide in half and knead each half a few times. Shape into 2 loaves. Place at least 4 inches apart on cookie sheet. Let rise again until double in bulk. Preheat oven to 375°F and bake loaves for 35-50 minutes, or until they sound hollow when rapped. Turn onto wire racks.

Easy (No Fail) Pizza Dough

Preparation time: 1½-2½ hours (total)
Cooking time: 12-15 minutes
Degree of difficulty: moderate
Calories: 3,264 (total)
1,088 (⅓)

YEAST MIXTURE

2½ cups lukewarm water

2 teaspoons sugar

2 packages active dry yeast

Dissolve sugar in lukewarm water. Sprinkle yeast on top of water. Let stand in a warm place for 10 minutes.

DOUGH

5½-6 cups all-purpose flour

Pinch salt

½ cup corn oil

In a large deep bowl, make a well in 5 cups of the flour mixed with the salt. Pour the corn oil and the prepared yeast mixture (stirred with a wooden spoon) into the well. Gradually stir in the remaining flour with a wooden spoon for a soft but not sticky dough, adding more flour if needed. Knead on a floured board until smooth, about 4-5 minutes. Allow to rest, covered, for 10-15 minutes (this makes it easier to work with). Cut into 3 equal parts. Use 1 part for pizza squares. Roll out remaining ⅔ dough ¼-inch thick to make 2 12-inch pizzas. Then place dough in oiled pizza pans leaving an outside lip of dough. Lightly oil top of dough to prevent sogginess. Add toppings of your choice. Let stand (covered) in a warm place to rise, 1-2 hours. Preheat oven to 400°F and bake pizzas for 12-15 minutes. Serve piping hot.

Apricot Date Nut Bread

Preparation time: 20 minutes
Standing time: 20 minutes
Cooking time: 1¼ hours
Degree of difficulty: simple
Amount: makes about 16 slices
Calories per slice: 220

Slices of fruit-nut bread are a satisfying accompaniment to tea and coffee, and they can also double as a dessert.

½ cup diced dried apricots

3 cups all-purpose flour (use part
whole wheat flour if you like)

3 teaspoons baking powder

¼ teaspoon baking soda

1 teaspoon salt

1 cup brown sugar

½ cup chopped dates

1 cup chopped walnuts

1 cup milk

1 egg, well beaten

½ cup maple syrup

Preheat oven to 350°F. Cover diced apricots with boiling water and let stand 15 minutes. Drain. Sift together flour, baking powder, baking soda, and salt. Mix in brown sugar and dates, apricots, and nuts. Mix together the milk, beaten egg, and maple syrup. Beat into flour mixture. Pour into a well-greased 9-x-5-x-3-inch loaf pan. Let stand about 20 minutes. Bake for about 1¼ hours, or until a toothpick inserted in the centre comes out clean. Cool. Spread with cream cheese if you like, and decorate with nuts.

Always shake raisins, currants, and other dried fruits with flour before adding them to dough or puddings, or they will sink to the bottom during baking.

Monte Cristo Sandwiches

Preparation time: 15 minutes
Cooking time: about 15 minutes
Degree of difficulty: simple
Servings: 4
Calories per sandwich: 470

These big, luscious west coast sandwiches make a meal in themselves.

8 slices firm white bread
4 tablespoons butter
at room temperature
8 slices baked Virginia ham
8 slices Swiss or Gruyère cheese
4 slices turkey breast
5 eggs
½ teaspoon salt
3 tablespoons water
3 tablespoons butter

To make each sandwich, butter 2 slices of bread on 1 side only with about ½ tablespoon of butter. On the buttered side of 1 slice, place 1 slice of ham, cheese, turkey, another slice of cheese, then another slice of ham. Place the other slice of bread, buttered side down, on top.

In a bowl, beat eggs well with the salt and water. Dip each sandwich in the egg, turning several times to make sure each sandwich is well soaked. Set sandwiches on a plate until ready to cook (if preparing them more than an hour ahead, cover with plastic and refrigerate). Heat butter in a frying pan and fry sandwiches until brown on both sides.

Monte Cristo Sandwiches with Red Pepper Jelly (see recipe page 151)

Maple Breakfast Cake

Preparation time: 15 minutes
Cooking time: 45 minutes
Degree of difficulty: simple
Amount: makes about 16 slices
Calories per slice: 116

What a treat it is to start a weekend breakfast with the aroma of warm spices and maple syrup.

1½ cups cake and pastry flour
½ cup whole wheat flour
4 teaspoons baking powder
1 teaspoon salt
¼ teaspoon cinnamon
⅛ teaspoon nutmeg
1 egg, beaten
⅔ cup maple syrup
⅔ cup milk
1½ teaspoons melted butter
1 teaspoon cinnamon
¼ cup maple sugar

Preheat oven to 350°F. Sift together flours, baking powder, salt, and spices. Beat together the egg, maple syrup, milk, and melted butter. Add to dry ingredients and mix well. Turn into a greased, 9-inch-square cake pan and sprinkle top with cinnamon and maple sugar. Bake for 45 minutes, or until a toothpick inserted in the centre comes out clean.

Sour Cream Cinnamon Loaves

Preparation time: 10-15 minutes
Cooking time: 35-40 minutes
Degree of difficulty: simple
Amount: makes 2 loaves
(12 slices per loaf)
Calories per serving: 145

For a touch of sweetness to a summer meal, you can't beat these flavorful cakes.

2 cups all-purpose flour
1½ teaspoons baking powder
1 teaspoon baking soda
½ teaspoon salt
1¼ cups sugar
½ cup shortening
2 eggs
1 teaspoon vanilla extract
1 cup sour cream
¼ cup milk
2 teaspoons cinnamon
1½ teaspoons finely grated orange peel

Preheat oven to 350°F. Stir together flour, baking powder, baking soda and salt, set aside. In a large bowl cream together 1 cup of the sugar and the shortening until light and fluffy. Add eggs and vanilla and beat well. Blend in sour cream and milk, add flour mixture and blend well. Spread ¼ of the batter in each of two greased 9-x-5-x-3-inch loaf pans.

Combine remaining sugar, cinnamon, and orange peel. Sprinkle all but 1 tablespoon of the sugar-cinnamon mixture over the batter in pans. Top each with half the remaining batter. Gently cut through batter with a spatula to make a swirling effect with the cinnamon. Sprinkle with remaining sugar-cinnamon mixture. Bake for 35-40 minutes, or until a toothpick inserted in the centre comes out clean. Cool in pans 10 minutes, remove, and cool thoroughly on wire racks.

Sour Cream Cinnamon Loaf

Quebec Winter Carnival Trempette

Preparation time: 5 minutes
Degree of difficulty: simple
Calories per slice: 365

Heavy, admittedly — but gorgeous, and traditional.

1 thick slice hot bread, freshly made
3 tablespoons whipping cream
2 tablespoons grated maple sugar

Pour the cream over the bread and sprinkle with the maple sugar. Serve immediately.

Food is life: to live we must eat; it is a law that all must obey, a rule that has no exceptions. Food is fuel: it supplies the power and materials the body needs and must have. But food can and should also be fun: it has in its gift some of the joy that makes life worth living. *(André Simon)*

Basic White Bread

Preparation time: 3-3½ hours (total)
Cooking time: 35-40 minutes
Degree of difficulty: moderate
Amount: makes 2 loaves
(20 slices per loaf)
Calories per slice: 85

The tantalizing smell of homemade bread has been known to bring the kids from the baseball field half a block away. The trick is to let it cool off before they get at it.

½ cup lukewarm water (it should test barely warm on the inside of your wrist)

3 tablespoons sugar

1 package active dry yeast (check the date on the package)

2 cups milk

2 tablespoons butter or margarine

2 teaspoons salt

6-7 cups sifted, unbleached white flour, or 7-8 cups all-purpose flour

Warm a large mixing bowl by rinsing it with hot water. In the bowl, dissolve 1 teaspoon sugar in the lukewarm water. Sprinkle yeast on top and let stand for 10 minutes, then stir well.

Combine remaining sugar, milk, butter or margarine, and salt in a small saucepan. Heat until milk is lukewarm. Add to yeast mixture; then add flour, 2 cups at a time, beating with a wooden spoon to make a smooth, elastic dough. When you've added enough flour so that the dough leaves the sides of the bowl, turn it out onto a floured board. Continue adding flour and kneading until the ball of dough is smooth but not sticky. (You knead dough with the knuckles and heels of your hands, turning and folding all the time.) Total kneading time should be 5-10 minutes.

Place dough in a lightly buttered bowl and turn over to butter all surfaces. Cover with wax paper and a tea towel. Let rise in a warm place, out of drafts, until double in bulk (1-1½ hours). Punch down, turn out on lightly floured board, and divide in half. Cover and let rest for 10 minutes. Shape into 2 loaves, and place in greased 9-x-5-x-3-inch loaf pans. Cover with a tea towel and let rise again in a warm place until double in bulk (about 1-1½ hours). Preheat oven to 375°F and bake loaves for 35-40 minutes, or until they sound hollow when tapped with a knuckle. Transfer immediately from pans to wire racks and let cool.

Homemade Brown Bread

Preparation time: 3 hours (total)
Cooking time: 35 minutes
Degree of difficulty: moderate
Amount: makes 2 loaves
(20 slices per loaf)
Calories per slice: 70

Every woman who has ever made bread enjoys the respect this accomplishment gains from those who don't make it. Making bread is easy. Besides, it is wonderful therapy.

1½ cups warm water

2 teaspoons sugar

2 envelopes active dry yeast

¾ cup milk

4 tablespoons butter or salad oil

6 tablespoons dark brown sugar

2 teaspoons salt

½ cup wheat germ

4 cups whole wheat flour

1-2 cups all-purpose flour

Warm a large bowl and pour the warm (not hot) water into it. Dissolve white sugar in the water. Sprinkle yeast over it and cover bowl with a clean tea towel. Let stand 10 minutes. Heat milk to boiling; add butter or oil, sugar, and salt and allow to cool to room temperature.

Combine 1 cup of white flour with 1 cup of whole wheat. Combine milk mixture with yeast mixture. If the yeast doesn't "work" and become frothy, pour it out and start afresh with two more packages of yeast. Add the two cups of flour and stir with a big wooden spoon. Add remaining combined flour and wheat germ (you may find you cannot work it all in — it depends on the weather). Use white flour on the board or pastry cloth, and form a round ball of dough on it. Knead by folding the ball forward and turning it clockwise a quarter-turn. Continue kneading for 10 minutes or until the dough feels elastic and smooth, and doesn't stick to your hands.

Place ball of dough in a warmed greased bowl somewhat smaller than the one you mixed the dough in. Cover and set in a warm place (a slightly heated oven, even an electric heating pad, is perfect). When the dough has risen (whole wheat dough takes anywhere from 1-2 hours) punch it down and form two balls. Cover and allow to rest on the board for 10 minutes. Then press each ball into an oblong shape with your fist until it is three times as wide as your bread pan but the same length. Fold over the two extra widths and form a seam down the middle. Place each envelope of dough, seam-side down, in a lightly greased 9-x-5-x-3-inch loaf pan. Cover and put to rise for an hour. Preheat oven to 400°F. When the bread comes up over the edge of the pan, bake for 35 minutes. Look at it after 10 minutes and if it's browning too much, cover with foil or reduce the heat.

Honey, Cheese, and Pepper Bread

Preparation time: 3-3½ hours (total)
Cooking time: 50 minutes
Degree of difficulty: moderate
Amount: makes 2 loaves
(20 slices per loaf)
Calories per slice: 86

Pepper has been a common spice since Roman times, when it was used both in recipes and for medicinal purposes. Here, mixed with honey and cheese, it produces a sweetly spicy and delicious bread.

1¾ cups lukewarm water
1 teaspoon sugar
1 package active dry yeast
1½ teaspoons salt
1½ teaspoons freshly ground black pepper
½ cup skim-milk powder
5½ cups sifted, all-purpose flour (approx.)
2 tablespoons soft butter
1 large egg, slightly beaten
5 teaspoons honey
2 cups grated sharp Cheddar cheese

Dissolve sugar in ¼ cup lukewarm water, sprinkle yeast over and let stand 10 minutes. Combine salt, pepper, milk powder, and 1½ cups of the flour. Add 1½ cups lukewarm water, butter, egg, and honey, then the dissolved yeast. Mix until smooth. Add enough of the remaining flour to make a moderately stiff dough. Turn out onto a floured board and knead until smooth and elastic (about 20 minutes). Place in a greased bowl and grease the top surface of the dough. Cover with a damp tea towel and let rise in a warm, draft-free place until double in bulk, about 1 hour.

Turn out onto a lightly floured surface, press to flatten, and cover with half the cheese. Knead in the cheese and then repeat with remaining cheese.

Shape into 2 loaves and place into 9-x-5-x-3-inch greased loaf pans. Grease the tops, cover and let rise until double in size, about 1½ hours.

Preheat oven to 400°F and bake loaves for 15 minutes. Lower temperature to 350°F and bake 35 minutes longer, or until the bread shrinks from the sides of the pan and is well browned.

Jack O'Hare's Wonderful Irish Soda Bread

Preparation time: 10 minutes
Cooking time: 50 minutes
Degree of difficulty: simple
Amount: makes 1 loaf (24 slices)
Calories per slice: 92

Soda bread is extraordinarily good, takes seconds to mix and only 50 minutes to bake. Your friends and family will be dazzled, and if any is left over, it makes great toast the next morning.

Jack O'Hare, general manager of CP Hotels' Chateau flight kitchens in the company's Vancouver head office, whips up a loaf of his bread at the drop of a begorra. If you serve unsalted butter, you can add ¾ teaspoon of salt to the recipe; otherwise omit it.

4 cups whole wheat or graham flour
1 cup unbleached white flour
2 teaspoons baking soda
Pinch of cream of tartar
Salt (optional)
2¼ cups buttermilk or
2 cups skim or 2% milk, soured with ¼ cup vinegar

Preheat oven to 375°F. Thoroughly combine flours. Add baking soda, cream of tartar, salt if required; mix very well. Add buttermilk and mix lightly (depending on the weather you might have to add a little more flour). Do *not* knead. Shape in a biggish circle on a baking sheet, cut a large cross across the middle with a sharp knife, and bake 50 minutes, or until loaf sounds hollow when tapped.

Hot Cross Buns

Preparation time: 2½ hours (total)
Cooking time: 10 minutes per cookie sheet
Degree of difficulty: moderate
Amount: makes 2½ dozen
Calories per bun: 100

Served hot and steaming, these flavorful buns are a traditional Easter treat.

¼ cup warm water
½ teaspoon sugar
1 package active dry yeast
1 cup milk
2 tablespoons butter
4 cups all-purpose flour
⅓ cup sugar
¾ teaspoon each cinnamon and salt
¼ teaspoon each nutmeg and cloves
1 cup currants
2 eggs, well beaten
1 egg yolk mixed with 1 teaspoon water (for glaze)
3 tablespoons icing sugar
1 tablespoon lemon juice

Dissolve yeast in warm water. Scald milk, add butter, and cool to lukewarm. Sift dry ingredients together and combine with currants. Stir in eggs, cooled milk, and yeast: blend thoroughly. Turn the dough onto a lightly floured board and knead until smooth. Place in a greased bowl, cover with a damp cloth, and let rise 1½ hours or until doubled in bulk.

Punch the dough down. Form smooth balls about 1¼ inches in diameter. Place on a greased baking sheet 2 inches apart and brush with the egg-and-water glaze. Let rise again until doubled in bulk (about 30 minutes). Meanwhile, preheat oven to 400°F. Bake for 10 minutes or until lightly browned. Cool for 5 minutes on a rack. Make lemon frosting by mixing the icing sugar with the lemon juice. Add water, if necessary, to make a smooth paste. Spread frosting on top of buns. Cut a small cross in the top of each, to a depth of about ⅛ inch.

Picnics, from the French *pique-nique*, which in turn came from an obsolete word meaning a trifle, are invariably happy times. We get away from routine meals and disciplines, wiggle our toes in the grass, and perhaps cool our wine in a running steam. The edibles of a picnic haven't changed all that much in Canada since the late 1800s, when it was an occasion for eating out of doors after a barn-raising, or on a sunny Sunday afternoon after church. Even then, salmon and watercress sandwiches were the "in" thing, as were devilled eggs, fried chicken, and applesauce cake. But the Victorians drank more wine than we do today at picnics, including lots of champagne.

**Avocado Bacon
Club Sandwiches**

Avocado Bacon Club Sandwiches

Preparation time: 20 minutes
Degree of difficulty: simple
Servings: 6
Calories per sandwich: 410

The smoothness of avocado is an interesting contrast to crisply cooked bacon slices, and curry powder adds extra zip. Use bread cut quite thickly, or the filling will be squashed rather than contained when you bite into it.

¼ cup lemon juice
30 thin slices peeled avocado
1 teaspoon curry powder
¼ cup homemade mayonnaise
18 slices white bread, toasted
6 lettuce leaves
12 thin slices tomato
12 slices crisply cooked bacon

Pour lemon juice over avocado slices and let stand. Combine curry powder and mayonnaise. Spread 1 teaspoon of mixture over each of 6 toast slices and top each with a lettuce leaf and 2 tomato slices. Spread 1 teaspoon mayonnaise each over 6 more slices of toast and place spread side down over tomatoes. Spread 1 teaspoon mayonnaise over top of each toast slice. Drain avocado well; top each slice with 5 slices of avocado and 2 slices of bacon. Spread remaining mayonnaise over remaining toast; place spread side down over bacon. Cut sandwiches into 4 triangles.

Curds 'n' Sprouts Pita Bread Pockets

Preparation time: 15 minutes
Degree of difficulty: simple
Servings: 2
Calories per serving: 375

For a delicious lunch or snack, stuff spiced cheese curds into a pita pocket, then top it with homemade dressing and fresh vegetables.

1 cup Cheddar or Friulano cheese curds
2 tablespoons fresh chopped chives
1 pita bread, halved
1 cup plain yogurt
1 clove garlic, minced
10 thin slices English cucumber
2 cherry tomatoes, sliced
½ cup loosely packed alfalfa sprouts
Freshly ground pepper

In a small bowl, combine the cheese curds with the chives and place in the bottom of the pita pockets. Mix together the yogurt and the garlic and spoon over the curds in each of the sandwiches. Top with slices of cucumber, cherry tomatoes, and sprouts. Season with pepper.

Combo Special

Preparation time: 15 minutes
Degree of difficulty: simple
Servings: 6
Calories per sandwich: 350

The rye bread should be light, large and without caraway seeds. A food processor will make short work of the chopping. For perfect hard-cooked eggs, add to gently boiling water, cook 9 minutes, cool quickly in cold water, and refrigerate.

1½ cups finely chopped
delicatessen corned beef

½ cup finely chopped celery

⅓ cup homemade mayonnaise

2 tablespoons Dijon mustard

Salt and freshly ground
pepper to taste

6 slices buttered rye bread

Lettuce

3 hard-cooked eggs, sliced

12 pimento-stuffed olives, sliced

Combine first 4 ingredients in a bowl and mix thoroughly. Add salt and pepper to taste. For each sandwich, top a slice of bread with lettuce and about ⅓ cup corned beef mixture. Garnish with egg and olive slices.

The Britannia

Preparation time: 10 minutes
Degree of difficulty: simple
Servings: 1
Calories per serving: 690

Hearty and satisfying, this sandwich is a splendid accompaniment to a bowl of hot soup.

2 slices Irish soda bread

Horseradish mayonnaise (1 table-
spoon prepared horseradish mixed
into ¼ cup homemade mayonnaise)

2-3 slices cooked turkey breast

1 hard-cooked egg, sliced

½ cup grated
Canadian Cheddar cheese

Chutney to taste

Spread mayonnaise evenly and generously over one side of each slice of bread. Place turkey on 1 slice and

PHOTO BY SKIP DEAN

arrange slices of egg on top; sprinkle with cheese, add chutney, and cover with the other slice of bread. Serve with pickled onions and half a pear stuffed with quince jelly.

Combo Special
with Cream of
Fennel Soup
(see recipe
page 171)

Capers are strange little buds of flavor used in hot and cold sauces, especially tartar sauce and mayonnaise remoulade. They're the small, immature flower buds of a shrub that grows throughout the Mediterranean, the Orient, and the East Indies, and are usually found bottled and pickled in vinegar. Their peppery flavor goes well with cold meats, seafood, and salads. Mock capers, or Canadian capers, are the pickled seeds of nasturtiums, which have a more mustardy overtone, but are quite similar and are also cheaper. Old herbal cookbooks often include recipes for them.

Scottish Scones

Preparation time: 15 minutes
Cooking time: 10-15 minutes
Degree of difficulty: simple
Amount: makes 12 scones
Calories per scone: 125

Scones are so versatile they can be served at the breakfast, lunch, or tea table, and can even do duty as dessert for a family dinner.

2 cups all-purpose flour
2½ teaspoons baking powder
¼ teaspoon baking soda
½ teaspoon salt
2 tablespoons sugar
¼ cup butter or margarine
1 egg
¾ cup buttermilk

Preheat oven to 375°F. Mix together flour, baking powder, baking soda, salt, and sugar. Cut in butter or margarine until mixture is like coarse meal. Beat egg slightly and combine with buttermilk. Mix quickly into dry ingredients with a fork. Divide dough in 2 and pat into circles about ½-inch thick. Slice each circle into 6 wedges. Prick tops with a fork. Bake on a buttered cookie sheet for 10-15 minutes. Serve hot with butter and jam.

VARIATIONS

Add ¼ cup currants and brush with slightly beaten egg white before baking, or add ¼ cup seedless raisins and 1 teaspoon grated orange peel.

Garlic Tomato Bread

Preparation time: 15 minutes
Cooking time: 15 minutes
Degree of difficulty: simple
Servings: 6
Calories per slice: 240

1 French stick, cut into 1½-inch slices
¼ cup butter
¼ cup olive oil
4 cloves garlic, minced
4 medium tomatoes, finely chopped
Chopped parsley

Preheat oven to 350°F. Place the bread slices on a cookie sheet. In a saucepan, melt the butter and add the oil. When bubbly, sauté the garlic until soft — about 5 minutes. Stir in the tomatoes and cook 5 minutes more. Spoon the tomato-garlic mixture onto the bread and bake for 15 minutes. Garnish with chopped parsley.

Italian Sandwich

Preparation time: 15 minutes
Chilling time: overnight
Degree of difficulty: simple
Servings: 6-8
Calories per slice: 430 (1/6)
325 (1/8)

The recipe for this flattened spicy sandwich was submitted to our Cuisine '85 recipe contest by Montreal's Monique Fernandes.

1 9-inch-round loaf of Italian bread
¼ pound sliced spicy salami
¼ pound sliced Provolone cheese
¼ pound sliced ham

FILLING

1½ cups sliced black Calamata olives
⅔ cup olive oil
⅓ cup minced parsley
1 cup chopped red pimentos
1 1.75-ounce can anchovies, minced
3 tablespoons capers
1 tablespoon minced garlic
1 tablespoon fresh thyme or 1 teaspoon dried
Freshly ground pepper to taste

Mix together all the filling ingredients except pimento oil and let stand overnight at room temperature. Slice off the top ⅓ of the bread and scoop out most of the interior, leaving ½-inch of bread all around. Brush the inside of the bread with the reserved pimento oil. Drain the filling and place half in the bottom of the loaf, then layer the cheese and meats over it: top with remaining filling. Replace top of bread, wrap well in foil, place a weight on top and chill. To serve, cut in wedges.

Whole Wheat Raisin Bread

Preparation time: 1½-3 hours (total)
Cooking time: 35 minutes
Degree of difficulty: moderate
Amount: 4 loaves (20 slices per loaf)
Calories per slice: 120

This hearty bread flavored with molasses and studded with raisins makes wonderful toast.

1 cup lukewarm water
1 tablespoon white sugar
2 tablespoons active dry yeast
⅓ cup corn oil
4½ cups warm water
1 cup molasses
1½ cups brown sugar
1 tablespoon salt
2 teaspoons cinnamon
4 cups whole wheat flour
1½ cups raisins
11 cups all-purpose flour

In a small bowl, dissolve white sugar in lukewarm water. Sprinkle the yeast over the water, stir briskly with a fork and let stand for 10 minutes in a warm place. In a large bowl stir together the corn oil, the remaining warm water, molasses, brown sugar, salt, and cinnamon. Add the yeast mixture. Beat in the whole wheat flour and raisins. Gradually beat in the white flour, adding a little more if necessary to make the dough easy to handle. Turn dough onto a lightly floured board and knead for about 5 minutes. Shape into a smooth ball, place in a lightly buttered bowl, and butter the top sparingly. Cover and let rise in a warm place until double in bulk. Punch down the dough and turn onto a lightly floured board. Cut into 4 equal pieces and form each into a smooth ball. Cover and let rest for 15 minutes. Preheat the oven to 375°F. Shape each ball of dough into a loaf. Place in buttered 9- x 5- x 3-inch loaf pans and butter the tops. Cover and let rise until almost double in bulk. Bake for about 35 minutes or until nicely browned.

Honey Pumpkin Loaf

Preparation time: 15 minutes
Cooking time: 1 hour
Degree of difficulty: simple
Amount: makes about 18 slices
Calories per slice: 190

Pumpkin adds a lovely flavor to soups, breads, and cookies.

2 eggs
½ cup liquid honey (if starting with solid, just warm it)
½ cup brown sugar
½ cup vegetable oil
1 cup pumpkin (either canned or fresh cooked)
1½ cups sifted all-purpose flour (use some whole wheat flour if you like)
1 teaspoon baking powder
1 teaspoon baking soda
¼ teaspoon salt
¼ teaspoon allspice
¼ teaspoon nutmeg
½ teaspoon cinnamon
1 cup chopped walnuts

Preheat oven to 325°F. Beat eggs. Add honey, brown sugar, oil, and pumpkin. Beat well. Sift together flour, baking powder, baking soda, salt, allspice, nutmeg, and cinnamon. Add to liquid mixture and mix until blended. Fold in nuts. Pour batter into a 9-x-5-x-3-inch loaf pan and bake for about 1 hour, or until a toothpick inserted in the centre comes out clean. Cool 10 minutes before removing from pan.

Yogurt Blueberry Bran Muffins

Preparation time: 15 minutes
Cooking time: 35 minutes
Degree of difficulty: simple
Amount: makes 2 dozen
Calories per muffin: 194

Raisins, dates, or nuts may be substituted for the blueberries — nothing could affect these delicious muffins.

2 cups plain yogurt
2 teaspoons baking soda
1½ cups brown sugar
2 eggs
1 cup oil
2 cups bran
2 teaspoons vanilla extract
2 cups all-purpose flour
4 teaspoons baking powder
½ teaspoon salt
1 cup unsweetened blueberries, fresh or frozen

Preheat oven to 350°F. Measure yogurt into a large bowl and mix in baking soda. Set aside. In a large mixing bowl beat together sugar, eggs, and oil. Add the bran and vanilla. Sift together the flour, baking powder, and salt. Add to the sugar mixture alternately with the yogurt. Fold in berries. Pour into muffin tins and bake for 35 minutes.

Oatcakes

Preparation time: 15-20 minutes
Cooking time: 12 minutes per cookie sheet
Degree of difficulty: simple
Amount: makes about 3 dozen
Calories per oatcake: 50

Warm oatcakes and cold butter are one of the better after-school snacks. Oatcakes are good with jam and cheese, too.

1 cup all-purpose flour
½ teaspoon baking powder
½ teaspoon salt
1 teaspoon sugar
1¾ cups rolled oats
½ cup butter or margarine
1 egg
2 tablespoons water

Preheat oven to 400°F. Mix together flour, baking powder, salt, sugar, and 1½ cups rolled oats in a bowl. Cut in butter until mixture is like coarse meal. Beat egg together with water and mix into dry ingredients. Work into a stiff dough. Sprinkle remaining oats on a lightly floured board and roll out dough as thin as possible. Cut into triangles. Bake on a greased cookie sheet for about 12 minutes.

NOTES

CAKES AND COOKIES

Although there's been a lot written and said about dieting and fitness (much of it is true and we're all the better for it), it's still true that the chocolate cheesecake and strawberry shortcake with whipped cream disappear first from the dessert tray. Perhaps it's because we're so fitness-conscious these days that we feel we deserve an occasional sweet treat after a thinner dinner.

Whatever the reason, cake making and decorating, and cookie baking, have never been more popular. There's something magical about going into a kitchen that smells of sugar and spice and everything nice, which seems to remind us of winter days after school, when we came home and reached for — what else? — a cookie or a piece of cake.

You have to use the very best ingredients in cakes and cookies and, even if you don't want to use all butter when it's called for, use at least part butter — you'll really notice the difference in flavor. Your cakes and cookies will be easier to handle and have better texture if you have the ingredients at room temperature. Don't open the oven door and let in cold air before the cake has time to set; test quickly, and never slam the oven door.

Cheesecakes, one of Canada's most loved sweet finales, have always maintained a certain mystique. Jeraldene Ballon, owner of Toronto's Dr. Cheese and the Cake Lady bakery, says there are only a few things to remember, including paying close attention to pan sizes. Manufacturers measure pans from the outside edges, while you and I tend to measure from the inside — in cheesecake, ½ or 1 inch can make a lot of difference to the batter. A cheesecake is done when the edges are slightly raised and puffy, and the inside custardy — any more and the cake will be overdone and liable to crack. Ballon leaves her cakes in the oven for half an hour, cools them to room temperature, and refrigerates them overnight, since she believes that a cheesecake should be ripened before being eaten.

Poppy Seed Cake with Lemon Butter Filling and Coffee Whipped-Cream Icing (see recipe page 42) and Thin Butter Cookies (see recipe page 45)

Hazelnuts are most easily peeled by placing them in a single layer on a baking sheet and toasting in a preheated 350°F oven for about 10 minutes. Transfer hot nuts to a metal sieve and rub with a cloth kitchen towel. The mesh of the sieve will scrape off almost all the skin.

Black Forest Cake

Preparation time: 30 minutes
Degree of difficulty: simple
Servings: 8-12
Calories per serving: 683 (1/8)
547 (1/10)
456 (1/12)

A traditional dessert cake.

2 9-inch chocolate sponge-cake layers
½ cup kirsch
2 cups pitted halved cherries (black are best)
2 cups whipping cream
1 tablespoon sugar
½ teaspoon vanilla extract
1 tablespoon kirsch
Chocolate curls

BUTTER CREAM FILLING
½ cup sweet butter, softened
3½ cups icing sugar, sifted
Pinch of salt
1 teaspoon strong coffee
Light cream

Make the butter cream filling: Cream butter until fluffy. Beat in sugar, salt, and coffee, adding enough cream to give icing a heavy spreading consistency.

Split and level the sponge cake layers. Sprinkle each of the 4 layers with kirsch. Spread the bottom layer with ⅓ of the filling. Press ⅓ of the cherries lightly into the butter cream. Top with one of the layers, and repeat the cream and cherry step. Add another layer, and top with remaining butter cream and cherries. Then press fourth layer firmly in place on top. Whip the cream, sugar, vanilla, and kirsch, and spread over top and sides of the sponge-cake layers. Decorate with chocolate curls or grated chocolate. (Chocolate curls are easily made using a potato peeler to peel off curls of chocolate from semisweet chocolate squares.)

Poppyseed Cake with Lemon Butter Filling and Coffee Whipped-Cream Icing

Preparation time: 30 minutes
Cooking time: 30 minutes
Assembly time: 15 minutes
Degree of difficulty: simple
Servings: 8-10
Calories per serving: 825 (1/8)
660 (1/10)

Cuisine '85 Semifinalist
Thanks to Debby Lexier of Winnipeg for sharing this cake: it's the kind we think our readers love to serve for Sunday tea or following a special dinner. Decorate the cake as you wish — with the icing piped into rosettes or with chopped nuts and chocolate shavings.

CAKE
¾ cup poppy seeds
1 cup milk
⅔ cup butter
1½ cups sugar
4 extra-large eggs, separated
2 cups cake and pastry flour
2½ teaspoons baking powder

LEMON BUTTER FILLING
¼ cup butter, softened
¼ cup cream cheese
1¼ cups icing sugar
2 tablespoons lemon juice

COFFEE WHIPPED-CREAM ICING
1 cup whipping cream
2 tablespoons instant coffee granules
3 tablespoons sugar

Preheat oven to 350°F. Butter and flour 2 9-inch-round layer pans and line with wax paper. Combine the poppyseeds with the milk and set aside. Cream the butter and sugar together until light and fluffy. Beat in the egg yolks one at a time, beating well after each addition. Sift together the flour and the baking powder. Add the flour mixture and the poppyseed mixture alternately to the butter-sugar mixture, mixing well after each addition. Beat the egg whites until stiff and fold into the batter. Pour the batter into the prepared cake pans. Bake for 20-30 minutes, or until a cake tester inserted into the centre comes out clean and the tops spring back when touched. Set cakes aside to cool before inverting onto a cake rack. For the filling, blend together the butter, cream cheese, icing sugar, and lemon juice until the mixture is smooth and thick (if the butter cream is too thin, add more icing sugar; if too thick, thin with drops of boiling water). Place 1 cake on a serving plate, spread with lemon butter filling and place the other layer on top. To prepare the icing, combine the cream and instant coffee granules. Whip, adding sugar gradually, until the cream stands in stiff peaks. Frost top and sides of cake with coffee whipped-cream icing. Chill.

Hazelnut Cake

Preparation time: 10 minutes
Cooking time: 1 hour
Degree of difficulty: simple
Servings: 4-6
Calories per slice 340 (1/4)
225 (1/6)

The Aberthnau Nut Farm in Rosedale, British Columbia, often offers tea to groups of tourists. This simple recipe for hazelnut cake is a favorite of owners John and Hazel Spencer.

3 eggs
⅔ cup sugar
1½ cups finely ground hazelnuts

Preheat oven to 325°F. Thoroughly butter a 9-inch-square baking pan. Beat the eggs. Add sugar and continue beating until the mixture becomes quite thick. Add the nuts. Pour in the batter and bake for 1 hour, or until the cake is golden and springy to the touch.

Dingle Cake

Preparation time: 45 minutes
Cooking time: 1 hour (total)
Degree of difficulty: moderately challenging
Servings: 12
Calories per serving: 355

MERINGUES

| 3 egg whites |
| 1 cup fruit sugar |

For meringues, beat the 3 egg whites until foamy and double in volume, using an electric beater. Add the sugar, a tablespoon at a time, beating all the time, until the meringue really stands up in firm peaks. (This should take about 5 minutes.) Preheat oven to 300°F. Dust 2 cookie sheets with flour. Take a plate about 8 inches in diameter and with it trace a circle on each of the cookie sheets. Divide meringue in half, put half on each cookie sheet within the circle, spreading evenly so it is as thick at the edges as in the middle. Bake 30-40 minutes until firm and lightly golden. Let cool 5 minutes, then remove meringues from the cookie sheets carefully and set aside.

WHIPPED CHOCOLATE FILLING

| ⅔ cup whipping cream |
| 7 squares semisweet chocolate |
| 3½ squares unsweetened chocolate |
| 4 tablespoons butter |
| 4 egg whites |
| 1 cup sugar |

To prepare the filling, heat cream in top of double boiler and add the 2 kinds of chocolate. Stir frequently with a wooden spoon, add butter and stir. Set aside. Beat the 4 egg whites until foamy and double in volume. Add sugar until egg whites peak and are glossy.

Fill bottom of the double boiler with cold water and lots of ice. Set chocolate mixture back on top of double boiler and beat at a high speed until light and fluffy and almost double in volume. It will be slightly thicker than whipped cream, but stop beating before you get fudge. Fold the chocolate mixture into the egg whites and mix slowly with a spatula. Put one of the meringue rounds on a pretty plate, spread 1½ cups of chocolate mixture over it, then put other meringue round on top. Ice top and sides with the rest of the chocolate mixture. Refrigerate. About 30 minutes before serving, remove from refrigerator and sprinkle lightly with sifted icing sugar. You can also decorate with chocolate bits sliced with a very sharp knife, or curls shaved with a potato peeler.

Coconut Cake Mary Darcy

Preparation time: 10 minutes
Cooking time: 1½-1¾ hours
Mellowing time: 24 hours
Degree of difficulty: simple
Servings: 10-12
Calories per serving: 750 (1/10)
625 (1/12)

This rich macaroon-like cake must be kept for at least 24 hours before serving to allow the flavors and texture to develop.

| 2 cups butter |
| 2 cups sugar |
| 2 cups all-purpose flour |
| 6 eggs |
| 2 teaspoons almond extract |
| 3 cups packaged coconut |
| 1 orange, peeled and sliced |
| 2 tablespoons Grand Marnier liqueur |

GLAZE

| 1 cup sugar |
| ½ cup water |
| 1 teaspoon vanilla extract |

Preheat oven to 375°F. Cream butter and sugar. Add 1 cup of flour. Mix well. Add the eggs and almond extract. Mix the remaining cup of flour with the coconut and add to the batter, blending well. Bake in a buttered, greased and floured 9-inch tube pan for 1½ to 1¾ hours, watching carefully. Make glaze by mixing sugar, water, and vanilla, simmer for 10 minutes. Remove hot cake from pan and brush glaze on until it sinks in. Cover the cake loosely with foil and keep at least 24 hours before serving. Decorate the platter with orange slices marinated in Grand Marnier. Serve in thin slices (this cake is *rich*).

Cold Water Orange Cake

Preparation time: 10 minutes
Cooking time: 35 minutes
Degree of difficulty: moderate
Servings: 8-10
Calories per serving: 230 (1/8)
184 (1/10)

This is a sponge cake that never fails — for a birthday cake perhaps.

| 2 cups cake and pastry flour |
| 1 teaspoon cream of tartar |
| ½ teaspoon baking soda |
| 5 egg yolks |
| 5 egg whites, beaten stiffly |
| 2 cups sugar |
| Juice of 1 orange |
| ½ cup ice water |

Preheat oven to 350°F. Sift together the flour, cream of tartar, and soda. Beat the egg yolks until lemon yellow and gradually add the sugar and the orange juice. Beat well and add the ice water. (Measure the water and put it in the freezer for a few minutes.) Add the flour mixture to the egg batter and beat well again. Fold in the stiffly beaten egg whites. Pour batter into 2 buttered 8-inch-square cake pans and bake for 35 minutes.

BOILED ICING

| 1 egg white |
| ¾ cup brown sugar |
| 1 teaspoon corn syrup |
| 2 tablespoons water |
| ½ teaspoon baking powder |
| 1 teaspoon vanilla extract |

Meanwhile, make the icing: put first 4 ingredients in the top of a double boiler over boiling water. Beat with eggbeater or electric mixer 7 minutes, or until thick enough to spread. Remove from heat, beat in baking powder and vanilla. Cool, remove from pans, and spread boiled icing between layers and on top of cake.

Use solid vegetable shortening when greasing a cake pan, since oil tends to burn, especially on any surface the batter doesn't cover, and imparts an unpleasant flavor. Don't invert a freshly baked cake on a plate until thoroughly cooled, since it will probably stick to the plate and tear when you try to move it.

Beet and
Ginger
Fruit Cake

Beet and Ginger Fruit Cake

Preparation time: 20 minutes
Cooking time: 1½ hours (total)
Degree of difficulty: moderate
Amount: makes 2 cakes
Servings: 12 slices per cake
Calories per slice: 210

This nontraditional fruit cake is healthy and delicious. A little bit goes a long way.

2 cups peeled and julienned fresh beets

3 oranges, unpeeled

1 grapefruit, peeled

1½ cups sugar

2½ cups all-purpose flour

1¼ teaspoons baking powder

½ cup heavy cream

½ cup slivered crystallized ginger

1 teaspoon nutmeg

½ teaspoon allspice

½ teaspoon cinnamon

½ teaspoon ground cloves

1 teaspoon vanilla

3 egg yolks

1 cup coarsely chopped pecans

1 cup chopped walnuts

1 cup raisins

ORANGE GLAZE

Juice of 1 orange

¾ cup icing sugar

4 tablespoons orange-flavored liqueur

Steam beets until tender. Set aside. Preheat oven to 350°F. Cut off ends of oranges and place in the bowl of a food processor along with grapefruit; process until coarsely chopped. Transfer mixture into a large bowl and add 1 cup of sugar. Add the flour, baking powder, and cream to the citrus mixture. Mix well and add the remaining ingredients including the remaining ½ cup sugar and the beets. Pour the batter into 2 7-inch greased stainless steel mixing bowls. Bake for about 80 minutes or until a tester inserted in the centre comes out clean. Turn cakes out on a wire rack. Blend together orange-glaze ingredients and brush cakes while still warm with glaze every 15 minutes until all the glaze is used. Cool, wrap and refrigerate.

Cardamom Cookies

Preparation time: 10-15 minutes
Cooking time: 10-12 minutes per cookie sheet
Degree of difficulty: simple
Amount: makes about 4 dozen
Calories per cookie: 58

These look like peanut butter cookies and at first bite taste quite mild. Then comes the cardamom kick.

½ cup butter

1 teaspoon baking soda

½ teaspoon ground cardamom

¼ teaspoon salt

1 cup brown sugar

1 egg

2¼ cups all-purpose flour

1 teaspoon cream of tartar

Preheat oven to 350°F. Cream butter and add baking soda, cardamom, and salt; mix well. Gradually blend in the sugar; then beat in the egg. Sift together flour and cream of tartar and gradually stir into the butter mixture. Shape the dough into ½-inch balls. Place on unbuttered cookie sheets. Dip a fork into flour and press into each cookie in crisscross style. bake 10-12 minutes.

The Best Chocolate Chip Cookies

Preparation time: 15 minutes
Cooking time: 12-15 minutes per cookie sheet
Degree of difficulty: simple
Amount: makes 2 dozen
Calories per cookie: 250

1 cup butter

1 cup brown sugar

2 eggs

1 teaspoon vanilla extract

2 cups all-purpose flour

1 teaspoon baking powder

½ teaspoon salt

½ teaspoon baking powder

1 12-ounce package chocolate chips

1 cup chopped walnuts

2 cups rolled oats (not instant)

Preheat oven to 350°F. Cream the butter and beat in sugar, eggs, and vanilla. Combine the flour, baking soda, salt, and baking powder and add the flour mixture to the butter mixture. Fold in the chocolate chips, walnuts, and rolled oats. Drop by teaspoonfuls onto buttered cookie sheets. Bake for 12-15 minutes or until browned.

Double Chocolate Malt Brownies

Preparation time: 10 minutes
Cooking time: 20-25 minutes
Degree of difficulty: simple
Amount: makes 12 brownies
Calories per brownie: 340

American mystery writer Virginia Rich includes recipes in her mystery stories.

½ cup shortening

¾ cup sugar

½ teaspoon vanilla extract

2 eggs

1 square semisweet baking chocolate, melted

1 cup all-purpose flour

½ cup malted milk powder or malted food drink base

¾ cup cocoa

½ teaspoon baking powder

½ teaspoon salt

½ cup broken walnuts

FROSTING

2 tablespoons butter, softened

¼ cup cocoa

¼ cup malted milk powder

1 cup icing sugar

Pinch of salt

3-4 tablespoons hot water

Preheat oven to 350°F. Combine the shortening, sugar, vanilla, eggs, and chocolate; cream until fluffy. Sift together flour, malted milk powder, cocoa, baking powder, and salt. Stir in the walnuts. Spread in a greased 8-inch-square pan. Bake 20-25 minutes. Cool. To prepare frosting, combine frosting ingredients and spread over brownies.

Double Chocolate Malt Brownies

Cheesecake

Preparation time: 15 minutes
Cooking time: 1 hour
Degree of difficulty: Simple
Servings: 10-12
Calories per slice: 300 (1/10)
250 (1/12)

This is a popular Jewish cheesecake.

1 cup matzoh meal

1 teaspoon cinnamon

1 cup sugar

¼ cup butter

4 eggs, well beaten

1¾ tablespoons lemon juice

⅛ teaspoon salt

1 cup milk

3 cups creamed cottage cheese

2 tablespoons potato starch

2 teaspoons grated lemon rind

Preheat oven to 350°F. Combine the matzoh meal, cinnamon, ¼ cup of the sugar, and the butter. Press into bottom and sides of unbuttered 9-inch springform pan.

Beat remaining sugar into eggs; add lemon juice, salt, milk, cottage cheese, and potato starch. Stir in lemon rind and pour mixture into crust. Bake for approximately 1 hour, or until it is "set" in the middle. Cool, and then chill.

Thin Butter Cookies

Preparation time: 10 minutes
Cooking time: 10-15 minutes per cookie sheet
Chilling time: several hours
Degree of difficulty: simple
Amount: makes about 8 dozen, depending on thickness
Calories per cookie: 40

For afternoons around the fire, these simple cookies can be made ahead of time and frozen, or the dough can be kept in the the refrigerator, then sliced and baked just before serving.

1 cup butter

1 cup sugar

4 tablespoons light cream

2¼ cups all-purpose flour

1 teaspoon vanilla extract

Cream butter and sugar. Add cream and stir in remaining ingredients. Combine and make into two rolls or one large one. Chill for several hours. Preheat oven to 350°F. Slice dough into thin rounds and bake 10-15 minutes until lightly browned. The cookies may be sprinkled with sugar, cinnamon, or cardamom just before baking.

Mascarpone, the darling of Italian cooks, is a mild, rich, and buttery cheese rather like soft cream cheese but more acidic in flavor. It can be mixed with grated chocolate or a liqueur and used as a filling in cakes and pastries, or as a topping for fresh berries and fruit.

Christmas Jam Cookies

Preparation time: 30 minutes
Chilling time: 4 hours
Cooking time: 15 minutes per cookie sheet
Degree of difficulty: moderate
Amount: makes about 7 dozen 2-to 3-inch cookies
Calories per cookie: 60

A real treat for family and friends.

1½ cups unsalted butter, softened
1¾ cups icing sugar
1 egg
2 cups sifted all-purpose flour
1 cup cornstarch
1 cup finely chopped walnuts
1 cup finely chopped pecans
½ cup red raspberry jam
1 tablespoon orange juice

In a large bowl, cream together the butter and 1 cup of the sugar until light and fluffy. Stir in the egg. Sift together the flour and the cornstarch and add to the creamed mixture. Stir in nuts. Wrap the dough in wax paper and chill for 4 hours. Roll dough out ¼-inch thick and, using Christmas cookie cutters, cut out shapes and place on lightly oiled cookie sheets. Bake cookies 15 minutes until lightly browned. Cool on wire racks with wax paper underneath for easy cleanup. Heat the raspberry jam with the orange juice and stir until melted. While cookies are still warm, lightly brush with raspberry jam mixture, then sprinkle with some of the remaining icing sugar. Sprinkle again when cool.

Three-Tiered Lemon Curd Cake

Preparation time: 30 minutes
Cooking time: 35 minutes (total)
Assembly time: 15 minutes
Degree of difficulty: simple
Servings: 8-10
Calories per slice: 815 (1/8)
650 (1/10)

Cuisine '85 Semifinalist
Milly Weizl contributed this luscious dessert.

CAKE

1¾ cups cake and pastry flour
2 teaspoons baking powder
¾ teaspoon salt
¾ teaspoon baking soda
1¼ cups sugar
Peel of 1 lemon
3 large eggs
¾ cup unsalted butter at room temperature, cut into 6 pieces
¾ cup sour cream
⅓ cup orange juice
2 tablespoons lemon juice
1 teaspoon lemon extract

LEMON CURD FILLING

1 cup sugar
Peel of 1 lemon
5 egg yolks
½ cup lemon juice
½ cup melted butter

LEMON BUTTER CREAM ICING

3 cups icing sugar
5 tablespoons softened butter
3-5 tablespoons sour cream
2 tablespoons lemon curd filling
¼ teaspoon lemon extract
Lemon twists and mint sprigs for garnish

Preheat oven to 350°F. Combine the first 4 ingredients in the bowl of a food processor fitted with a steel blade. Process 2 seconds. Transfer to another bowl and set aside. Put the sugar and lemon peel in the food processor bowl and process until peel is finely minced. Add the eggs and process 1 minute more. Add the butter and process another minute. Add the sour cream, juices and lemon extract and process 10 seconds. Spoon the flour mixture over the batter and combine, using 4 on-off pulses. Divide the batter into 3 greased and floured 8-inch-round cake pans. Bake for about 20 minutes or until cake begins to pull away from the sides. Set aside to cool before turning out of pans.

To prepare lemon curd filling, combine the sugar and peel in the bowl of a food processor fitted with a steel blade and process until peel is finely minced. Add the egg yolks and juice and process 5 seconds. While the machine is running, slowly pour in the melted butter. Transfer the mixture to a heavy saucepan and stir over medium heat until the curd is thickened and begins to boil — about 10-12 minutes. Set aside, cool to room temperature, then refrigerate.

To prepare icing, combine the sugar, butter, 3 tablespoons of the sour cream, the curd filling, and the lemon extract in the bowl of a food processor fitted with a steel blade and process for about 5 seconds. If the icing is too thick, add 1-2 more tablespoons of sour cream.

To assemble, place 1 layer on a plate and spread with half the curd filling; add the next layer and spread with the remaining curd. Top with the third layer and cover the top and the sides of the cake with the butter cream icing. Garnish with lemon twists and sprigs of mint.

Rich Dark Fruit Cake

Marinating time: overnight
Preparation time: 1 hour
Cooking time: 1½-4½ hours
Degree of difficulty: challenging
Calories: 120 per ½-x-2-inch slice

Eileen (Edith Adams) Norman contributed this recipe, which her grandmother gave her. Although not cheap to make, it is the kind of specially good cake most people like to bake at Christmas and for weddings.

1 cup blanched almonds, slivered

Juice of 1 orange

2½ cups washed seedless raisins

2 cups washed sultana raisins

2 cups candied pineapple, cut

2 cups candied red cherries, cut or whole

2 cups candied green cherries, cut or whole

2 cups candied citron peel, cut finely

1 cup grape juice or ½ cup each grape juice and rum

2 cups butter

2 cups sugar

12 medium egg yolks, beaten thoroughly

1 6-ounce jar grape jelly

1 1-ounce square unsweetened chocolate, melted

2 cups all-purpose flour

1 teaspoon baking powder

2 cups pecans, halved

12 medium egg whites, stiffly beaten

Prepare almonds; soak overnight in orange juice. Prepare fruit; soak overnight in grape juice.

Sprinkle a little flour over fruit. Cream butter at room temperature, but not too soft, until like whipped cream. Add sugar gradually, creaming until no sugar grains remain. Beat in beaten egg yolks thoroughly. (All steps must be followed as given, to prevent butter oozing out of cake during baking.)

Stir in jelly and chocolate. Blend in flour and baking powder. Add fruit, a small amount at a time, mixing thoroughly. Add almonds and pecans. Fold in stiffly beaten egg whites.

Preheat oven to 275°F. Line Christmas cake pan set, plus 1 extra, with 3 layers brown paper. Butter side next to batter or use 1 layer unbuttered heavy-duty foil. Fill pans ⅔ full and bake until cake tests done. (Test by pressing finger in centre; if no dent, press harder; it should be firm to touch, or slightly springy.) Approximate baking times: 4-x-4-inch pan, 1½ hours; 6-x-6-inch, 3 hours; 8-x-8-inch, 4½ hours.

NOTES

DESSERTS

This is the best part of the meal, according to many people, and it's a fact that, along with weight-loss diets, desserts are the most popular item in mass-circulation magazines. Certainly they can be the most fun to make for either family or friends, and provide a variety of approaches to end either a simple supper or a formal dinner for eight.

Consider the possibilities of a warm apple crisp sprinkled with crunchy oats and laced with cinnamon or cardamom, with thick cream trickled down the sides; or cool, fresh-tasting orange charlotte, sharp with citrus flavor and gentled with ladyfingers and whipped cream; or a smooth chocolate mousse melting easily on the tongue.

There's much to be said for old (and new) England, with their steamed puddings filled with all manner of dried fruits and always a sauce to accompany them, perhaps made with brown sugar and cream laced with brandy or rum; or a simple baked custard sprinkled with nutmeg, elevated by sprinkling tiny flowers on the surface before serving. Fruit fools are simple but delicious desserts made with equal parts of fresh fruit and heavy cream; and syllabubs, a felicitous mixture of wine, brandy, whipping cream, and sugar, are enjoying a resurgence of interest.

But there's nothing to forbid the serving of a plate of, say, three cheeses (perhaps an aged Canadian Cheddar, French Brie from a dealer who can be trusted, and a block of snowy goat cheese), with the best fruit you can buy — red and green seedless grapes, apples (preferably not controlled storage), and meltingly ripe pears. Divine.

Frozen Grand Marnier Mousse (see recipe page 50)

PHOTO BY SKIP DEAN, FOOD STYLING BY KATE BUSH

Pure vanilla extract has a much better flavor than artificial vanilla. It's made by soaking and preserving the vanilla bean in alcohol, and you can make your own by splitting 4-5 beans and adding them to 2 cups of brandy, bourbon, or vodka. Cover the jar tightly and let stand for 2 weeks or longer before using. It will keep indefinitely.

Frozen Grand Marnier Mousse

Preparation time: 20 minutes
Freezing time: overnight
Degree of difficulty: moderate
Servings: 12
Calories per serving: 230

A variation on a traditional dessert.

6 egg whites

¼ teaspoon cream of tartar

1½ cups sugar

1½ cups whipping cream

Red and yellow food coloring (optional)

1 teaspoon vanilla extract

Grated zest of 3 oranges

¼ cup Grand Marnier

Chocolate shavings for garnish

In a large bowl, beat egg whites and cream of tartar until frothy. Add sugar gradually and beat until stiff but not dry. Place whipping cream in a separate bowl and add 4 drops of red food coloring and 12 drops of yellow (optional). Add vanilla and beat until thick. Fold in orange zest and Grand Marnier. Gently fold the beaten egg whites into the whipped cream. Pour into a glass serving bowl, cover with plastic wrap and freeze overnight. Remove from freezer 15-20 minutes before serving and garnish with chocolate shavings.

Banana Ginger Soufflé

Preparation time: 20 minutes
Cooking time: 30 minutes (total)
Degree of difficulty: moderate
Servings: 4-6
Calories per serving: 435 (1/4)
290 (1/6)

Light as a cloud, warm as a kiss, a heavenly combination of smooth and spicy.

4 tablespoons butter

2 ripe but firm bananas, sliced

3 pieces candied ginger, chopped

3 tablespoons all-purpose flour

1 cup milk

6 tablespoons rum

4-6 tablespoons apricot jam

4 large eggs

1 extra egg white

3 tablespoons grated bittersweet chocolate bar

Preheat oven to 375°F. Melt the butter in a saucepan; add the banana slices and the chopped ginger and cook over medium-low heat 2 minutes. Remove pan from heat; stir in the flour and mix. Add the milk a little at a time, stirring to form a smooth sauce. Return mixture to medium-low heat and cook until thickened. Add rum and apricot jam; stir. Taste for sweetness and allow to cool to room temperature. Separate eggs, taking care not to get any yolk in the white. Stir the yolks into the banana mixture. Butter a 5-cup soufflé dish and tie a 4-inch parchment paper collar firmly around the top, leaving about 2 inches above the rim. Whisk the egg whites to stiff peaks. Lighten the banana mixture by stirring in a dollop of the whisked whites, then gently fold in the rest of the whites, taking care not to overfold. Turn oven up to 400°F and bake for 18-20 minutes. Remove from oven and carefully remove the collar. Sprinkle top of soufflé with grated chocolate and serve immediately.

Authentic English Trifle

Preparation time: 1 hour (including cooking time)
Chilling time: 12 hours
Degree of difficulty: moderate
Servings: 6-12
Calories per serving: 460 (1/6)
383 (1/12)

Everybody murders trifle; this is the way it *should* be.

4 egg yolks

2 cups light cream

¼ cup sugar

1 tablespoon orange-flower water or vanilla

2-layer sponge cake

¾-1 cup raspberry jam

½ cup sherry

2 cups whipping cream

½ cup icing sugar

Vanilla extract to taste

12 toasted almonds

1 tablespoon angelica

First, make a soft rich custard: beat egg yolks until light and pale yellow. In the top of a double boiler, heat light cream with sugar and orange-flower water or vanilla. Add beaten egg yolks, while beating very hard. Then cook without boiling, stirring continuously until custard coats the spoon. Remove to a bowl. Cover and refrigerate until well chilled.

Cut 1 2-layer sponge cake (that you bake or buy) into finger-length pieces. Spread each one on one side with raspberry jam and quickly dip them in sherry. Place half of these sponge fingers in the bottom of a deep cut-glass bowl. Cover with half the custard.

Whip cream, sweeten with icing sugar, and add vanilla to taste. Cover custard with half the whipped cream. Place another layer of sponge fingers on top of all this. Top with 12 toasted almonds, standing them upright in the cream, and a few slivers of angelica. Or use small roses instead of almonds and angelica. Refrigerate at least 12 hours.

Almond Soufflé

Preparation time: 15 minutes
Cooking time: 35-40 minutes
Degree of difficulty: moderate
Servings: 6-8
Calories per serving: 180 (1/6)
135 (1/8)

Satisfying taste, yet light in texture. This dessert is good after almost any main course.

½ cup finely ground toasted almonds
½ tablespoon butter
1 tablespoon sugar
3 tablespoons all-purpose flour
¾ cup milk
⅓ cup white sugar
4 egg yolks
2 tablespoons butter
5 egg whites
Pinch of salt
¼ teaspoon cream of tartar
1 tablespoon sugar
2 tablespoons vanilla extract
¼ teaspoon almond extract

Preheat oven to 325°F., then toast almonds on a cookie sheet for about 10 minutes. Grind in coffee grinder or blend. Raise oven temperature to 400°F. Butter the inside of a 6-cup charlotte or soufflé mold. Roll 1 tablespoon sugar around in the mold and tap out excess. In a large saucepan, beat flour with a little milk. Beat in the rest of the milk and ⅓ cup sugar. Stir over moderate to high heat until mixture comes to the boil. Boil for 30 seconds, stirring constantly. Remove from heat and beat for 2 minutes. Gradually beat egg yolks into mixture. Beat in 1 tablespoon butter; dot surface with remaining tablespoon of butter to prevent mixture from forming a skin.

In a separate bowl, beat egg whites and salt. Add cream of tartar and beat until soft peaks are formed. Add sugar. Beat to stiff peaks. Add flavorings and almonds to the custard base. Spoon a quarter of the egg-white mixture into the custard and fold in. Carefully spoon the rest of the egg-white mixture on top of the custard and gently fold together. *Do not overmix.* Turn into the mold (there should be at least 1¼ inches between top of soufflé and rim of mold). Place in centre of oven and lower temperature to 375°F. Bake for 35-40 minutes, or until a long knife inserted in the centre comes out clean. Serve immediately.

Baklava

Preparation time: 20 minutes
Cooking time: 45 minutes
Degree of difficulty: moderate
Servings: 12
Calories per serving: 570

Rich and satisfying — not quite traditional, but perhaps even better.

1 pound phyllo pastry
1½ cups butter, melted
1½ cups chopped walnuts
2½ tablespoons sugar

SYRUP

1½ cups honey
Juice and finely chopped peel of 1 lemon
1 small can unsweetened frozen orange juice

Butter a large baking dish (a 9-x-13-inch cake pan will do). Fit one sheet of phyllo pastry into the dish, overlapping and folding where necessary. Brush with melted butter. Add more sheets, brushing each with butter, until half the pastry has been used. Mix together nuts and sugar and spread evenly over pastry. Cover with remaining sheets, brushing each with butter. Cut into pieces with a sharp knife.

Preheat oven to 350°F. Simmer syrup ingredients together until thick enough to coat a spoon. Cool and refrigerate. Bake pastry for 30 minutes, then raise heat to 450°F and continue cooking until puffed and golden (about 15 minutes). Remove from oven and quickly pour cooled syrup over. Allow to cool.

Chestnut Bavarian Cream with Kiwi Fruit

Preparation time: 20 minutes
Cooking time: 15 minutes
Chilling time: 4 hours (minimum)
Degree of difficulty: moderate
Servings: 4-6
Calories per serving: 710 (1/4)
475 (1/6)

Chestnut cream makes a smooth dessert to end a heavy meal.

2 envelopes unflavored gelatine
½ cup cold water
1 cup milk
1 cup sugar
1 teaspoon vanilla extract
2 tablespoons dark rum
6 egg yolks
Pinch of salt
1 8-ounce can chestnut purée
1 cup whipping cream
2 kiwi fruit, peeled and sliced

Lightly oil a 1-quart tin mold and chill in refrigerator. Soak gelatine in water. Scald milk, sugar, vanilla, and rum. Beat egg yolks and salt lightly. Over hot water in a double boiler, gradually add milk mixture to egg yolks, stirring constantly until the custard thickens enough to coat a spoon. Add gelatine and cook until very thick. Remove from heat and beat in chestnut purée. Cool. Whip the cream and fold into mixture. Pour into the chilled mold, cover with wax paper, and chill 4 hours or overnight. To unmold, dip mold into very hot water for 3-4 seconds, then turn out onto a platter. Decorate with slices of kiwi.

When making meringues or soufflés, a rotary beater or an egg beater with small wires will produce a smaller volume but finer texture, while a whisk with heavy wires gives a larger volume of looser texture, such as for angel cake, and you will have to give double, or more the number of strokes.

Bread and Butter Pudding, the Dorchester Grill

Bread and Butter Pudding, The Dorchester Grill

Preparation time: 20 minutes
Cooking time: 1 hour
Degree of difficulty: simple
Servings: 6-8
Calories per serving: 645 (1/6)
483 (1/8)

An update of a classic favorite, this pudding somehow manages to be rich but light. Nobody has failed to ask for a second helping.

4 tablespoons golden raisins

4 tablespoons currants

8 slices stale French bread, 1/3-inch thick

3 tablespoons unsalted butter, melted

2 large eggs

1 large egg yolk

1/4 cup plus 1 tablespoon sugar

3 cups whipping cream, scalded

Preheat oven to 300°F. In a buttered oval 9-x-6-x-3-inch tin dish sprinkle 2 tablespoons each of the raisins and currants. Arrange the slices of bread over the dried fruit, covering the bottom of the dish. Cut little bits to fill any holes. Drizzle melted butter over the bread.

In a large bowl, beat the eggs and egg yolk until combined. Gradually add 1/4 cup of the sugar, and beat until mixture ribbons when the beater is lifted. Whisk in scalded cream and strain the mixture over the bread. Sprinkle the pudding with remaining raisins and currants. Set the dish in a baking pan, and pour enough hot water into the pan to reach halfway up the sides of the dish. Bake for 1 hour. Remove dish from the pan. Sprinkle pudding with 1 tablespoon sugar, and place under broiler for 1-2 minutes, or until the top is golden brown and the sugar is caramelized.

Brown Sugar Ice Cream

Preparation time: 5 minutes
Degree of difficulty: simple
Servings: 6
Calories per serving: 285

Brown sugar adds another dimension to a dessert topping that's basically an "iced cream."

1 pint whipping cream

1/3 cup brown sugar

Beat the whipping cream until it forms firm peaks. Fold in brown sugar. Freeze until ready to serve. Delicious as a topping for fresh fruit. The same method can be used with sour cream, but it cannot be frozen.

Blueberry Mousse

Preparation time: 10 minutes
Chilling time: 4 hours (total)
Degree of difficulty: simple
Servings: 8-10
Calories per serving: 460 (1/8)
                    370 (1/10)

This fresh-tasting dessert makes an elegant finale for any dinner.

3 10-ounce packages frozen, unsweetened blueberries, thawed

¾ cup sugar

1 tablespoon lemon juice

2 envelopes unflavored gelatine

½ cup water

3 cups whipping cream

Place 1 package of the blueberries in a blender and blend at high speed for 30 seconds. Pour into a bowl and repeat with second package. Add sugar and lemon juice to puréed berries and stir until sugar dissolves. Sprinkle gelatine over water in the top of a double boiler; place over simmering water and heat until gelatine is dissolved, stirring frequently. Stir gelatine into blueberry mixture. Chill until mixture is slightly thickened and has the consistency of unbeaten egg whites. Whip 2 cups of the cream; fold into blueberry mixture and pour into a 2- to 2½-quart mold. Chill for several hours, or until set. Unmold on a plate and garnish with the remaining package of blueberries, drained. Whip the remaining cream and spread over the mousse.

Blueberry Trifle with Raspberry Jam

Preparation time: 30 minutes
Cooking time: 20 minutes
Degree of difficulty: moderate
Servings: 10-12
Calories per serving: 400 (1/10)
                    333 (1/12)

There are trifles, and there are trifles. This is a good adaptation of a traditional favorite.

1 10-ounce package frozen unsweetened blueberries, partially thawed

1 tablespoon cornstarch

3 tablespoons water

1 tablespoon grated lemon peel

2 cups milk

2 whole eggs

2 egg yolks

¼ cup sugar

1-inch piece vanilla bean

1 pound cake, cut into ½-inch slices

1 cup raspberry jam

½ cup sherry

2 bananas, thinly sliced

1 cup whipping cream, whipped

2 tablespoons toasted slivered almonds

Put blueberries in a saucepan. Combine cornstarch with water. Stir half the cornstarch mixture into the blueberries and cook over low heat until thickened (if still too thin, add the rest of the cornstarch). Cool, then stir in the lemon peel. In the top of a double boiler bring the milk to a boil. Beat the whole eggs and the egg yolks in a mixing bowl, adding sugar gradually, until lemon-colored. Take milk off heat; slowly add egg mixture, stirring constantly. Return to low heat, add vanilla bean and, stirring constantly, cook until mixture is thickened and coats the back of a spoon. Remove from heat; remove vanilla bean. Cool. Spread pound-cake slices with the raspberry jam. Pour sherry over cake. Pour half the blueberry mixture into the bottom of a large glass serving bowl. Top with pound-cake slices, then with banana slices, then with custard, and finally with remaining blueberry mixture. Chill. Just before serving, top with whipped cream and garnish with almonds.

Kitchen hint: Custard-type desserts that need to be cooled quickly and evenly should be strained into metal bowls. Set the bowl in ice water and stir frequently. The mixture will set rapidly and there won't be any lumps. You'll also be able to fold in whipped cream or eggs at exactly the right moment before setting.

Blueberry Grunt

Preparation time: 10 minutes
Cooking time: 20-25 minutes
Degree of difficulty: simple
Servings: 6
Calories per serving: 315

The odd name of this classic Nova Scotia dessert must refer to the noisy gratitude of its recipients. Baked blueberries are topped with heavy dumplings and served hot with ice cream. This recipe was contributed by Winnie Allen.

3 cups fresh or frozen blueberries
1 cup sugar
½ cup water
Pinch of allspice
2 cups all-purpose flour
¼ teaspoon salt
4 teaspoons baking powder
2 teaspoons sugar
1 cup water

Bring blueberries, sugar, water, and allspice to a boil in a saucepan. Meanwhile, blend the flour, salt, baking powder, and sugar together in a bowl. Add 1 cup of water to make a soft dough, adding a few extra tablespoons if necessary. Using a tablespoon, drop the dough on top of the boiling blueberries. Cover and reduce heat slightly. Cook, without uncovering, for 15 minutes. Serve piping hot with ice cream.

Cold Chocolate Soufflé

Preparation time: 1 hour
Chilling time: 4 hours (minimum)
Degree of difficulty: moderate
Servings: 6-8
Calories per serving: 290 (1/6)
218 (1/8)

This rich, cold dessert is excellent after a light main course.

1 cup milk
4 squares semisweet baking chocolate, broken
3 eggs, separated
4 tablespoons fruit sugar
5 tablespoons cold black coffee
1 envelope gelatine
¾ cup whipping cream

Put ½ cup of the milk and the broken chocolate in the top of a double boiler over hot water. Stir frequently so that the chocolate melts evenly and smoothly. Add the remaining milk to the pan and bring to the scalding point.

Whip the egg yolks with the fruit sugar until thick and lemon-colored. Pour the chocolate mixture into the yolks, stir, and return to the double boiler. Stir constantly over gentle heat until the mixture thickens and coats the back of a wooden spoon. Strain into a metal bowl and allow to cool.

Put the cold coffee into a small saucepan and sprinkle with gelatine. When the gelatine has softened, cook over low heat until dissolved, 3-5 minutes. Stir it quickly, but firmly, into the cold custard.

Lightly whip the cream. Whisk the egg whites until stiff. Prepare a 5-cup soufflé dish by wrapping a double thickness of wax paper (with the fold at the bottom of the dish) around the dish, leaving 2 inches above the rim. Secure the collar with string.

Fold the whipped cream and egg whites into the custard and pour into the soufflé dish. The recipe amount will be more than the dish can hold and the surplus mixture will be held by the wax paper. Refrigerate.

To remove the paper collar, hold a palette knife in boiling water for a few seconds and then run it between the double thickness of paper. The heat loosens the paper from the soufflé and it will peel away without hurting the appearance of the dessert.

Top the cold soufflé with a little whipped cream and serve in the soufflé dish.

Cold Cherry Soufflé

Preparation time: 1 hour (including cooking time)
Freezing time: 4-5 hours
Degree of difficulty: moderate
Servings: 6-8
Calories per serving: 310 (1/6)
232 (1/8)

This frozen soufflé is ideal for a busy hostess because it can be made ahead. Serve it in a large soufflé dish, or 6-8 small individual custard or demitasse cups.

¾ cup sugar
1¼ cups water
2½ cups fresh cherries, pitted
1 tablespoon unflavored gelatine
4 egg whites at room temperature
1 cup whipping cream

Butter a double piece of wax paper and tie it around the top of a buttered 1-quart soufflé dish (or make similar collars for small dishes) so that it stands about 2 inches above the top.

Combine sugar and 1 cup of water in a saucepan. Bring to the boil and simmer 5 minutes. Add pitted cherries (reserving a few for garnish) and cook for 10 minutes. Purée mixture in a blender or force it through a sieve. Soften gelatine in remaining ¼ cup water and place over hot water until dissolved. Combine dissolved gelatine and cherry mixture and cool. Place over ice or cold water and beat with rotary beater for 5 minutes. Beat egg whites until stiff but not dry. Fold egg whites and cream into cherry mixture. Pour into dish(es) and freeze for 4-5 hours. Remove from freezer 5 minutes before serving; remove paper collar(s) carefully (see Cold Chocolate Soufflé for instructions). Garnish with whole cherries.

Chestnut-Stuffed Poached Pears with Chocolate Cream and Custard Sauce

Preparation time: 20 minutes
Cooking time: 20 minutes (total)
Degree of difficulty: moderate
Servings: 6
Calories per serving: 655

It's hard to know which ingredient is the star in this wonderful combination of pears, chocolate, and chestnuts. A challenge for a compulsive cook and an excellent reward for the audience.

6 firm, ripe Bartlett pears

2 cups unsweetened pineapple juice

12 bottled chestnuts in syrup, finely chopped (available in specialty food stores)

CUSTARD SAUCE

1 cup milk

1 cup whipping cream

5 tablespoons sugar

6 egg yolks

1 teaspoon vanilla extract

1 tablespoon unsalted butter

CHOCOLATE CREAM

4 squares semisweet chocolate

1 cup whipping cream

Peel and core the pears, using a melon ball scoop to remove the core from the bottom end, leaving the pear intact, stem on. Bring pineapple juice to a boil and immerse pears; simmer for 5 minutes or until tender but not too soft. Drain and chill. Stuff the pears with the chopped chestnuts.

In the top of a double boiler, combine milk and cream. Scald. Combine sugar and egg yolks in a mixing bowl and beat until light yellow and thickened. Gradually pour the milk and cream mixture into the egg yolk mixture, stirring vigorously with a whisk. Return to double boiler and stir constantly until custard coats the spoon. *Do not overcook or custard will curdle.* Add vanilla and butter and chill.

Do not proceed to the next step until close to serving time. Melt semisweet chocolate over very low heat. Cool slightly, add to whipping cream and whip until set. Quickly spoon into individual serving dishes. Place chilled pear in the centre of each and pour custard over.

Crème Caramel à l'Orange

Preparation time: 10 minutes
Cooking time: 1 hour (total)
Degree of difficulty: moderate
Servings: 6
Calories per serving: 445

A classic dessert, easy to make and a delicious finale to any festive meal, with family or friends.

1 cup sugar

2 tablespoons water

1 large orange (or 2 medium)

4 cups milk

8 eggs

1/3 cup Cointreau or Grand Marnier liqueur

Almonds and whipping cream to garnish

Preheat oven to 300°F. Place 1/4 cup sugar and 2 tablespoons water in a saucepan; dissolve over low heat stirring constantly, then boil rapidly until caramelized to a medium brown color, being sure not to burn. Pour into an 8- to 10-inch soufflé mold; set aside to cool. Grate the peel of half the orange and add it to the milk. Heat milk until boiling, then remove from the heat. Mix eggs with remaining sugar; add the juice of the orange and the orange liqueur. Pour on hot milk, whisk thoroughly, strain, and pour into the mold. Place in a large pan containing 1/2 inch of water. Place in oven for 35-40 minutes (or about 12 minutes if you use individual molds). The custard is done when a knife inserted in the centre comes out clean. Leave in the pan to cool, then refrigerate. When ready to serve, loosen edges and unmold onto a plate. Garnish with orange slivers, almonds, and/or whipping cream.

Cinnamon Ice Cream with Raspberry Sauce

Preparation time: 20 minutes
Freezing time: 30 minutes with ice-cream maker or 6 hours in freezer
Degree of difficulty: simple
Servings: 6-8
Calories per serving: 380 (1/4)
285 (1/8)

Cinnamon marries beautifully with strawberries or raspberries (better than chocolate, in some experts' opinion) — a taste surprise.

ICE CREAM

4 egg yolks

1 cup granulated sugar

1 rounded tablespoon ground cinnamon

1 cup whipping cream

SAUCE

1 10-ounce package frozen unsweetened raspberries

1/2 cup icing sugar

Beat egg yolks, gradually adding sugar mixed with cinnamon. Beat until mixture is very thick. Whip cream, not too stiffly. Fold the mixtures together and freeze in an ice-cream maker according to the manufacturer's instructions. If you don't have a machine, freeze, and beat a couple of times at intervals of about 2 hours. To make sauce, combine raspberries and sugar in a blender until well mixed. Strain mixture through a sieve to remove seeds. Serve over ice cream.

Pour 1/2 cup hot honey over 3-4 cups of fresh or whole frozen and thawed strawberries and let rest for 1 hour before using on a strawberry shortcake.

Rice Pudding Creole

Rice Pudding Creole

Preparation time: 1 hour
Cooking time: 1 hour (total)
Setting time: 3 hours
Degree of difficulty: challenging
Servings: 10-12
Calories per serving: 580 (1/10)
                        483 (1/12)

This elegant dessert, developed by Pastry Chef Morand Dare, is scrumptious and spectacular. This adapted version is worth the extra time it takes.

CHAMPAGNE OR WINE JELLY

7 packages unflavored gelatine
2 cups cold water
½ cup sugar
Zest and juice of 1 lemon
Zest and juice of 1 orange
2 cups Canadian champagne or Canadian white wine

FRUIT SALAD

1 banana, peeled
2 oranges, peeled
1 pineapple, peeled and cored
1 mango, peeled
1 pint strawberries, hulled
1 kiwi fruit, peeled
2 tablespoons lemon juice
½ cup rum

RICE PUDDING

½ cup rice
1 vanilla bean, split in half
4 cups milk
¼ cup sugar
1 package unflavored gelatine, soaked in ¼ cup water
½ cup raisins
¼ cup rum
1 cup whipping cream, lightly whipped
½ teaspoon cinnamon

COFFEE CUSTARD SAUCE

2 cups milk
1 vanilla bean, split in half
¾ cup sugar
6 egg yolks
¾ cup coffee-flavored liqueur

Make the champagne or wine jelly. In a noncorroding pan, soak the gelatine in the water. Add the sugar, lemon, and orange juices and zests and bring to a boil. Cover, remove from heat, and let stand for 10 minutes. Return to heat and bring to a boil again. Add champagne or white wine and mix. Strain through a damp cloth that has been squeezed to remove excess water. Coat a savarin or ring mold with half the jelly and refrigerate until set; refrigerate leftover jelly to set.

Meanwhile, cut up fruit; add lemon and rum; refrigerate.

To make rice, blanch the rice in boiling water for 2 minutes; drain. Add vanilla bean to milk, stir in rice, bring to a boil, and simmer for about 45 minutes, or until the rice is cooked and has absorbed all the milk. Remove rice from heat, add the sugar and the gelatine; mix well and refrigerate until cold. Plump raisins by soaking in rum to cover; set aside.

When rice mixture is cool, fold in the lightly whipped cream, the drained raisins, and the cinnamon. Transfer the rice mixture to the jelly-lined mold; refrigerate for 3 hours or until set.

To prepare the sauce, bring the milk and the vanilla bean to a boil. Whisk the sugar and egg yolks together. Remove milk from heat and slowly whisk in the egg-yolk mixture. Return to heat and stir over low heat until thickened (the custard should be thick enough to coat the back of a spoon). Strain the mixture; cool, add liqueur and refrigerate until ready to serve.

To serve, dip mold in warm water to loosen and unmold onto a serving dish. Fill the central cavity with the fruit salad. Garnish plate with remaining jelly, chopped. Serve with coffee custard sauce.

Dessert Crêpes Filled with Chestnut Purée

Preparation and cooking time: about 1 ½ hours
Degree of difficulty: challenging
Amount: makes 25-30 crêpes
Calories per serving: 550 (2 crêpes)

CRÊPES

2 ¼ cups milk

4 large eggs

Pinch of salt

2 tablespoons sugar

1 ½ cups all-purpose flour

4 tablespoons unsalted butter, melted

CHESTNUT PURÉE

1 cup unsalted butter, softened

1 15-ounce can chestnut purée

1 cup icing sugar

2 egg yolks

2 tablespoons bourbon, rum or brandy

Sliced strawberries or kiwi for garnish

CRÈME ANGLAISE

1 ½ cups milk

1 teaspoon cornstarch

4 egg yolks

½ cup sugar

1 tablespoon bourbon, rum, or brandy

Sliced fruit for garnish

To prepare crêpes, place milk, eggs, salt, and sugar in the bowl of a food processor or blender and process until smooth. Add flour and butter, process again, and refrigerate for 1 hour. Lightly brush the bottom of a 6-inch crêpe pan with a little melted butter. Ladle 2-3 tablespoons of the batter into the crêpe pan and tilt so that the batter will spread evenly. Cook crêpe over medium heat for a few seconds or until batter is set; flip once, remove, and set aside. Repeat. Crêpes may be prepared a day ahead and stored in the refrigerator, separated by sheets of wax paper (they may also be frozen).

To prepare chestnut purée, place the butter, chestnut purée, icing sugar, egg yolks, and liquor in the bowl of a food processor or blender and process until well blended. Refrigerate about 30 minutes. Place 1 heaping tablespoon of the chestnut purée on each crêpe, roll up cigar-fashion and place seam side down on a cookie sheet lined with wax paper; place in freezer.

To prepare the crème anglaise, put the milk and cornstarch in a medium saucepan and cook, stirring over medium heat, until it boils. Whisk together the egg yolks and sugar. When the milk mixture boils, remove from heat and slowly whisk in the egg yolk mixture, stirring constantly. Place the mixture back on the stove and cook over low heat until thickened. (If the mix-

ture curdles, pass it through a sieve and return it to the heat if necessary.) Stir in the liquor. Remove crêpes from freezer at least 30 minutes before serving, garnish with sliced fruit, and serve with warm crème anglaise.

Lemon Ice Cream

Preparation time: 10 minutes
Freezing time: overnight
Degree of difficulty: simple
Servings: 6
Calories per serving: 338

Light and zingy; this easy dessert rated 15 with food testers when they were asked to grade it on a scale of 0 to 10:

3 lemons

1 ¼ cups whipping cream

1 cup milk

1 cup sugar

Grate the peel of the lemons. Mix the cream, milk and sugar thoroughly, and add the peel. Place in a covered bowl in the freezer until almost firm, about 5 hours. (It can be left overnight and then put in a warm room until it's easy to handle.) Mash with a potato masher, wooden spoon, or food processor, add the juice of 2½-3 lemons (depending on taste), mix very well, cover, and return to the freezer until firm.

Dessert Crêpes
Filled with
Chestnut Purée
(far left);
Lemon Ice
Cream

Lemon Syllabub

Soaking time: 1 hour
Preparation time: 10 minutes
Degree of difficulty: simple
Servings: 8
Calories per serving: 660

For the fainthearted whose appetites have bogged down after a heavy meal and can't summon any enthusiasm for pie.

Peel of 1 lemon, thinly cut (outer skin only)
1 cup cream sherry
1 cup Madeira wine
4 cups whipping cream
1/3 cup lemon juice
3/4 cup sugar
Nutmeg

Soak lemon peel in sherry and Madeira for at least 1 hour. Whip cream until it just begins to hold its shape. Remove peel from sherry and discard; gradually beat wine mixture, lemon juice, and sugar into cream until mixture thickens. Pour into parfait or sherbet glasses and sprinkle with nutmeg.

Marquise au Chocolat

Preparation time: 20 minutes
Cooking time: a few minutes
Chilling time: 12 hours
Degree of difficulty: moderate
Servings: 8
Calories per serving: 640

This genteel concoction of rich chocolate surrounded by ladyfingers earns its royal name from its flavor and eye appeal.

1 large package ladyfingers
1 cup strong coffee
5 ounces bitter chocolate
7 egg yolks
1 cup sugar
1 cup plus 2 tablespoons unsalted butter
1 cup cocoa
7 eggs whites, stiffly beaten
2 cups whipping cream
2 tablespoons fine sugar
1 teaspoon vanilla extract

Dip ladyfingers in the coffee and line sides and bottom of a lightly buttered 9- or 10-inch springform pan. Melt chocolate in a double boiler. Beat egg yolks and sugar until thickened and light. Cool chocolate slightly and mix into egg yolks. In a separate bowl, beat the butter until fluffy and slowly beat in cocoa. Beat together the butter mixture and the egg yolk mixture, then fold in the egg whites. Spoon into the pan and chill for 12 hours. Before serving, whip cream with fine sugar and vanilla. Remove sides from pan and spread cream over top.

Orange Charlotte

Preparation time: 1 hour
Cooking time: 5 minutes
Chilling time: 3-4 hours or overnight
Degree of difficulty: simple
Servings: 6
Calories per serving: 360

This is light and refreshing after a heavy meal.

1 envelope unflavored gelatine
1 cup fresh orange juice
1/2 cup sugar
1/2 cup water
1 generous tablespoon grated orange peel
3 tablespoons orange liqueur
2 oranges, peeled and sectioned
21 ladyfingers (or 18 3-by-1-inch slices sponge cake)
1 cup whipping cream
2 egg whites
Orange twist for garnish

Sprinkle gelatine into the orange juice to soften. Heat sugar and water in a pan until sugar is dissolved. Add orange juice mixture; place over low heat and stir constantly until gelatine dissolves, about 3 minutes. Remove from heat, stir in grated orange peel and orange liqueur. Cool and place in the refrigerator until the mixture has the consistency of unbeaten egg whites, about 30-45 minutes.

Remove all skin from the orange sections. Butter well an 8-inch mold or soufflé dish; cover the bottom with orange sections and line the sides with ladyfingers. When the orange mixture is chilled, beat it until frothy. Whip the cream until firm and beat egg whites separately until stiff. Gently fold the orange mixture into the cream, then fold in the egg whites. Carefully spoon the mixture into the mold and chill at least 3 hours. Trim any protruding ladyfingers. Garnish with an orange twist.

Middle Eastern Pancake Dessert

Preparation time: 15 minutes
Cooking time: 1 hour (total)
Degree of difficulty: moderate
Servings: 6-8
Calories per serving: 520 (1/6)
390 (1/8)

Many national cuisines include sweet pancakes, although they may be called crêpes or blintzes. This recipe is for the Middle Eastern version.

½ cup butter, melted
1 cup all-purpose flour
2 cups milk
2 eggs
½ teaspoon salt
1 tablespoon sugar
4 tablespoons melted butter

SAUCE
1 cup honey
½ cup water
1 stick cinnamon
2 tablespoons orange peel

FILLING
2 tablespoons sugar
1 cup finely chopped walnuts

Mix the ½ cup melted butter, the flour, milk, eggs, salt, and sugar in a mixing bowl with a wire whisk.

Heat a crêpe pan or 7-inch skillet and brush with butter. Pour in a thin layer of batter to just cover the bottom. Cook briefly and turn. Cook the second side briefly and turn out onto a plate. Continue until all the batter is used (depending on the size of your skillet and how thick you pour the batter, this will make about 16 pancakes).

Preheat oven to 325°F. Combine the honey, water, cinnamon, and orange peel and boil for 5 minutes. Set aside. Combine the nuts and sugar. Put a tablespoon of nut mixture in each pancake. Fold in half and place in a large, shallow baking dish or on a cookie sheet; drizzle the melted butter over. Bake for 15 minutes. Remove from the oven and drizzle with the syrup, using about 2 tablespoons for each pancake. Serve slightly warm.

Spiced Fruit in Savory Syrup

Preparation time: 20 minutes
Cooking time: 2½-3 hours
Degree of difficulty: simple
Servings: 30
Calories per serving: 175

By the time the fruit has poached in the sugar and vinegar for several hours, it's barely recognizable, but the taste is stunning. This is an excellent accompaniment for goose or turkey.

30 large peaches or pears
½ cup whole cloves (approx.)
10 cups sugar
2 cups cider vinegar
4 sticks cinnamon

Preheat oven to 325°F. Peel the peaches by dropping them into boiling water for 1 minute — the skins will slip off easily. Peel the pears with a sharp knife. Stud each piece of fruit with 3 whole cloves and place in a large roasting pan.

Combine the sugar and cider vinegar in a large bowl, pour the mixture over the fruit. Add the cinnamon sticks to the roasting pan, and bake for 2½-3 hours, or until fruit is reduced to half its original size. It will be golden to dark brown in color and quite candied in texture. Bottle in clean containers while still slightly warm. Serve with roast meat. (Will keep in the refrigerator for 2 to 3 weeks.)

Oranges in Red Wine

Preparation time: 20 minutes
Cooking time: 5 minutes
Degree of difficulty: simple
Servings: 6
Calories per serving: 345

This recipe is prepared from ingredients you can easily have on hand for last-minute dinners.

1 cup dry red wine
1 cup water
⅓ cup honey
2 cinnamon sticks
4 cloves
2 slices lemon
6 large oranges
½ pint whipping cream, whipped

Combine wine, water, honey, cinnamon, cloves, and lemon. Bring to a boil and simmer 3 minutes. Remove cloves; keep syrup hot. Peel the oranges, reserving the peel. Section the oranges, keeping the segments as whole as possible. Discard fibrous membrane. Drop orange sections into the hot syrup.

Pare away the white part of the orange peel and cut peel into very fine julienne strips. Sprinkle over the oranges; chill. Serve with sweetened whipped cream.

If eggs are stored in a refrigerator, warm them a little in your hands or bring to room temperature before trying to cook with them. Egg whites for cakes and pastry are better if they're beaten warm rather than cold.

Dropped Yorkshire Pudding with Fresh Fruit (right); Fresh Peach and Banana Sweet (below)

Dropped Yorkshire Pudding with Fresh Fruit

Preparation time: 5 minutes
Standing time: 1 hour
Cooking time: 17-23 minutes
Degree of difficulty: simple
Servings: 4-6
Calories per serving: 305 (1/4)
203 (1/6)

Usually served as an accompaniment to roast beef, Yorkshire pudding becomes an excellent dessert in this creative recipe contributed by Ann Bartok.

1 cup milk

3 eggs

2 tablespoons vegetable oil

1 cup sifted all-purpose flour

1/2 teaspoon salt

1 tablespoon lard or butter

1-1 1/2 cups fresh strawberries and kiwi or other soft fruit

In a blender or food processor combine milk, eggs, oil, flour, and salt. Blend or process for 1 minute. Let stand for 1 hour. Meanwhile, preheat oven to 400°F. Grease a 9-inch metal pie plate with lard. Heat pie plate in oven until very hot. Remove from oven, pour in batter, then arrange fruit on top. Bake for 2-3 minutes. Lower temperature to 350°F and bake for 15-20 minutes longer. Serve sprinkled with icing sugar or maple syrup.

Whole Oranges

Preparation time: 5 minutes
Steeping time: 10 days
Maturing time: 3-4 weeks
Degree of difficulty: simple
Servings: 16 (4 cups)
Calories per serving: 120

Time-consuming, but not labor-intensive — and worth it, in any case.

3 sweet oranges with peel, cut in wedges

1/2 lemon, cut in wedges

2 whole cloves

3 cups vodka

1 cup sugar

1 cup water

Place oranges, lemon, cloves, and vodka in a jar (the vodka should cover the fruit) and steep 10 days. Strain and filter. Combine sugar and water and simmer for 5 minutes. Add to fruit mixture. Mature 3-4 weeks. Place in individual bottles for gift-giving.

PHOTO BY SKIP DEAN

Fresh Peach and Banana Sweet

Preparation time: 20 minutes
Degree of difficulty: simple
Servings: 6-8
Calories per serving: 395

4 large firm bananas

4 large eggs, separated

1 tablespoon sugar

1 cup whipping cream

3 medium firm ripe peaches, peeled and sliced

1/2 cup flaked almonds, lightly toasted

Put bananas in a large bowl, add egg yolks and sugar, and mash with a fork, combining evenly. Whip cream until stiff and carefully fold half into the banana mixture. Whip egg whites until stiff and fold into remaining whipped cream. Arrange sliced peaches over the bottom of a serving dish, add banana mixture, smoothing evenly, then the egg-white-and-cream mixture. Sprinkle with almonds, cover with plastic wrap, and chill thoroughly before serving.

Kiwi Sorbet

Preparation time: 5 minutes
Freezing time: 5 hours in freezer; follow instructions for ice-cream maker
Degree of difficulty: simple
Servings: 6
Calories per serving: 142

Clean, fresh and totally ravishing to see.

4 kiwi fruit

2/3 cup simple syrup (see Note)

2 teaspoons fresh lemon juice

Peel kiwis and purée in a food processor or blender. Stir in syrup and lemon juice, pour into an ice-cream maker; freeze according to manufacturer's instructions.

To make sorbet in the freezer, pour into a metal bowl, cover, freeze until mixture is frozen 2 inches in from the sides, about 2 hours. Remove from freezer, scrape down, beat with an electric mixer until smooth. Cover bowl, return to freezer, repeat procedure 3 times at 45-minute intervals, allowing sorbet to freeze solid after final mixing. Soften at room temperature if necessary before serving.

Note: Simmer equal parts sugar and water until sugar dissolves, and cool.

The best apples for baking are firm and should hold their shape well, such as Spy, Idared, Rome, and Golden Delicious, and the best pies are also made with Spy and Idared. Gravenstein apples are good for applesauce because they mash easily, and Cortland apples are good in salads and as garnishes, since they stay white when cut.

Apple and Raisin Crisp

Preparation time: 15 minutes
Cooking time: 30-40 minutes
Degree of difficulty: simple
Servings: 6
Calories per serving: 385

Comforting, warming, and just plain good.

6 medium tart apples, peeled, cored, and sliced
3/4 cup raisins
1 cup rolled oats
1/2 cup all-purpose flour
3/4 cup brown sugar
Pinch of salt
Pinch of cinnamon
1/3 cup butter
Vanilla ice cream or whipped cream (optional)

Preheat oven to 350°F. Arrange sliced apples in a lightly buttered 8-inch-square baking pan. Sprinkle with raisins. In a small bowl, combine oats, flour, brown sugar, and seasonings. Cut in butter until mixture is crumbly and well blended. Spread mixture over apples. Bake for 30-40 minutes, or until apples are tender and topping is brown and crisp. Serve warm with ice cream or whipped cream.

Pears in Red Wine with Peppercorns

Preparation time: 10 minutes
Cooking time: 30 minutes
Degree of difficulty: simple
Servings: 8
Calories per serving: 238

Pears have been a favorite fruit for centuries, and black peppercorns were often added to stewed fruits in medieval times. In this new twist on traditional poached pears, the syrup is sweet but also has a bite.

8 firm, ripe pears, peeled, stems left on
Juice of 1 lemon
2 cups dry red wine
2 cups water
1/2 cup honey
12 whole cloves
3 cinnamon sticks
40 black peppercorns
1 piece candied ginger

In a saucepan large enough to hold the pears, combine lemon juice, wine, water, honey, cloves, cinnamon, peppercorns, and candied ginger. Bring to a boil. Add pears and poach over medium heat for 10-15 minutes, or until tender. Remove pears carefully with a slotted spoon. Strain syrup, then boil to thicken slightly. Spoon syrup over; serve warm or cold.

Pumpkin Pudding

Preparation time: 20 minutes
Cooking time: 1 hour (total)
Degree of difficulty: moderate
Servings: 6
Calories per serving: 300

Dark rum lends good flavor and a grown-up touch to this traditional Thanksgiving custard.

1 1/2 pounds fresh pumpkin
2 eggs, separated
3/4 cup light cream
4 tablespoons dark rum
1/2 cup light brown sugar, packed
1/2 teaspoon each ground ginger, cloves, and nutmeg
1/4 teaspoon cinnamon
1 cup whipping cream, whipped and flavored with additional rum

Preheat oven to 350°F. Remove the seeds and rind from the pumpkin and cut meat into small pieces. Cook in boiling water until tender. Drain, cool slightly, then purée in a blender or food processor. Beat the egg yolks until thick and lemon-colored. Beat the egg whites until stiff. Combine the yolks with the pumpkin purée, cream, rum, brown sugar, and spices. Mix thoroughly and fold in the beaten egg whites. Place the mixture in a buttered 5-cup soufflé dish and bake for 40-45 minutes. Serve at once with sweetened, flavored whipped cream.

Silvia Wilson's Frozen Lemon Mousse with Sauce Cardinale

Preparation time: about 30 minutes
Chilling time: 8 hours or overnight
Degree of difficulty: simple
Servings: 6
Calories per serving: 568

Cuisine '85 Winner

It wasn't only our judges for the 1985 culinary contest who enjoyed this lovely dessert, but also *Homemaker's* staffers, who declared it number one after tasting more than a dozen possible semi-finalist desserts.

1 tablespoon vegetable oil
2-3 tablespoons ground almonds
4 egg yolks
½ cup fresh lemon juice
¼ cup sugar
1½ tablespoons grated lemon peel
4 egg whites
⅛ teaspoon cream of tartar
⅛ teaspoon salt
¾ cup sugar
1½ cups whipping cream, whipped
Fresh fruit such as kiwi and strawberries for garnish

SAUCE CARDINALE

1 15-ounce package frozen unsweetened raspberries, thawed
⅔ cup sugar
2 tablespoons kirsch or Cointreau

Oil the bottom and sides of an 8-inch springform pan and sprinkle with ground almonds, shaking the pan so that the almonds cover the bottom and sides completely. Combine the egg yolks, lemon juice. ¼ cup sugar and lemon peel in a large bowl and mix well: set aside. Beat the egg whites until foamy. Add the cream of tartar and salt and continue beating until soft peaks form. Gradually add the ¾ cup sugar, beating until egg whites are glossy and stand in stiff

peaks. Gently fold the egg whites and whipped cream into the egg-yolk mixture. Carefully spoon into the pan. Cover with foil and freeze at least 8 hours.

To prepare the sauce, press the berries through a sieve to remove the seeds. Place berries in the jar of a blender; add the sugar and kirsch and blend until smooth. (For a thicker sauce, omit some of the raspberry syrup.) Chill. At serving time, remove frozen mousse from pan and garnish with sliced fruit. Spoon sauce over individual servings.

Apple and Raisin Noodle Pudding

Preparation time: 20 minutes
Cooking time: 45 minutes
Degree of difficulty: simple
Servings: 4-6
Calories per serving: 550 (1/4)
*   367 (1/6)*

This traditional recipe is good hot or cold. Serve with sour cream or yogurt.

½ pound dried egg noodles
½ cup raisins
6 eggs, slightly beaten
¼ cup butter, melted
¼ teaspoon cinnamon
3 tart apples, peeled, cored, and chopped
Salt and freshly ground pepper to taste

Preheat oven to 375°F. Cook noodles according to package instructions, drain in a collander, and rinse well with cold water to remove excess starch. Soak raisins in a cup of boiling water to soften. Let stand for 10 minutes, then drain. Combine the remaining ingredients with the noodles, including the raisins, mix well, and pour into a buttered casserole dish. Bake for 45 minutes, or until crisp and browned on top.

Chocolate Orange Mousse

Preparation time: 30 minutes
Cooking time: 30 minutes
Chilling time: 5 hours
Degree of difficulty: simple
Servings: 6
Calories per serving: 486
(without whipped cream)

12 ounces semisweet chocolate
⅓ cup orange liqueur
2 tablespoons grated orange peel
6 eggs, separated
Pinch of cream of tartar and/or salt
½ cup superfine sugar
Whipped cream (optional)
Grated orange peel for garnish

Melt the chocolate in the top of a double boiler, or use microwave. Stir in the liqueur and orange peel; add the egg yolks 1 at a time, mixing constantly to prevent scrambling the eggs. Set mixture aside to cool to room temperature. Beat the egg whites until frothy; add the cream of tartar and/or salt and beat until the egg whites are almost stiff. Add the sugar and continue beating until stiff. Gently fold the egg whites into the chocolate mixture. Pour into an attractive serving bowl or individual dessert dishes and chill at least 5 hours. Top each serving with whipped cream and orange peel if desired.

Microwave short cuts
heat milk, water, or stock in a measuring cup or microwave-safe cup, rather than messing up a pan on the stove; liquefy crystallized honey by removing jar lid and heating 30-60 seconds; melt butter, ¼ cup will take 20-40 seconds; melt chocolate, using half power and heating only until soft, when sweet or semisweet chocolate will not have lost its shape; reheat coffee, taking care not to boil it and lose the delicate flavor — a large mug takes about 1½-2 minutes.

Two-Liqueur Strawberries

Preparation time: 10 minutes
Degree of difficulty: simple
Servings: 6
Calories per serving: 150

The combination is synergistic — the total effect is more than the sum of the two acting independently.

4 cups strawberries, hulled and washed (or thawed)

6 tablespoons sugar

4 tablespoons crème de cacao

4 tablespoons orange liqueur

Two or 3 hours before serving, gently toss all ingredients together lightly in a serving bowl. Let stand at room temperature; do not chill. The strawberries may be served on their own or as a topping for cheesecake.

PHOTO BY GARY WHITE

Toffee Berries

Preparation time: 5 minutes
Cooking time: 5-10 minutes
Degree of difficulty: moderate
Servings: 2-3
Calories per serving: 630 (1/2)
*   420 (1/3)*

Suzanne Demers of L'Âtre restaurant on the Île d'Orléans is responsible for this whimsical approach to strawberries.

10-12 large strawberries

1½ cups maple syrup

Wash berries carefully, leaving stems and hulls on, and thoroughly pat dry with paper toweling. Lightly oil a cookie sheet. Boil maple syrup in a small, deep saucepan until a candy thermometer registers 240°F. Remove pan from heat. Working quickly, dip berries into syrup, one at a time. Remove from syrup and put on cookie sheet to harden, making sure the berries do not touch each other. When cool, skewer each berry on a toothpick. Fresh cherries can be used, but do not make either version more than 2-3 hours before serving, or on a humid day.

PHOTO BY TIM SAUNDERS

White Chocolate Mousse with Raspberry Sauce

Preparation time: 15 minutes
Cooking time: a few minutes
Chilling time: overnight
Degree of difficulty: simple
Servings: 4
Calories per serving: 265

Plain chocolate may be substituted in this beautiful recipe from the William Tell Restaurant in Vancouver, but do try to find good white chocolate in a specialty store — the subtlety of taste and the contrast in color make a fascinating dessert.

3 ounces white Swiss chocolate
2 tablespoons plus 1 ½ teaspoons warm milk
1 egg white
Few drops fresh lemon juice
Pinch of salt
½ cup whipping cream, beaten until stiff
Chocolate shavings

RASPBERRY SAUCE

1 cup fresh or frozen raspberries
1 ½ teaspoons water
2 tablespoons sugar
1 tablespoon fresh lemon juice
1 ½ teaspoons light rum
A few fresh raspberries

Melt chocolate in the top of a double boiler or in a microwave oven. Add the milk, stirring until smooth. Cool the mixture to room temperature.

Beat the egg white with lemon juice and salt until it forms stiff peaks. Fold into the chocolate mixture, then fold in the ½ cup whipped cream (reserving 1 tablespoon for garnish). Divide the mousse into small soufflé dishes. Refrigerate, covered, overnight.

PHOTO BY TIM SAUNDERS

To make the sauce bring the raspberries and water to a boil. Remove from the heat and put in a blender. Add the sugar, lemon juice, and rum and blend until smooth. Strain through a sieve and chill.

Unmold the mousse onto individual chilled plates. Garnish each with a ring of shaved chocolate. Surround with raspberry sauce. Top with a cream rosette and a fresh raspberry.

White Chocolate Mousse with Raspberry Sauce

Dried Fruit Compote

Preparation time: 5 minutes
Cooking time: 15 minutes
Degree of difficulty: simple
Servings: 6-8
Calories per slice: 215 (1/6)
160 (1/8)

¼ pound each dried apples, apricots, prunes and figs
1 ½ cups water
4 thin slices lemon, seeds removed
¼ cup honey
2 tablespoons dry white wine, dark rum or brandy
½ cup whipping cream, whipped

Place fruit in a large saucepan. Add the water and bring to a boil. Reduce heat. Add lemon slices and honey and simmer 10 minutes until the fruit has swollen. Add the liquor and cook 5 minutes more. Remove lemon slices. Transfer fruit to a bowl and cool to room temperature. Serve with whipped cream.

For lovers of cream and whiskey liqueurs, here's a recipe to experiment with: In a blender, pour ¼ cup sweetened condensed milk, ¼ cup whipping cream, ⅓ cup blended whiskey, ½ teaspoon vanilla extract, ½ teaspoon chocolate syrup, ¼ teaspoon instant coffee. Whir until well mixed and chill in the refrigerator. It yields 6 1-ounce servings in small liqueur glasses, and can be adjusted to taste. If you like it, you could increase the quantities and bottle the mixture.

Iced Irish Coffee

Preparation time: 5 minutes
Degree of difficulty: simple
Servings: 4
Calories per serving: 200

2 cups cold double-strength coffee

8 teaspoons sugar

½ cup Irish whiskey

½ cup whipping cream, whipped

Put ½ cup coffee in each of 4 glasses. Add 2 teaspoons sugar to each, and stir to dissolve. Add 2 tablespoons or more whiskey to each, then fill glasses with ice cubes and top with whipped cream. (For hot Irish coffee, eliminate ice cubes and use hot coffee.)

Mexican Coffee

Preparation time: a few minutes
Degree of difficulty: simple
Servings: 4
Calories per serving: 125

4 teaspoons chocolate syrup

2 cups strong, hot coffee

½ cup whipping cream, whipped and lightly sweetened

Freshly grated nutmeg

4 3-inch cinnamon sticks or dash of ground cinnamon

For each serving: Put 1 teaspoon chocolate syrup into ½ cup strong, hot coffee. Top with sweetened whipped cream. Dust with freshly grated nutmeg and insert a cinnamon stick into each cup or lightly dust with cinnamon.

Cardinal Strawberries

Preparation time: 10 minutes
Cooking time: 2 minutes
Degree of difficulty: simple
Servings: 4
Calories per serving: 210

A red raspberry cloak adds festivity to this season's welcome strawberries.

1 quart fresh strawberries

¼ cup raspberry jam, pushed through sieve

2 tablespoons honey

¼ cup water

1 tablespoon kirsch

¼ cup slivered, blanched almonds

Wash and hull the strawberries. Combine the jam, honey and water in a saucepan and simmer about 2 minutes. Add the kirsch and chill. Arrange the strawberries in 4 individual serving dishes. Pour the chilled raspberry sauce over the fruit and sprinkle with the slivered almonds.

Stuffed Peaches

Preparation time: 15 minutes
Cooking time: 30 minutes
Degree of difficulty: simple
Servings: 6
Calories per serving: 195

These can be served warm or cold, with whipped cream.

6 ripe, firm peaches, unpeeled

7 almond macaroons (available in Italian stores, or substitute similar macaroons)

2 tablespoons sugar

2 egg yolks

3 tablespoons butter, melted

½ cup light rum

Preheat oven ot 350°F Halve the peaches and remove the pits. Finely chop macaroons, or crush with a rolling pin, and mix with the sugar, egg yolks, and a little butter. Fill the peach cavities with the mixture. Place peach halves in a buttered baking dish and drizzle with melted butter. Bake for 30 minutes, basting with rum and pan juices.

Fresh Strawberry Ice Cream

Preparation time: 5 minutes
Cooking time: a few minutes
Freezing time: 4 hours
Standing time: 2 hours
Degree of difficulty: simple
Servings: 4-6
Calories per serving: 380 (1/4)
253 (1/6)

It's the very best kind.

15 large marshmallows

1 cup crushed fresh strawberries

1 cup whipping cream

1 cup sliced strawberries

2 tablespoons of honey or 3 tablespoons strawberry jam

Quarter marshmallows and melt in top of double boiler with crushed strawberries. Cool. Whip cream and add to cooled strawberry mixture, then pour into refrigerator freezer tray and freeze, beating when half frozen, every 2 hours.

Sweeten sliced strawberries with honey or strawberry jam, and let stand a few hours. Serve as a sauce for the ice cream.

Ricotta Pears

Preparation time: 5 minutes
Degree of difficulty: simple
Servings: 6
Calories per serving: 115

The wide availability of this Italian cheese means a welcome '80s version of that dieter's favorite, cottage cheese and fruit.

3 ripe pears, cored and halved

3 tablespoons lime juice

1 cup ricotta cheese or low-fat ricotta

1 tablespoon vanilla extract

1 small piece candied ginger, sliced thinly into 6 pieces

1 tablespoon unsweetened shredded coconut, toasted

Rub cut surface of pear halves with lime juice to prevent discoloration. Combine ricotta with vanilla and spoon into the pear halves. Top with a candied ginger slice and toasted coconut.

Scented Geranium Floating Islands

Preparation time: 5 minutes
Cooking time: 20 minutes
Chilling time: 2 hours
Degree of difficulty: simple
Servings: 6
Calories per serving: 140

An unusual twist on the traditional custard and poached meringue dessert. Scented geraniums are now available in specialty garden centres — grow your own flavoring!

2 cups milk
3 rose geranium leaves
3 egg yolks
¼ cup sugar
⅛ teaspoon salt
1 teaspoon vanilla extract
3 egg whites
2 tablespoons icing sugar

For the custard, scald milk with geranium leaves. Beat egg yolks slightly and add sugar and salt. Gradually stir in the scalded milk. Cook over low heat, stirring until custard coats the spoon. Cool. Remove leaves and add vanilla. For the meringue, beat egg whites until very stiff, gradually adding icing sugar. Pour the custard into a bowl and place 6 islands of meringue on the custard. Serve well chilled.

NOTES

EGGS AND CHEESE

There is no food more versatile than the egg and, unless you have a particular aversion or an allergy to them, they can provide an infinite variety of dishes for your cooking repertoire.

Eggs are cooked in so many ways in different countries that it would take a computer to add them all up. As well, they provide substance in mayonnaise, cakes, and sauces; enrich ice creams and milkshakes; add to the food value of almost anything; and make the soufflé a possible dream. They're low in calories (about 80 per large egg). White and brown eggs are the same in flavor and nutrition content, although many people think brown eggs look prettier.

The freshest eggs are, of course, the best, unless you're a hard-cooker for potato salad and egg salad sandwiches, in which case use eggs a few days old — the shells won't stick to the egg when being peeled. The tiniest speck of yolk will prevent whites from beating properly, so remove any with a piece of paper towel. Egg whites beat light if they're at room temperature, and there's nothing to make better volume than a copper bowl and balloon whisk (next best is a rotary hand beater, but not a food processor).

Cheese and eggs go together like a horse and carriage, but cheese stands well enough on its own to make any number of interesting dishes, from Welsh rarebit made with beer, through cheese fondue (a wonderful supper dish served with crusty bread and a crisp green salad — don't forget, the person who eats the last piece of bread gets a kiss), main course soufflés, and, in the case of cottage and cream cheeses, desserts like blintzes and cheesecakes.

Sweet Red Pepper Tart (see recipe page 70)

Pie crusts get soggy when making custard and cream pies if the custard bakes at a lower temperature than is required by the pastry. If they're baked simultaneously, the custard makes the crust soggy before it has a chance to get crisp.

You can partially prebake the pastry shell at 425°F until golden, then cool and moisture-proof the shell with a glaze of 1 egg white beaten with 1 tablespoonful of water. Then add filling and bake at the temperature required in your recipe. Or you can prebake the pie shell, butter a pie plate the same size, bake the custard in the buttered plate, cool until lukewarm, and slide it into the prebaked crust (it will slide as long as it's still warm.)

Sweet Red Pepper Tart

Preparation time: 20 minutes
Cooking time: about 1 hour
Degree of difficulty: simple
Servings: 8
Calories per serving: 380

This makes a wonderful brunch or light supper dish, with a green salad accompaniment, and two of them would anchor a party buffet table.

1 10-inch pie crust
1 tablespoon Dijon mustard
3 tablespoons unsalted butter
2 onions, finely chopped
1 clove garlic, minced
3 large sweet red peppers, diced
1 green pepper, diced (optional)
1 cup grated Swiss cheese
3 tablespoons chopped fresh parsley or basil
4 eggs
1 cup whipping cream
1/2 cup cream
1 teaspoon salt
1/4 teaspoon freshly ground pepper
Pinch each nutmeg and cayenne pepper

Preheat oven to 450°F. Bake crust 10 minutes, remove and reduce heat to 350°F. Brush bottom of crust with mustard. Melt butter in a frying pan and sauté onions and garlic over medium heat until tender, about 10 minutes. Add peppers and cook 6 to 8 minutes longer, until tender. Cool slightly. Spread vegetable mixture in the pie shell and cover with cheese. Sprinkle with parsley or basil.

Beat eggs with both creams; add salt, pepper, nutmeg and cayenne. Pour over vegetable mixture. Bake 30 to 40 minutes, until top is golden brown and slightly puffy. Cool 10 minutes before serving.

Alsatian Onion Pie

Preparation time: 30 minutes
Cooking time: 50 minutes (total)
Degree of difficulty: moderate
Servings: 6
Calories per serving: 510

Customers at Le Crocodile in Vancouver won't let chef Michel Jacob take this flavorful entrée off the menu. It also makes a good supper dish accompanied by a mixed green salad.

PASTRY

1 cup all-purpose flour
1/2 cup cold butter
1 egg yolk
4 to 6 tablespoons ice-cold water

To prepare the pastry, place the flour in a bowl and gradually cut in butter with a pastry blender or 2 knives until it is in small pieces. Lightly beat egg yolk with 2 tablespoons of the cold water. Sprinkle 1 tablespoon at a time over the flour mixture, stirring lightly with a fork, using only as little additional cold water as necessary to form a smooth dough. Roll out dough, fit into a 9-inch deep-dish pie plate, and chill.

FILLING

3 medium onions, sliced
1 tablespoon butter
1 tablespoon vegetable oil
2 slices bacon, cut into 1-inch pieces
1 cup thick béchamel sauce
Salt and freshly ground pepper to taste
Ground nutmeg to taste
1/2 cup whipping cream
1/3 cup dry white wine
4 eggs

For the filling, sauté onions in butter and oil in a skillet over low heat for 20 minutes, stirring frequently, until they are soft but not brown. Preheat oven to 400°F.

While onions are cooking, bring 2 cups of water to a boil in a small saucepan. Add bacon pieces and cook for 2 minutes. Drain immediately and set aside. Remove onions from heat and add béchamel sauce, salt, pepper, nutmeg, whipping cream and white wine. Stir until smooth. Beat in eggs, one at a time. Stir in bacon pieces. Pour mixture into pastry shell and bake for 25-30 minutes, or until pie is golden brown.

THICK BÉCHAMEL SAUCE

Preparation time: 1 minute
Cooking time: 5 minutes
Degree of difficulty: simple
Amount: makes 1 cup

3 tablespoons butter
3 tablespoons all-purpose flour
1 cup milk
Salt and freshly ground white pepper to taste

For the béchamel sauce, melt butter in a small saucepan over medium heat. Remove from heat and stir in flour. Return to heat and cook 2-3 minutes, stirring constantly. Gradually add milk off the heat, whisking constantly until sauce is smooth. Cook over low heat for 3 minutes until thick. Season with salt and pepper.

Beggars' Purses

Preparation time: 20 minutes
Cooking time: 1 hour (total)
Standing time,
  crème fraîche: 28 hours
  crêpe batter: 1 hour
Degree of difficulty: moderate
Servings: 8-10 generously, as an appetizer or first course
Calories per serving: 440 (1/4)
                      352 (1/10)

These little crêpe pouches, filled with crème fraîche and caviar, are tied with chives. The recipe is from Jeraldene Ballon of Toronto's Dr. Cheese and the Cake Lady bakery.

| 1 cup whipping cream |
| 1 cup sour cream |
| 3 eggs |
| ¼ teaspoon salt |
| 2 cups all-purpose flour |
| 2 cups milk |
| ¼ cup butter, melted, or vegetable (not olive) oil |
| 2 tablespoons vegetable (not olive) oil |
| 1 small (3½ ounce) jar Canadian black caviar or Danish lumpfish caviar |
| 12 fresh chives, each at least 6 inches long and split lengthwise (the green part of green onions may be substituted) |

To prepare crème fraîche, whisk together the heavy cream and sour cream. Cover loosely with plastic wrap and let stand in a warm place overnight or until thickened (this may take up to 24 hours). Refrigerate for at least 4 hours.

To prepare crêpes, combine eggs, salt, flour, milk, and melted butter in a blender. Blend until smooth (about 1 minute). Refrigerate batter at least 1 hour; if it is too thick, thin with 1-2 tablespoons milk. Place a small skillet or crêpe pan over medium to high heat. Brush with a little of the 2 tablespoons vegetable oil. When the pan is hot, pour in approximately 2 tablespoons of the crêpe batter, tilting the pan to spread the batter thinly over the surface. Cook 1-2 minutes, then turn and cook other side. Repeat until all the batter is used up. Store crêpes by stacking them in a pile, each separated by either wax paper or aluminum foil.

To assemble, place 1 heaping teaspoon of crème fraîche in the centre of each crêpe. Place a smaller amount (about ½ teaspoon) of caviar on top of the crème fraîche. Carefully draw up the crêpe around the mixture to form a purse or pouch. Wrap the split length of 1 chive twice around the top of each pouch; tie with a double knot. Trim the tops of each crêpe; snip the loose ends of the chives. The pouches should be small. Arrange 2-3 on individual dishes with wedges of lemon.

Baked Brie

Preparation time: 15 minutes
Cooking time: 45 minutes
Degree of difficulty: moderate
Servings: 75
Calories per serving: 170

Leona Chase is a cheese expert and caterer. She suggests choosing slightly underripe Brie (baking the cheese ripens it) and looking for a firmer centre and a snow-white rind.

| 1 wheel Brie (5-6 pounds) |
| ½ cup sweet butter |
| 1 cup demerara or dark brown sugar |
| ½ cup chopped walnuts |
| ½ cup raisins |
| 1 package frozen puff pastry, thawed |
| 2 apples (preferably Northern Spy), peeled, cored, and sliced |
| 2 eggs, beaten |
| 2 tablespoons whipping cream |

Preheat oven to 350°F. Melt butter in a saucepan. Mix in sugar, walnuts, and raisins; stir well. Roll out puff pastry until it is large enough to completely enclose the cheese. Spread aluminum foil on a cookie sheet. Drape pastry over cookie sheet and place Brie in centre. Pat sugar mixture on top of cheese. Top with sliced apples. Enclose in pastry by bringing pastry ends up and over top of Brie. Seal well by pinching pastry, decorate with leftover cut-out pastry shapes. Mix eggs and cream together and paint pastry with the mixture. Bake about 45 minutes or until pastry is puffed and golden.

Cheese and Mushroom Frittata

Preparation time: 30 minutes
Cooking time: 15 minutes
Degree of difficulty: simple
Servings: 4
Calories per serving: 332

An admirable example of a supper dish. Just add a green salad.

| ½ ounce dried porcini or cèpe mushrooms |
| ½ cup boiling water |
| 2 tablespoons light olive oil |
| 1 slice bread |
| 7 large eggs, beaten |
| 2½ tablespoons minced onion |
| 1 small red pepper, finely chopped |
| 4 ounces Mozzarella cheese, diced |
| ½ teaspoon salt |
| ⅓ cup minced parsley |

Combine mushrooms, water, and 1 teaspoon of the olive oil in a small bowl. Soak 20 minutes or until soft. Drain, reserving liquid; chop mushrooms and set aside. Preheat oven to 400°F. Soak bread in mushroom liquid, then mash with a fork. Place eggs in a bowl and add bread and mushrooms.

Meanwhile, heat 2 teaspoons of remaining oil in a small skillet, add onion and red pepper, and sauté 1 minute. Let cool and add to egg mixture with Mozzarella, salt, and ¼ teaspoon of the parsley. Heat remaining oil in a nonstick 9-inch omelet pan or skillet with an ovenproof handle. Pour in egg mixture. Set on the top rack of the oven and bake until set, about 12 minutes. Gently loosen edges with a rubber spatula and slide frittata onto a serving dish. Sprinkle with parsley, cut into wedges, and serve at once.

Marriages have been swayed by the arguments surrounding the eating of cheese rind, particularly Brie: should you or shouldn't you? The French cheese authority *Larousse des Fromages* says it's simply a question of personal taste. Pierre Androuët, head of a prestigious cheese store and restaurant in Paris, disagrees. The rind, he says, holds the developing mold and yeast of the cheese, and can give off an alkaline odor. It's up to you, except that the rind of such hard cheeses as Emmenthal and Gruyère should always be trimmed off.

Smoked Salmon and Onion Cheesecake

Smoked Salmon and Onion Cheesecake

Preparation time: 20 minutes
Cooking time: 1 hour 40 minutes
Cooling time: 3 hours
Degree of difficulty: moderate
Servings: 12-20
Calories per serving: 400 (1/12)
240 (1/20)

Savory cheesecakes are a trend. Delicious and easy to make. We suggest it as an *hors d'oeuvre*, but it's also wonderful for lunch with a salad.

3 8-ounce packages plus 4 ounces cream cheese at room temperature

4 large eggs

⅓ cup whipping cream

⅓ cup fine breadcrumbs

¼ cup plus 3 tablespoons freshly grated Parmesan cheese

3 tablespoons butter

½ cup chopped onion

½ cup chopped green pepper

⅓ pound smoked salmon, diced

½ cup grated Gruyère cheese

Salt and freshly ground pepper to taste

Preheat oven to 300°F. Place the cream cheese, eggs, and cream in the bowl of an electric mixer. Beat ingredients until blended and smooth. Set aside. Butter the inside of an 8-inch springform pan; sprinkle the inside with breadcrumbs combined with ¼ cup Parmesan cheese. Shake the crumbs around the bottom and sides until coated; shake out excess crumbs. Heat butter in a frying pan and sauté onion and green pepper. Fold the salmon, Gruyère, remaining Parmesan, and sautéed onion and green pepper into the cheesecake mixture; salt and pepper to taste. Pour batter into the pan and shake gently to level the mixture. Make a bain-marie: place the pan in a slightly larger pan and pour boiling water into the larger pan to about 2 inches. Bake 1 hour and 40 minutes, turn oven off, and leave cheesecake in oven 1 hour more. Lift springform pan out of its water bath and place on a rack to cool at least 2 hours. Unmold.

Smoked Salmon and Onion Cheesecake

Hasty Cheese Loaf

Preparation time: 10 minutes
Cooking time: 10-15 minutes
Degree of difficulty: simple
Servings: 6-8
Calories per serving: 260 (1/6)
195 (1/8)

Serve with scrambled eggs for brunch, or with soup for supper.

1 cup shredded Cheddar cheese

¼ cup mayonnaise

1 loaf French bread

Preheat oven to 425°F. Slice bread into thick slices, not cutting through bottom crust. Moisten cheese with mayonnaise. Spread cheese between slices and wrap loaf in aluminum foil. Heat in oven for 10-15 minutes.

Scrambled Eggs New Orleans

Preparation time: 5 minutes
Cooking time: 5-10 minutes
Degree of difficulty: simple
Servings: 2
Calories per serving: 315

1 small green pepper

1 small tomato

1 tablespoon butter or margarine

1 cup drained canned corn kernels

4 eggs

Salt and freshly ground pepper to taste

Dice pepper and tomato. Sauté in butter or margarine for 1-2 minutes. Add corn kernels. Beat eggs with salt and pepper. Pour on top of vegetable mixture and scramble together. Serve with buttered rice or a green salad.

Ruffled Cheese Torte

Preparation time: 15 minutes
Cooking time: 45 minutes (total)
Degree of difficulty: simple
Servings: 6
Calories per serving: 830

Beautiful with its undulating ruffles of pasta and oozing with melting cheese, this excellent recipe from the Dino De Laurentiis Foodshow in New York may be served with a green salad dressed with the freshest of olive oil, garlic, and lemon juice.

1 pound ruffled lasagna

5 tablespoons butter

¼ pound thinly sliced Gruyère cheese

¼ pound thinly sliced Fontina cheese

¼ pound thinly sliced Mozzarella cheese

¼ pound freshly grated Parmesan cheese

WHITE SAUCE

4 tablespoons butter

4 tablespoons all-purpose flour

3 cups milk

Salt and freshly ground pepper to taste

Freshly grated nutmeg

2 teaspoons kirsch

Cook lasagna in a large amount of boiling salted water until *al dente*. Drain and coat with butter. Place in a deep, buttered pan, alternating a layer of lasagna and a layer of cheese; first the Gruyère, second the Fontina, third the Mozzarella, and last, the Parmesan.

Preheat oven to 375°F. Make a thin white sauce by melting butter and stirring in the flour. Cook for 2 minutes, then add milk off the heat. Stir and heat until thickened and season with salt, pepper, and nutmeg. Add the kirsch.

Pour the sauce over the layered lasagna and bake in oven until the cheeses have melted and the topping is golden (about 25 minutes).

PHOTO BY TIM SAUNDERS

Ruffled Cheese Torte

Cheese Crêpes

Preparation time: 45 minutes
Cooking time: 30 minutes
Degree of difficulty: moderate
Amount: makes about 1½ dozen
Calories per crêpe: 225

Delicious but, alas, fattening. On occasion, calories are worth it.

9 eggs

2 cups milk

¼ cup light cream

6 tablespoons butter

1½ cups all-purpose flour

1 teaspoon salt

4 cups cottage cheese (2 cups creamed and 2 uncreamed)

2 egg yolks

½ teaspoon salt

2 teaspoons chopped dill

1½ cups whipping cream

1 tablespoon chopped onion or chives

1 teaspoon chopped fresh dill

Beat eggs; add milk, ¼ cup light cream, and 4 tablespoons melted butter. Add flour and salt. Beat well. Pour batter into pitcher. Mix together cheese, egg yolks, salt, and 2 teaspoons dill.

Pour batter into crêpe pan (or onto heavy griddle), about 2 tablespoonfuls at a time. Swirl pan to make crêpes spread and become thin. When very light brown on one side, turn and cook 1 minute on other side. Spread cheese filling on each crêpe. Roll up and place in a large buttered casserole. Dot with remaining butter. Preheat oven to 350°F. Heat together cream, chopped onion, and dill. Spoon over crêpes. Bake for 30 minutes.

Eggs should be cooked slowly, since their high protein content will toughen over a high heat. Scrambled eggs are creamier if cooked in a double boiler.

Crab and Bacon Quiche

Preparation time: 30 minutes
Cooking time: 40 minutes (total)
Degree of difficulty: simple
Servings: 6
Calories per serving: 550

One-batch single-crust pie dough: the richer the pastry, the more luscious the quiche.

1 cup milk

1 cup whipping cream

½ pound grated Swiss cheese

4 eggs

Salt and freshly ground white pepper to taste

Dash of cayenne

6 slices bacon, partially cooked and diced

½ cup canned crabmeat, drained and crumbled

Preheat oven to 450°F. Roll out pastry and line a quiche pan or 9-inch pie plate. Bake crust for 10 minutes. Remove and set aside.

Reduce oven temperature to 350°F. Scald the milk and cream and seasonings; reduce the heat and blend in the cheese. Remove from heat and beat in the eggs one at a time. Arrange the bacon pieces and crabmeat over the pie shell and pour on the cheese mixture. Bake for 30 minutes or until a knife inserted in middle comes out clean.

Eggs Florentine

Preparation time: 20 minutes
Cooking time: 5-10 minutes
Degree of difficulty: simple
Servings: 2
Calories per serving: 575

The yellow yolk and the green spinach make this dish of quite common ingredients special. Serve for breakfast or brunch with fresh orange juice and warm rolls with fresh butter.

3 tablespoons butter

3 tablespoons all-purpose flour

½ cup milk

½ cup light cream

Salt and freshly ground pepper to taste

1 pound spinach, cooked and puréed

Pinch of nutmeg

4 poached eggs

¼ cup grated Parmesan cheese

Preheat oven to 400°F. In a saucepan melt the butter, add the flour, and whisk until blended. Scald the milk and cream and add to the butter-flour mixture, stirring vigorously with the whisk until thickened. Season to taste with salt and pepper. Combine the hot, drained spinach with ⅓ cup of the sauce and season with nutmeg. Pour the spinach mixture into a shallow oven-proof casserole and arrange the eggs on top. Spoon the remaining sauce over the eggs, sprinkle with grated Parmesan and bake until brown, or brown lightly under the broiler.

Cheddar Eggs in Tomatoes Florentine

Preparation time: 45 minutes
Cooking time: 7 minutes
Degree of difficulty: simple
Servings: 6
Calories per serving: 205

A perfect dish for Easter brunch.

6 firm, ripe tomatoes

Salt

6 teaspoons butter, melted

6 eggs

6 tablespoons grated Cheddar cheese

1 pound fresh spinach

Preheat oven to 400°F. Cut a slice from the top of each tomato and, using a grapefruit knife, release the pulp. Remove pulp, salt the insides lightly, and invert on a rack. Let drain for 30 minutes. To prepare spinach, trim stems and wash leaves thoroughly. Place in a 2-quart saucepan and cook for about 5 minutes without adding any water (the water that clings to the leaves is sufficient). Add salt and pepper to taste. Don't add butter — the butter, egg yolk, and cheese in the tomato are ample flavoring. Put ½ teaspoon butter in each tomato and arrange in a lightly buttered baking dish. Bake for 10 minutes. Break 1 egg into each tomato; pour ½ teaspoon melted butter over each egg, and salt the egg whites lightly. Cover loosely with foil.

Bake tomatoes for 7 minutes, or until the egg whites are just set (don't overcook, or the yolks will become hard). Top each egg with 1 tablespoon of grated Cheddar and a dot of soft butter. Place under a preheated broiler for 1 minute, or until the cheese is melted and the whites are set. Serve on a bed of cooked spinach.

Tomato Cheese Soufflé

Preparation time: 10 minutes
Cooking time: 1 hour
Degree of difficulty: moderate
Servings: 6
Calories per serving: 450

Soufflés are splendidly awe-inspiring, so don't tell anyone how easy this one is. With a tossed salad, it makes a wonderful supper.

1 28-ounce can tomatoes
½ cup butter or margarine
½ cup all-purpose flour
2 teaspoons salt
½ teaspoon paprika
Pinch of cayenne
2 cups grated sharp Cheddar cheese
8 eggs, separated

Drain tomatoes and put through a food mill or blender, adding some of the drained liquid if necessary to make 2 cups tomatoes. Melt butter in the top of a double boiler over simmering water. Add flour and seasonings, mix well, and cook a few minutes until flour is absorbed. Add cheese gradually and stir until melted. Stir in tomatoes and cook, stirring, until sauce is thick and smooth. Remove from heat.

Preheat oven to 475°F. Beat egg yolks until light and vigorously stir in a small amount of tomato-cheese sauce. Stir yolks into remaining sauce. Beat egg whites until stiff but not dry, and carefully fold sauce into whites. Pour mixture into a generously buttered 3-quart casserole or soufflé dish. Bake for 10 minutes, lower temperature to 400°F and bake about 25 more minutes. The soufflé should be firm but not dry.

Gnocchi

Preparation time: 30 minutes
Standing time: 1 hour
Cooking time: 15 minutes
Degree of difficulty: moderate
Servings: 6
Calories per serving: 390

Serve these spinach and cheese dumplings as a first course with cherry tomatoes baked with fresh grated Parmesan and drizzled with butter.

2 pounds fresh spinach
5 tablespoons butter
1 medium onion, finely chopped
1 cup ricotta cheese
3 eggs, lightly beaten
8-10 tablespoons all-purpose flour
1 cup freshly grated Parmesan cheese
1 teaspoon salt
¾ teaspoon freshly ground black pepper
8 quarts water
4 tablespoons melted butter

Wash the spinach and steam in a saucepan for about 8 minutes. Do not overcook. Drain spinach in a collander, and when cool, squeeze very dry. Chop it and pat *very* dry with paper towels. Melt 5 tablespoons butter in a skillet and fry the spinach and onion, stirring constantly, until the moisture is gone — about 3 minutes. Add the ricotta and stir-fry a further 3 minutes.

Transfer mixture to a mixing bowl and add the eggs, flour, ½ cup Parmesan, salt and pepper. Mix thoroughly, cover, and place in the refrigerator for at least 1 hour.

Bring the water to a boil in a large pot, flour your hands, and shape dumpling mixture into small balls, 1 tablespoonful at a time. Drop the balls into the water and cook, uncovered, for about 8 minutes. Remove with a slotted spoon and drain on paper towels.

Just before serving, place the gnocchi in an ovenproof 3-cup serving dish, drizzle with melted butter, and decorate with cherry tomatoes (optional). Sprinkle with the remaining Parmesan and place under a hot broiler until the cheese melts (about 3 minutes). Serve immediately. These are also good at room temperature. If serving cool, use less butter in the final step.

A food mill is a good utensil to have in your kitchen for the odd job that can't be done well by either a food processor (sometimes it can't get certain ingredients quite smooth enough), a blender (which occasionally can't handle certain fibrous ingredients), or by pressing through a sieve (which can demand more time than you might want to spend). Consider a food mill.

Camembert with Herbs

Bake for 25 minutes, without opening the door. Then, if not sufficiently brown, bake another 5 minutes. Cut in wedges. Garnish with broiled or pan-fried bacon and serve with thick slices of generously buttered black bread or giant popovers and a steaming hot cup of café au lait.

Brunch Omelet

Preparation time: 5 minutes
Cooking time: 5 minutes
Degree of difficulty: simple
Servings: 2
Calories per serving: 580

There are no limits to what you can put into an omelet — it inspires creative imagination. Fillings such as onion, shrimp, tomatoes, bacon, sausage, salami or green pepper (even sauerkraut and corned beef) may be cooked ahead. Think of it as an envelope for your favorite fillings.

2 tablespoons butter

6 eggs

Salt and freshly ground pepper to taste

¼ cup sautéed mushrooms

½ cup grated cheese

3 slices diced ham

Heat butter in a heavy frying pan or omelet pan. Beat eggs, salt and pepper until blended. Pour half of egg mixture into pan and cook until set on bottom. With wooden spatula, gently draw sides of omelet up, and, tilting the pan, let the uncooked portion slide underneath. When top is almost set, add half the mushrooms, cheese and ham to half of the omelet. Gently fold other half on top and cook just 1 minute longer to allow cheese to melt. Slide onto a plate. Place in oven to keep warm; cook second omelet the same way.

Camembert with Herbs

Preparation time: 5 minutes
Degree of difficulty: simple
Servings: 24
Calories per ounce: 84

A wheel of Camembert from Quebec is pressed with a selection of fresh garden herbs.

1 large wheel Camembert cheese
Fresh herbs of various shapes (parsley, thyme, rosemary, tarragon, mint)

Gently wash and pat dry herbs. Cut off stems and discard bruised or torn leaves. Using a small sharp knife, remove the top rind of the cheese. Design a pattern of your choice by pressing the herbs, gently but firmly, into the top of the cheese, and place a ring of fresh herbs around the edge. Serve with fresh fruit and crackers. (The same effect may also be achieved with fewer herbs and a smaller wheel of cheese; Brie may be substituted.)

Baked Cheese Omelet

Preparation time: 15 minutes
Cooking time: 25-30 minutes
Degree of difficulty: simple
Servings: 4
Calories per serving: 420

Easy to make, the old-fashioned baked omelet always satisfies, especially on a cold winter's day.

½ pound Canadian Cheddar or Gruyère, grated

½ cup light cream

½ teaspoon salt

Freshly ground pepper to taste

6 eggs, separated

8 slices bacon, cooked

Preheat oven to 325°F. Melt cheese over very low heat. Gradually stir in cream, salt, pepper to taste. Remove from heat. Beat egg whites until stiff, beat egg yolks until fluffy and light in color. Fold the yolks into the cheese mixture, then fold in the whites until just blended. Pour into a 10-inch soufflé dish.

Chopped Egg and Caviar Spread

Preparation time: 15 minutes
Chilling time: 4 hours or overnight
Degree of difficulty: simple
Servings: 8-10 as spread,
4-6 sandwich filling
Calories per serving: 305 (1/4)
203 (1/6)
152 (1/8)
122 (1/10)

This sophisticated version of an egg salad sandwich is equally good on crackers or bagels.

¼ teaspoon vegetable oil

1 Spanish onion or large red onion, finely chopped

6 hard-cooked eggs, shelled and finely chopped

1 cup sour cream

1 1¾-ounce jar black Danish lump-fish caviar or red Canadian caviar

2 tablespoons chopped scallions, green and white parts

Oil an 8½-inch springform pan. Spread chopped onions on bottom of pan and top with a layer of chopped egg. Gently spread sour cream on top. Sprinkle surface with caviar and scallions. Refrigerate at least 4 hours or overnight. Remove springform sides. Serve spread on crackers or as a sandwich filling.

Mozzarella in Carrozza

Preparation time: 10 minutes
Cooking time: 10 minutes
Degree of difficulty: simple
Servings: 4
Calories per serving: 545

Of course, this will only work if you like anchovies.

4 slices Mozzarella cheese

8 slices fresh Italian bread, ½-inch thick

2 eggs, lightly beaten

4 tablespoons olive oil

4 tablespoons butter

PHOTO BY TIM SAUNDERS

ANCHOVY SAUCE

4 tablespoons olive oil

4 tablespoons unsalted butter

2 2-ounce cans anchovies, drained

10 cloves garlic, coarsely chopped

Put each slice of Mozzarella between 2 slices bread. Dip in egg and set aside. In a large skillet, heat olive oil. Melt butter in oil. Sauté sandwiches on both sides in this mixture until they are golden brown and cheese begins to ooze out.

To prepare the anchovy sauce, heat oil and butter in a saucepan. Add anchovies and garlic; cook until anchovies dissolve and garlic is golden. Pour over sandwiches and serve hot.

Lox and Onion Omelet

Preparation time: 10 minutes
Cooking time: 30 minutes
Degree of difficulty: simple
Servings: 4
Calories per serving: 260

As the onions cook, they become slightly caramelized and lend this dish its unique and wonderful flavor.

3 medium cooking onions, chopped

2 tablespoons butter

6 eggs

6 slices smoked salmon, cut in pieces

In a large, heavy pan, sauté the onion very slowly in the butter until brown (about 20 minutes). Beat the eggs with a fork and add the salmon slices. Pour into a medium-hot frying pan and cook slowly until the eggs are set. If you prefer the omelet more broken, like scrambled eggs, stir it as it cooks.

Chopped
Egg and
Caviar
Spread

To hard-cook eggs, put in a pan and cover with cold water. Bring to a boil and remove pan from heat. Cover and let stand 20 minutes. Immediately rinse with cold water. The eggs will be tender with no grey ring. For easy shelling, roll the eggs back and forth gently in the pan containing a little cold water. The water seeps into the cracks that develop and facilitates peeling.

Scotch Eggs

Preparation and cooking time: about 45 minutes
Degree of difficulty: simple
Servings: 6
Calories per serving: 560

A favorite snack food is this surprise package: a hard-cooked egg wrapped in a seasoned sausage crust. It is fried and eaten cold — an old-fashioned treat that makes lovely make-ahead picnic fare and is perfect with cold beer, salad, and an herbed bread.

6 eggs
1 pound pork sausage
1 tablespoon breadcrumbs
3 tablespoons finely chopped parsley
1 medium onion, minced
1 tablespoon chervil
2 tablespoons tarragon
½ teaspoon salt (optional)
Freshly ground pepper
¼ cup all-purpose flour
Vegetable oil for frying

Cook the eggs until hard (approximately 10 minutes), then immerse in cold water; peel and pat dry with paper towels. Mix together the sausage, breadcrumbs, parsley, onion, chervil, tarragon, salt and pepper. Divide the sausage mixture into 6 portions and pat evenly around the eggs. Roll the eggs lightly in flour and fry in hot oil, turning to brown evenly on all sides. Drain on paper towels; cool.

Crêpes Suzette

Preparation time: 15 minutes
Standing time: overnight
Cooking time: 1 hour
Degree of difficulty: moderate
Servings: 8 (40 9-inch crêpes)
Calories per serving (5 crêpes and sauce): 655

A version of the classic French dessert — and eternally impressive.

8 large eggs
3¾ cups all-purpose flour
3 cups warm milk
¾ cup sugar
1 teaspoon salt
1 teaspoon active dry yeast
4 tablespoons brandy
2 tablespoons orange-flower water (you can substitute grated orange peel and add 2 tablespoons of milk)

Separate the eggs and beat egg whites until stiff. Mix the flour and egg yolks. Add the warmed milk in which you have dissolved the sugar, salt, and yeast. Add the brandy, orange-flower water and mix well. Fold in egg whites. The batter will be fairly thin. Refrigerate overnight.

Beat batter again. Lightly butter a 9-inch cast-iron griddle or crêpe pan. Pour a small ladle (2-3 tablespoons) of batter onto the griddle and spread rapidly, tilting the pan until the crêpe is as thin as possible. As soon as one side is cooked, lift the crêpe by one edge and flip it over. Brown lightly on the other side. Wipe the griddle before making the next crêpe. Brush with butter when necessary to keep the griddle surface just coated. Keep the crêpes hot in a covered pan in the oven.

SAUCE

Preparation time: 5 minutes
Cooking time: 15 minutes
1 cup plus 3 tablespoons unsalted butter
7 ounces lump sugar
Peel from 4 oranges
1 cup brandy with a dash of curaçao

Melt the butter in a heavy frying pan at 400°F. Add the sugar which has been rubbed in the orange peel. Stir until it dissolves and carmelizes slightly. Add about half the brandy and curaçao. Fold the crêpes in 4 (or roll them) and place in the butter mixture to warm. Then add the rest of the brandy and heat for a few moments. Ignite the brandy and flame the crêpes.

Arrange crêpes on a heated serving platter and pour sauce over.

Mexican Eggs

Preparation time: 10 minutes
Cooking time: 15 minutes
Degree of difficulty: simple
Servings: 6
Calories per serving: 235

Fun for brunch with friends, or breakfast with someone you love.

3 tablespoons butter or margarine
6 tortillas (canned or frozen)
1 medium onion, finely chopped
½ teaspoon chili peppers
1 clove garlic
2 tablespoons tomato paste
1 large tomato, finely chopped
Salt and freshly ground pepper to taste
6 eggs
Butter for frying

Melt the butter in a heavy frying pan and brown the tortillas. Put in a 250°F oven to keep warm. Mix the onion, chili peppers, garlic, tomato paste, tomato, and seasonings in the same pan and bring to a simmer. Fry the eggs in a separate pan. Remove tortillas from oven. Place one egg on each tortilla and cover with the sauce.

Ham and Egg Pie

Preparation time: 20 minutes
Cooking time: 40 minutes
Degree of difficulty: simple
Servings: 6-8
Calories per serving: 335 (1/6)
250 (1/8)

Served with fresh asparagus and a romaine salad, this makes a great springtime brunch — especially when there's leftover ham from Easter.

½ onion, diced

½ green pepper, diced

2 tablespoons butter or margarine

2 tablespoons flour

¾ cup milk

1 10-ounce can cream soup (chicken, mushroom or celery)

2 teaspoons prepared mustard

1½ cups cubed cooked ham

4 or 5 hard-cooked eggs, quartered

2 tablespoons mayonnaise

Pastry for 1 deep 10-inch double crust pie

Sauté onion and green pepper in hot butter for 1 or 2 minutes. Stir in the flour, then add milk and cook until thick. Add the next 5 ingredients and taste for seasoning. Cool.

Preheat oven to 425°F. Roll out pastry and fit half into a deep 10-inch pie plate. Trim and dampen edge. Add the filling and cover with top crust. Crimp edges together and gash the top. Brush with milk, cream or slightly beaten egg. Bake for 20 minutes. Reduce heat to 375°F and bake until pastry is golden. Cool slightly before cutting.

NOTES

FISH AND SEAFOOD

here are countless ways to cook fish: you can steam it, fry it, poach, bake, grill, or marinate it. None of it will be worth the trouble unless your fish is of the highest quality because, if it isn't, there's no way to disguise the fact.

Most fish is seasonal. Learn the best varieties available in your area and buy at the right time. You can tell fresh fish from foul by sight (they should look slightly pop-eyed), by nose (saltwater fish should smell like an ocean wave and freshwater of hardly anything — neither should be "fishy"), and by touch (when poked, the flesh should offer some resistance and should never by slimy).

Microwave cooking is good for fish, since it cooks quickly from the inside out. Steaming and poaching are both good methods: a poaching mixture of milk and water for white-fleshed fish seems to make it even whiter, as well as adding subtle flavor. For the cholesterol-conscious, most shellfish isn't considered the villain it once was — lobster has no more cholesterol than chicken. Shrimps do contain a high level, but they're low in fat and so wonderful to eat that moderation rather than abstinence might be the best way to go.

If you're lucky enough to be on the west coast when Dungeness crabs are available, you'll find them a treat — big and sweet, with firm flesh, they're wonderful steamed and served simply dressed with butter, or piled in a cold, snowy mound on a lettuce leaf, with dollops of home-made mayonnaise on the side.

On the other side of Canada, Prince Edward Island Malpeque oysters are large and meaty, as are their cultured mussels. As for salmon, you can choose between the richer of the two from B.C. or the lighter texture of the Atlantic fish.

Baked Trout with Lemon (see recipe page 82)

Recent studies show that a preventive measure against heart disease may be to eat more seafood, especially oil-rich fish, such as sardines. Fish oil lowers blood cholesterol and actually thins blood, decreasing the chance of dangerous clotting. One 3¾-ounce tin of sardines has more calcium and phosphorous than an 8-ounce glass of milk.

Broiled Mackerel with Mustard

Preparation time: 5 minutes
Cooking time: 10 minutes
Degree of difficulty: simple
Servings: 2
Calories per serving: 420

Mackerel is a relatively inexpensive, yet underrated fish. The mustard-lemon sauce lends tangy flavor to this easily prepared dish.

1-2 pounds mackerel, clean and split for broiling
2 tablespoons melted butter
1 tablespoon mustard, mild or hot according to taste
2 tablespoons lemon juice
Salt and freshly ground pepper to taste
Minced parsley or dill for garnish

Preheat broiler. Combine butter, mustard, lemon juice, salt, and pepper. Rub over fish and place on broiler rack, skin side down (if broiling over charcoal, place skin side up), and broil for 5 minutes. Brush with remaining seasoning mixture and broil another 5 minutes, or until fish flakes easily with a fork. Sprinkle with parsley or dill and serve.

Baked Trout with Lemon

Preparation time: 20 minutes
Marinating time: 2 hours
Cooking time: 30 minutes
Degree of difficulty: simple
Servings: 6
Calories per serving: 350

A handsome offering at a party or family supper.

6 fresh, cleaned medium rainbow trout
½ cup butter
⅓ cup lemon juice
½ cup chopped parsley
Salt and freshly ground pepper to taste
¼ cup chopped almonds
Grated peel of 1 lemon
2 cups fresh breadcrumbs
1 egg, beaten
3 tablespoons all-purpose flour
1 cup fish stock
1 egg yolk
⅓ cup whipping cream
Lemon slices and fresh tarragon

Wash trout and pat dry. Slash fish about ¼-inch deep on either side. Place side by side in a lightly greased shallow casserole. Melt ⅓ cup of the butter in a pan, cool, then mix in lemon juice, ⅓ cup of the parsley, salt and pepper, and pour over fish. Cover with plastic wrap and leave in a cool place (not the refrigerator) 2 hours, turning and basting once.

Preheat oven to 375°F. Combine almonds, lemon peel, breadcrumbs, salt, pepper, remaining parsley and egg. Stuff cavities of fish with mixture. Cover dish with foil and bake for about 30 minutes.

To make sauce, melt remaining butter in a small saucepan, add flour, and cook, stirring, 1-2 minutes. Remove from heat and gradually stir in stock. Bring to a boil, reduce heat, and continue to cook, stirring constantly until sauce thickens. Remove from heat, blend egg yolk with cream and stir into sauce. Season with salt and pepper, reheat gently *without* boiling, and serve with fish. Garnish with lemon slices and tarragon.

Alex Colville's Sole Florentine

Preparation time: 15 minutes
Cooking time: 30 minutes (total)
Degree of difficulty: simple
Servings: 6
Calories per serving: 385

Light in texture, creamy in flavor, this is an easy dish for family or friends.

6 sole fillets
1 teaspoon butter
½ cup finely chopped mushrooms
½ cup white wine
1 pound fresh spinach
1 tablespoon butter
½ teaspoon grated nutmeg
2 tablespoons whipping cream
2 tablespoons butter
2 tablespoons all-purpose flour
1 cup hot fish stock or clam juice
½ cup whipping cream
½ cup grated Swiss or Parmesan cheese (optional)
2 tablespoons parsley, chopped
Salt and freshly ground pepper to taste

Preheat oven to 375°F. Butter a 10-12-inch shallow baking/serving dish. Line bottom with mushrooms. Arrange fish in 1 layer on top; pour wine over. Bake for about 20 minutes, or until the fish is milky and can be pierced easily with a fork.

Meanwhile, trim and wash the spinach. Place in a large saucepan and cook with the water that clings to the leaves, stirring frequently. Remove from heat when wilted, about 4 minutes. Add butter, nutmeg, and cream. Mix; set aside. To make sauce, melt 2 tablespoons butter in a small saucepan. Mix in 2 tablespoons flour to make a roux. Slowly stir in hot fish stock and cook over low heat until thickened. Stir in cream; keep warm.

To assemble, remove fish from dish in which it was cooked; set aside. Turn on broiler. Spread the spinach over the mushrooms on the bottom of the fish baking dish and arrange fillets on top. Cover with hot sauce, sprinkle cheese and parsley on top, and broil until bubbly and lightly browned. Serve with rice.

Chilled Whole Fish with Avocado Dressing

Preparation time: 20 minutes
Cooking time: 50 minutes (total)
Chilling time: overnight
Degree of difficulty: simple
Servings: 12
Calories per serving: 350

This colorful dish is designed for a buffet table. Decorate with black olives and strips of red pepper and serve with crusty white bread.

2 4-pound whole fish, white snapper, or whitefish, cleaned, with head and tail left on, or 1 7-pound fish
3 large onions, sliced
1 teaspoon salt
½ teaspoon peppercorns
1 bay leaf
1 teaspoon thyme
Juice of 2 lemons
2 quarts water
4 large, ripe avocados
Juice of 1 lemon
Salt and freshly ground pepper to taste
Dash of Tabasco sauce
3 green onions, finely chopped
Sliced black olives, and strips of red pepper or pimentos

Preheat oven to 375°F. Simmer the sliced onions, salt, peppercorns, bay leaf, thyme, lemon juice and water for 20 minutes. Wrap the fish in cheesecloth and place in a large roasting pan. Pour the mixture over it. Cover the pan and bake for 30 minutes or until the fish is almost done. (Don't overcook.) Allow to cool in the broth in the refrigerator overnight, if possible. Lift the fish onto a platter, remove the cheesecloth and skin carefully. Drain off moisture.

Peel and mash avocados and combine with lemon juice, seasonings, and green onion. Coat the fish with a thick layer of the dressing. Decorate with sliced olives and strips of red pepper or pimento. Serve immediately or refrigerate, tightly covered with plastic wrap, until ready to serve.

Baked Whitefish with Grapefruit

Preparation time: 15 minutes
Cooking time: 1 hour
Degree of difficulty: simple
Servings: 4-6
Calories per serving: 365 (1/4)
325 (1/6)

An easy recipe for a succulent summer dinner. Use fresh fish rather than frozen.

1 4-5 pound whitefish
Salt
6 tablespoons butter
½ small onion, minced
1 cup stale breadcrumbs or bread cubes
½ cup fine cracker crumbs
½ teaspoon dried or 1 teaspoon fresh dill
2 teaspoons chopped parsley
¼ teaspoon salt
Freshly ground black pepper to taste
1 grapefruit, sectioned, with its juice

Preheat oven to 350°F. Sprinkle the fish inside and out with salt. In a frying pan heat 4 tablespoons of the butter, add the onion, and cook until transparent. Add the breadcrumbs and cracker crumbs, the dill, parsley, ¼ teaspoon salt, the pepper, and mix. Stuff the fish with the mixture, and place in a greased, foil-lined pan. Bake for 50-60 minutes, or until fish flakes easily. Melt the remaining butter and mix with the grapefruit juice. Brush mixture frequently over the fish as it cooks. Three minutes before removing fish from the oven, arrange the grapefruit sections on top and brush with the remaining mixture or with additional butter.

Chilled Salmon Soufflé

Preparation time: 20 minutes
Cooking time: 5-10 minutes
Degree of difficulty: simple
Servings: 6-8
Calories per serving: 375 (1/6)
280 (1/8)

This is an unexpected and delicious addition to a supper table or a buffet.

1 15½-ounce can salmon, drained and flaked
1½ envelopes unflavored gelatine
½ cup cold tomato juice
1 10-ounce can cream of shrimp soup
¾ cup milk
4 eggs, separated
¼ cup lemon juice
1½ teaspoons prepared horseradish
1½ teaspoons salt
1 cup whipping cream
1 tablespoon snipped parsley

Sprinkle gelatine over tomato juice and let stand 5 minutes to soften. Add soup and milk, and heat to a simmer, stirring constantly, until gelatine is dissolved. Stir a little of the hot mixture into well-beaten egg yolks. Return to saucepan and cook 2 minutes longer. Add lemon juice, horseradish, and salt. Chill until partially set. Beat egg whites until stiff but not dry. Whip cream until softly stiff. Fold egg whites, cream, and salmon into chilled mixture. Turn into a 5-cup soufflé dish that has been extended with a 2-inch paper collar. Chill until set. Remove collar and garnish with parsley.

To defrost 1 pound of frozen fish, microwave at low (30%) for 4-6 minutes, let stand for 5 minutes, or until thawed. If there's an automatic defrost, use that instead. To defrost only half a package of frozen food, wrap aluminum foil completely around the portion you don't want to defrost. When soft enough, cut off the portion you need and put the rest back in the freezer in its foil wrap. There's no danger defrosting in the microwave as long as the foil doesn't touch the sides or walls of the oven.

Fresh Salmon Scallops Georgia Straits

Fresh Salmon Scallops Georgia Straits

Preparation time: 30 minutes
Cooking time: 15-20 minutes (total)
Degree of difficulty: moderate
Servings: 4
Calories per serving: 990

Fresh oysters and sorrel leaves provide delicious accents for this special dish from the William Tell Restaurant in Vancouver. Serve with boiled potatoes and chilled white wine.

1³⁄4 pounds fresh salmon, centre cut, skinned and boned
8 medium fresh oysters
³⁄4 cup fish stock
²⁄3 cup dry white wine
²⁄3 cup dry vermouth
2 shallots, finely chopped
1³⁄4 cups crème fraîche (recipe follows)
2 cups finely chopped fresh sorrel leaves
1 tablespoon finely chopped parsley
1 teaspoon fresh thyme leaves
3 tablespoons unsalted butter, cut into small pieces
Fresh lemon juice
Salt and freshly ground white pepper to taste
6 cups fresh leaf spinach, blanched
2 tablespoons peanut oil

Cut salmon lengthwise into 4 scallops and flatten slightly with a meat cleaver between sheets of wax paper. Carefully open the oysters, strain juice into a bowl, and set aside.

Combine fish stock, vermouth, wine, and shallots in a heavy saucepan. Boil until reduced to about 4 tablespoons. Add the oyster juice and crème fraîche, and simmer gently until slightly thickened. Add sorrel, parsley, and thyme; cook for 30 seconds. Remove from heat and swirl in 2 tablespoons of the butter. Add lemon juice and season with salt and pepper.

Preheat oven to 275°F. Sauté the blanched spinach in remaining butter for 3 minutes; season with salt and pepper. Place spinach on a serving platter and arrange the oysters in their shells around it. Put in oven to keep warm.

Heat a large frying pan over high heat and lightly coat the bottom with peanut oil. Season the salmon with salt and pepper; sauté in the hot oil for about 20 seconds on each side (the salmon should be undercooked). Arrange salmon on the spinach, spoon some of the sauce over the oysters and salmon, and serve the rest in a sauceboat.

CRÈME FRAÎCHE

1³⁄4 cups whipping cream
2 teaspoons cultured buttermilk

Combine cream and buttermilk. Heat to 85°F and let stand at room temperature until thickened. Crème fraîche will tolerate a slightly higher temperature in cooking than sour cream before it curdles. Makes 1¾ cups.

Tomato-Crowned Cod

Preparation time: 15 minutes
Cooking time: 25 minutes in oven;
8-10 minutes in microwave
Degree of difficulty: simple
Servings: 6
Calories per serving: 184

Inexpensive cod becomes a party dish, cooked in either a conventional oven or a microwave.

| 2 pounds cod fillets |
| 2 tablespoons lemon juice |
| 1/8 teaspoon freshly ground black pepper |
| 2 large tomatoes, sliced 1/4-inch thick |
| 1/2 medium green pepper, finely chopped |
| 2 tablespoons chopped onion |
| 1/4 cup dry breadcrumbs |
| 1/4 teaspoon dried crumbled or 1 tablespoon chopped fresh basil |
| 1 tablespoon oil |

Preheat oven to 350°F. Place the fish in an oiled baking dish and season with lemon juice and pepper. Place tomato slices on the fish, then sprinkle with the green pepper and onion. In a small bowl, combine the breadcrumbs, basil, and oil. Spread the crumb mixture evenly over the tomatoes. Bake, uncovered, for 25 minutes. To microwave, arrange prepared fish in a microwave-safe dish and cover with wax paper. Cook 8-10 minutes on high (100% power) or until fish flakes easily. Let stand 5 minutes before serving.

Tomato-Crowned Cod, Wild Rice with Pine Nuts (see recipe page 113), and Chilled Asparagus with Yogurt Sauce (see recipe page 191)

Glorious Goldeye

Preparation time: a few minutes
Cooking time: 10 minutes
Degree of difficulty: simple
Servings: 4
Calories per serving: 80

The rare and delicate taste of Winnipeg goldeye is best enjoyed served cold, as a salad.

| 1 Winnipeg goldeye |
| 1/2 cup skim milk |
| 1/2 cup water |
| 1 head lettuce |
| Lemon juice |

Poach the goldeye gently in the skim milk and water in oven for about 10 minutes. Allow to cool, skin, and serve in bite-size pieces on a bed of lettuce. Sprinkle with lemon juice.

The Canadian Fisheries rule of thumb for cooking fish is adhered to around the world, unless you like fish almost raw. Simply lay fish on its side, measure it with a ruler at its thickest part, and, whatever cooking method you're using, calculate 10 minutes per inch of thickness for cooking. Don't forget, if you have a sauce to make for accompaniment, or other things to do, the fish will continue to cook internally for a few minutes after removal from heat.

Spanish Red Snapper

Preparation time: 15 minutes
Cooking time: 40 minutes
Degree of difficulty: simple
Servings: 4-6
Calories per serving: 450 (1/4)
300 (1/6)

This recipe is a favorite in the Canary Islands during Carnival.

2 2-pound red snappers, cleaned, head and tail left on
1½ teaspoons salt
1 lemon, cut in six wedges
2 black olives
¾ cup soft breadcrumbs
1 teaspoon finely chopped garlic
1 tablespoon parsley
2 tablespoons mild paprika
3 potatoes, thinly sliced
Salt and freshly ground pepper to taste
1 cup water
½ cup olive oil

Preheat oven to 350°F. Wash fish under cold water and pat dry inside and out. Sprinkle with salt, then score with 3 crosswise cuts. Insert a lemon wedge, skin side up, in each cut. Insert a black olive in the eye socket of each fish.

In a small bowl, combine breadcrumbs, garlic, parsley, and paprika. Spread the potato slices evenly in the bottom of a 10-x-16-inch baking dish; sprinkle with salt and pepper. Place fish side by side on top of the potatoes. Pour water down the side of the baking dish and pour olive oil over the fish. Sprinkle with the breadcrumb mixture. Bake for 40 minutes.

Fresh Fish Baked with Cheese

Preparation time: 15 minutes
Cooking time: 30 minutes
Degree of difficulty: simple
Servings: 6-8
Calories per serving: 511 (1/6)
383 (1/8)

The affinity of fresh fish for creamy sauces is well served by this excellent casserole. Serve with spinach noodles to mop up the plentiful sauce.

2 pounds cod, haddock, or halibut fillets
1 cup water
½ teaspoon salt
2 onions, thinly sliced
4 stalks celery, sliced
1 cup sliced fresh mushrooms
6 tablespoons butter
3 tablespoons all-purpose flour
2½ cups light cream
Salt and freshly ground pepper to taste
1 cup grated old Cheddar cheese

Bring water and salt to a boil in a large saucepan and add fish fillets. Reduce heat and simmer about 10 minutes, or until fish flakes easily. Meanwhile, sauté onion, celery, and mushrooms in 3 tablespoons of the butter until onion is transparent and celery tender.

Preheat oven to 375°F. Place vegetables in a bowl. Melt remaining butter in the same pan and stir in the flour. Cook for a few minutes and then add the cream. Stir constantly over medium heat until thickened. Season to taste with salt and pepper. Drain fillets and arrange in a buttered 2-quart casserole. Add vegetables and pour sauce over. Sprinkle with cheese and bake, uncovered, until hot and bubbly, about 10 minutes.

Sauté de Lotte aux Champignons Chinois et au Parfum de Gingembre

Preparation and cooking time: less than 1 hour
Standing time: 30 minutes
Degree of difficulty: moderately challenging
Servings: 6
Calories per serving: 220

1½ pounds lotte, filleted and cut in 2-inch-square pieces
Salt and freshly ground pepper to taste
¼ pound dried Chinese mushrooms (preferably brown)
3 tablespoons vegetable oil
1 clove garlic, pressed
½ pound snow peas, diagonally sliced
1 tablespoon ginger juice, squeezed from about 3 tablespoons grated fresh ginger
2 tablespoons rice wine (available at Chinese grocers)
2 tablespoons oyster sauce (available at Chinese grocers)
Fresh coriander or watercress for garnish

Salt and pepper the fish; set aside. Put the dried mushrooms in a bowl and add boiling water to cover; cover the bowl and set aside for 30 minutes. Discard mushroom stems; slice mushroom caps into thin strips and place on paper towels to drain. Heat the oil in a large pan; add the mushrooms and sauté 3 minutes. Add the garlic, snow peas, and ginger juice; stir-fry briefly; set aside and keep warm. Deglaze the pan with the rice wine; add the fish and fry over medium-high heat 3 minutes or until just cooked. Add the oyster sauce. To serve, divide fish among 6 plates, place snow-pea mixture around fish and decorate with coriander or watercress.

Kulibyaka

Preparation time: 20 minutes
Cooking time: 35 minutes
Degree of difficulty: moderate
Servings: 4 for lunch or 6 as
an appetizer for dinner
Calories per serving: 690 (1/4)
460 (1/6)

This recipe tastes much better and is easier than it sounds. The ingredients seem mundane, but they combine beautifully. The pie can be put together a few hours ahead and baked just before serving.

½ pound canned salmon, drained and flaked

1 small onion, finely chopped

½ cup finely chopped mushrooms

4 tablespoons butter

8 ounces rough puff pastry (or plain pastry)

⅓ cup cooked rice

1 tablespoon chopped parsley

Lemon juice

2 hard-cooked eggs, sliced

Salt and freshly ground pepper to taste

Preheat oven to 425°F. Sauté onion and mushrooms in half the butter for 5 minutes. Roll out the pastry and cut into 2 rectangles, 12 x 6 inches. Lay one piece of pastry on a baking sheet. Put the ingredients in layers on the centre of the pastry, seasoning each layer lightly with salt and pepper, and heaping ingredients so that the filling will be high in the centre. Spread the rice first, sprinkled with parsley, then the onions and mushrooms, then the salmon (add a little squeeze of lemon here), and finally the egg slices. Dampen the edges of the pastry and lay the second piece on top of the filling. The top pastry must be put on carefully to keep the filling from falling all over the place. Seal the edges of the pastry layers by fluting them on all four sides.

Just before baking, make 3 or 4 gashes in pastry top to allow the steam to escape, and bake for 30 minutes. Just before serving, melt the remaining 2 tablespoons butter and pour into the the steam holes.

Salmon in Sorrel Sauce

Preparation time: 10 minutes
Cooking time: about 10 minutes
Degree of difficulty: simple
Servings: 6
Calories per serving: 650

This elegant dish was developed for Toronto's King Edward Hotel by chef Casari. He uses sorrel in jars (from specialty shops) when fresh is not available.

6 large salmon fillets, ¼-½-inch thick

½ cup sorrel, drained

½ cup dry white wine

1 teaspoon shallots, finely chopped

2 cups whipping cream

½ cup butter

Salt

Freshly ground pepper

Purée the sorrel to yield ½ cup, then combine with the white wine and shallots in a large frying pan. Boil the mixture until it is almost dry (about 3 minutes). Add cream and boil again until it has the consistency of a sauce (3-5 minutes more). Continue to boil while adding 4 tablespoons soft butter with a wire whisk. Stop boiling and add salt to taste. Keep the sauce warm while you prepare the salmon. Melt remaining butter in a warm, not hot, frying pan. Salt and pepper the salmon fillets. Sauté over very low heat on each side for 2-3 minutes — be careful not to overcook or it will dry out. Spread the sorrel sauce on a serving platter and place the salmon on it. Serve with boiled potatoes.

Smoked Fish Soufflé

Preparation time: 20 minutes
(including cooking fish)
Cooking time: 30-40 minutes
Degree of difficulty: simple
Servings: 6
Calories per serving: 240

This blending of smoked fish and mashed potatoes yields a softly risen soufflé with a sophisticated flavor. Serve it for brunch with a green salad and light beer.

1 pound smoked haddock or whitefish, boned, cooked, and flaked

2 cups hot mashed potatoes (about 4 medium potatoes)

¼ cup light cream

3 eggs, separated

Salt and freshly ground pepper to taste

Juice of ½ lemon

½ teaspoon celery salt

¼ teaspoon thyme or summer savory

4 tablespoons melted butter

6 green onions, chopped

Preheat oven to 350°F. Beat cream, egg yolks, salt and pepper, lemon juice, celery salt, and thyme into mashed potatoes. Mix in butter, green onions, and fish. Beat egg whites until stiff and fold gently into the mixture. Pour into a buttered casserole and bake for 30-40 minutes, or until golden brown and puffy.

The term "Véronique" refers to a garnish of white Muscat grapes, usually used in sole Véronique, fillets of sole poached in fish stock and white wine. The poaching liquid is reduced and enriched with butter, and sometimes cream, the dish is garnished with grapes and quickly glazed under the broiler. Chicken can be used in this dish too. The method was originated by August Escoffier when he was chef at the Carlton Hotel in London in 1903, to honor a comic opera of the same name.

Moules Marinière

Preparation time: 10-15 minutes
Cooking time: 10 minutes
Degree of difficulty: simple
Servings: 6
Calories per serving: 384

The simplest and best known of the mussel stews, this forms the basis for many a variation. Try it with a Chablis or Sancerre.

6 pounds mussels
2 large onions, chopped
3 shallots, chopped
2 cloves garlic, chopped
1 tablespoon chopped parsley
1 cup dry white wine
4 tablespoons butter
Salt and freshly ground black pepper to taste
Parsley for garnish

Clean mussels in cold water, rubbing them together vigorously. Remove the beardlike threads (known as byssus) with a knife. Discard any mussels that are open. (A mussel may be full of mud and virtually vacuum-sealed. Test each mussel by pushing on the shells in opposite directions; discard any that slide open.) Put onions, shallots, garlic, parsley, and wine into a large saucepan. Simmer for 5-6 minutes. Add mussels, cover, and leave to steam open for a few minutes. Remove mussels to a collander to drain briefly, then transfer them to a large heated bowl. Discard any that have not opened. Carefully strain the mussel liquor into a saucepan and set over low heat. Whisk in the butter, taste, and correct seasonings. Pour sauce over the mussels, sprinkle with parsley, and serve immediately with lots of good bread.

Moules Marinière

Marinated Shrimp in Lime Juice

Preparation time: 30 minutes
Marinating time: 2-3 hours
Grilling time: 6-10 minutes
Degree of difficulty: simple
Servings: 4 as a main course or 6 as an appetizer
Calories per serving: 185 (1/4)
125 (1/6)

This dish, developed for *Homemaker's* by food consultant Barbara Pathy, has a tangy, tropical touch. For best results, use medium or large shrimp.

1½ pounds uncooked shrimp
½ cup fresh lime juice
1 tablespoon Dijon mustard
1 clove garlic, minced
2 teaspoons minced fresh ginger or ½ teaspoon powdered
Salt and freshly ground pepper to taste

Shell and devein shrimp. Place in a bowl and add lime juice, mustard, garlic and ginger. Refrigerate 2-3 hours, stirring occasionally. When ready to grill, divide the shrimp among 6 skewers. Place over coals, baste frequently with remaining marinade, and cook until flesh is no longer translucent — 3-5 minutes each side. Add salt and pepper to taste.

Quenelles of Scallops La Belle Auberge

Preparation time: 15 minutes
Chilling time: 90 minutes
Cooking time: 10 minutes
Degree of difficulty: moderate
Servings: 6
Calories per serving: 380

This is a simple preparation for an impressive result. Tablespoons of scallop mousse are poached in sauce, then decorated with slivers of vegetables. The recipe is from La Belle Auberge in Ladner, B.C., about a half-hour from Vancouver.

MOUSSE

| About 1 pound scallops |
| 1/4 cup white wine |
| Juice of 1/2 lemon |
| 1/3 cup whipping cream |
| 3 tablespoons butter |
| 3 eggs, separated |
| Salt and freshly ground white pepper to taste |

SAUCE

| 2/3 cup white wine |
| 1 cup whipping cream |

GARNISH

| 1 leek, julienned, steamed for 3 minutes |
| 1 carrot, julienned, steamed for 3 minutes |
| 1 sprig dillweed |

To prepare the scallop mousse, place scallops and 1/4 cup wine in a food processor or blender and chop finely at low speed. Add lemon juice, 1/3 cup cream, butter, egg yolks, salt, and pepper. Remove mixture to a bowl and chill for 90 minutes. Beat egg whites until stiff and fold into the scallop mousse.

For the sauce, bring 2/3 cup wine and 1 cup cream to a boil. Using a tablespoon, drop in spoonfuls of scallop mousse. Reduce heat, cover saucepan, and poach 4-5 minutes. Remove from sauce with a slotted spoon.

Arrange cooked quenelles in soup plates or a deep serving dish. Cover and keep warm. Boil the sauce until reduced by half. Pour over quenelles and decorate with julienned vegetables and dill.

Scallops Jambalaya

Preparation time: 10 minutes
Cooking time: 20 minutes
Degree of difficulty: simple
Servings: 6
Calories per serving: 275

This complete dish, which stars carefully simmered scallops, needs no accompaniment except a bottle of chilled white wine. Don't overcook the scallops or they'll be tough.

| 2 pounds scallops |
| 4 slices bacon, diced |
| 1 onion, minced |
| 1/2 cup sliced celery |
| 1 clove garlic, peeled and minced |
| 1/2 teaspoon thyme |
| Salt to taste |
| Tabasco sauce to taste |
| 1 28-ounce can whole tomatoes, drained |
| 2 cups frozen or fresh green peas |
| 2 cups cooked rice |

Place bacon, onion, celery, and garlic in a frying pan and cook on low heat until onion and celery are tender, but not brown. Add thyme, salt, Tabasco, scallops, tomatoes, peas, and rice. Cover and simmer slowly for 15 minutes. Serve immediately.

PHOTOS BY TIM SAUNDERS

FISH AND SEAFOOD

Cognac can be used in a number of ways to zing up food — a few drops in 1 or 2 tablespoons of water and a knob of butter will render carrots food fit for the gods. It does wonders for onion soup, party punches, and pâtés. Pernod is perfect with shellfish and Grand Marnier's personality fits so well with dark chocolate that a movie should be made about the relationship.

Semiahmoo Salmon

Preparation time: 10 minutes
Cooking time: 20 minutes
Degree of difficulty: simple
Servings: 4
Calories per serving: 435

Rich and elegant, this is from The Cannery, in Vancouver, a beautiful restaurant overlooking Burrard Inlet and the north shore mountains.

12 ounces smoked salmon, cut in thin strips
3 tablespoons butter
1 small shallot, diced
1 avocado, peeled and sliced
1 tablespoon brandy
1/4 cup whipping cream
1 green onion, chopped
Salt and freshly ground pepper to taste
4 slices French bread, toasted

Melt 2 tablespoons of the butter in a sauté pan. Add shallot and sauté until translucent. Add smoked salmon, sauté quickly and add the avocado. Add brandy and flame with a match. Add cream and remaining tablespoon of butter. Cook and stir until thickened. Add green onion and season to taste. Serve over toasted French bread.

Shrimp in Pernod

Preparation time: 15 minutes
Cooking time: 1 hour (total)
Degree of difficulty: moderate
Servings: 4 as a main course or 8 as an appetizer
Calories per serving: 860 (1/4) 430 (1/8)

The amount of Pernod seems large, but it cooks down to a smooth and elegant sauce. This is from *Cooks* magazine.

1 1/2 pounds shrimp, peeled, shells reserved
1/2 cup unsalted butter
2 tablespoons vegetable oil
2 shallots, minced
3 tablespoons Dijon mustard
2 tablespoons lemon juice
1 1/2 cups chicken stock
1 1/2 cups Pernod
1 cup unsalted butter, cut into 8 pieces
1/2 cup chopped scallions
Salt and freshly ground black pepper to taste

Place shrimp shells in a large frying pan with butter and cook over medium heat, turning often, until shells turn pinkish brown, 5-7 minutes. Transfer shells and butter to a food processor and process until shells are pulverized.

Line a strainer with several layers of cheesecloth cut large enough to drape over rim, and set over a small bowl. Pour shells and butter into cheesecloth, gather up corners and twist as tightly as possible to get out all the butter. Discard shells and cloth. This may be made ahead and refrigerated.

To prepare shrimp, heat 2 tablespoons of the shrimp butter with oil in a large frying pan. Add shrimp and sauté over medium-high heat until they turn pink on both sides and are just cooked, about 3 minutes (you may have to do this in batches, adding butter and oil as needed).

Remove shrimp and add shallots to pan. Sauté over gentle heat until soft. Stir in mustard, add lemon juice, chicken stock, and Pernod, turn heat to high, and bring to a boil. Boil 10-15 minutes or until mixture is reduced to about 1 cup. Reduce heat to low and whisk in butter, piece by piece. The butter should soften to form a creamy sauce, but shouldn't melt completely. You may have to move pan off and on heat to maintain temperature. Whisk in reserved shrimp butter, stir in scallions, add reserved shrimp, and return to medium-low heat to just warm the shrimp. Season to taste with salt and pepper. To serve, put a few tablespoons of sauce on warm plates, arrange shrimp on top and cover with more sauce. Serve immediately.

Tuna, Broccoli, and Mushroom Casserole

Preparation time: 15 minutes
Cooking time: 25-30 minutes
Degree of difficulty: simple
Servings: 4
Calories per serving: 410

A delicious one-dish meal that's packed with protein and other things that are good for your.

1 7-ounce can tuna, drained and flaked
2 pounds fresh broccoli, sliced into fine spears
1/2 pound mushrooms, sliced
5 tablespoons butter or margarine
4 tablespoons all-purpose flour
1 cup light cream
1 cup chicken broth
Salt and freshly ground pepper to taste
1 tablespoon chopped parsley
2 hard-cooked eggs, sliced
1/4 cup grated Parmesan cheese

Preheat oven to 300°F. Cook broccoli until barely tender and arrange in bottom of a shallow baking dish. Lightly sauté the mushrooms in 1 tablespoon butter. Melt remaining butter, blend in flour, then stir in cream and broth to make a smooth sauce. Season to taste. Gently stir in the parsley, tuna, eggs, and mushrooms. Pour carefully over the broccoli and top with the cheese. Bake 15-20 minutes, then put under the broiler for 1 minute and brown.

Gaspé Seafood Casserole

Preparation time: 30 minutes
Cooking time: 1¼ hours (total)
Degree of difficulty: moderate
Servings: 8
Calories per serving: 620

This hearty casserole is a regional tradition designed to show off the excellent local seafood. The recipe is from the family files of Michael and Marielle Sheehan of Gaspé, Quebec.

1 pound fresh cod, cut
in 2-inch pieces

1½ pounds fresh salmon,
cut in 2-inch pieces

1 pound shrimp, peeled
and deveined

1 pound scallops

1 can clams, drained

2 cooked lobsters or 1 large
can frozen lobster

⅓ cup butter

1 green pepper, chopped

1 large onion, chopped

1 cup chopped celery

¼ cup butter

¼ cup all-purpose flour

1½ cups milk, scalded

1 teaspoon salt

Freshly ground pepper to taste

6 slices Mozzarella or
Emmenthal cheese

In a medium-size soup pot, cover the cod and salmon with water and poach for 10 minutes. Add the shrimp, scallops, clams, and lobster meat and cook slowly for a few minutes more until the shrimp turns slightly pink. Remove the fish from the poaching liquid and set the fish and liquid aside separately.

Preheat oven to 325°F. Sauté the green pepper, onion, and celery in ⅓ cup butter until the onion is translucent. Add the vegetables to the fish and set aside. Melt ¼ cup butter in a saucepan and add the flour to make a roux. Cook for 1 minute to remove the floury taste. Slowly add the milk, stirring constantly with a wire whisk. Add 1 cup of the reserved poaching liquid and continue stirring over low heat until the sauce thickens. Season to taste with salt and pepper. Combine the sauce with the fish and vegetables in an ovenproof casserole. Bake, covered, for 45 minutes. Remove the casserole from the oven and top with slices of Mozzarella or Emmenthal cheese. Return to the oven and bake, uncovered, until the cheese melts.

Salmon Loaf

Preparation time: 5 minutes
Cooking time: 50 minutes (total)
Degree of difficulty: simple
Servings: 4
Calories per serving: 475

A "down home" dish that's just as good today as it was yesterday.

1 pound fresh salmon
(or 1 can salmon)

1 6-ounce can evaporated milk

½ cup soft breadcrumbs

3 tablespoons butter

½ cup chopped celery

2 eggs

2 tablespoons chopped parsley

½ tablespoon salt

2 tablespoons lemon juice

½ teaspoon prepared mustard

Preheat oven to 350°F. Put breadcrumbs and milk in the top of a double boiler. Cook for 5 minutes. Add other ingredients. Mix thoroughly. Pour in greased 8-x-4-inch loaf pan and bake for 45 minutes.

NOTES

MEAT

*M*eat in the '80s is a controversial topic, particularly among the health-conscious population. "Too much fat," they say, as well as "too expensive," and there's some truth in it, even though breeders today are producing pigs and cattle with more lean-meat proportion than ever before.

Most people do like a certain amount of meat in their diet, though, and the trick isn't to eliminate it altogether but to cut down on quantity, which will minimize both the fat content and the cost. After all, meat is a good source of protein, vitamins, and minerals, especially B vitamins and iron: why turn your back on such goodness? And there's a lot to be said for a standing rib roast in all its glory, wreathed with golden popovers or Yorkshire pudding — or a glorious rack of lamb, cooked briefly over glowing coals or in the oven, perhaps brushed with an orange-apricot glaze.

There's argument about the best way to cook lamb, with some plumping for steady low temperatures, others insisting it should be seared and the temperature then lowered, still others preferring a constant medium temperature. You'll have to find the way that suits you best — but always cook it to a medium-rare state, not well done, when it will be dry, gray, and unappetizing. If you visit the west coast, try to indulge yourself with some Salt Spring Island lamb, kissing cousin to the famed présalé lamb of Normandy: both feed on salt marshes and have a deliciously different flavor.

Times can never be more than approximate for roasting and broiling, since much depends on the oven, and the thickness, quality and shape of the meat (to say nothing of personal taste). Poking the meat with a finger is fairly reliable: a well-done steak will be firm to the touch, while one cooked to a rare state will give a little.

Don't turn up your nose at liver, sweetbreads, kidneys, or even tongue, served hot with Madeira or raisin sauce.

Spicy Steaks (see recipe page 94)

A fragrant, spicy mixture made famous by Hediard, in the famous food square of Paris on the Place de la Madeleine (just across from Fauchon's), has been translated by a number of people. Here's one inspired by supercook Madeleine Kamman. Use it as a seasoning in place of normal pepper.

1 tablespoon black peppercorns

1 tablespoon white peppercorns

1½ teaspoons whole allspice berries

Mix together, and grind to a powder in a pepper or spice mill.

Spicy Steak

Preparation time: 15 minutes
Cooking time: 7-8 minutes
Degree of difficulty: simple
Servings: 4
Calories per serving: 280

Fiery, but not painfully so, this surprise is from American cook Barbara Tropp.

4 8-ounce rib-eye steaks, trimmed

1 teaspoon coarse (kosher) salt

2 tablespoons black peppercorns, coarsely ground

1 tablespoon white peppercorns, coarsely ground

2 tablespoons fennel seeds, coarsely ground

1 teaspoon dried lavender, ground to a powder

3 tablespoons light olive oil

Sprinkle both sides of the steaks with salt and set aside for about 10 minutes. On a large, flat plate, mix seasonings and press both sides of the steaks into mixture to form a crust. Heat 2 large, heavy frying pans, preferably cast-iron, over high heat. Add 1½ tablespoons of oil to each frying pan. When oil is almost smoking, add steaks carefully so as not to disturb their crusts. Immediately reduce heat to moderate. Cook the first side until bottom crust browns, about 4 minutes. Turn and cook to desired doneness (3 minutes for medium-rare).

Chef Michel Clavelin's Blanquette de Veau Vermouth

Preparation time: 15 minutes
Cooking time: about 1 hour (total)
Degree of difficulty: simple
Servings: 6
Calories per serving: 560

This recipe is from Michel Clavelin, one of the members of British Columbia's team at the 1980 World Culinary Olympics.

2 pounds lean veal, cubed

3 tablespoons butter

½ pound shallots, peeled and coarsely chopped

½ pound fresh mushrooms, quartered

¼ cup dry vermouth

2 tablespoons demiglace or undiluted bouillon

1 tablespoon fresh or 1 teaspoon dried chervil

1 tablespoon fresh or 1 teaspoon dried oregano

1 tablespoon fresh or 1 teaspoon dried basil

Salt and freshly ground pepper to taste

1 cup whipping cream

Sauté the veal in the butter until brown. Add the shallots, mushrooms, vermouth, demiglace, and herbs. Cover and simmer slowly for 45 minutes. Season with salt and pepper. Remove the meat and vegetables to a warm platter. Reduce the pan juice by boiling for 1 minute, then simmer until the sauce thickens. Add the cream. Stir, scraping up any bits clinging to the bottom and sides. Taste, and correct the seasoning. Pour over the meat and serve immediately with hot rice.

Cod Jigger's Dinner

Preparation time: 20 minutes
Standing time: overnight (for salt beef)
Cooking time: about 3 hours (total)
Degree of difficulty: moderate
Servings: 10-12
Calories per serving: 726 (1/10)
605 (1/12)

This fisherman's meal of salt beef, vegetables, and pease porridge is part of a traditional Newfoundland lunch.

4 pounds salt beef, corned beef brisket, or cottage roll

1 8-ounce package yellow split peas

6 potatoes, peeled and quartered

6 carrots, scraped and chopped into large chunks

1 large turnip, peeled and sliced in 10-12 pieces

1 head cabbage, cut in wedges

Butter for vegetables

Salt and freshly ground pepper

Cut the meat into 2-inch pieces and remove excess fat. If you are using salt beef, soak it overnight in cold water. Do not soak corned beef or cottage roll. Place in a large soup pot and cover generously with fresh water. Put peas into a cotton bag or several layers of fresh cheesecloth tied into a bag. (Make sure the bag is secure, since the peas will be suspended in the boiling soup for the duration of the cooking.)

Suspend the bag in the water by hooking or tying the tied end onto the handle of the soup pot. Boil the meat and the peas for 2½ hours. Add the potatoes, carrots and turnip. Cook a further 15 minutes. Add cabbage and cook for 10 minutes more. Do not overcook or the cabbage will become too soft. While the cabbage is cooking, remove the peas from the water and turn them into a heated bowl. Mash them with butter and season with salt and pepper.

Remove vegetables and meat from the pot while water is boiling. Drain and chop the cabbage and add butter, salt, and pepper. Arrange the meat on the serving platter surrounded by the vegetables, and accompanied by mustard pickles or pickled beets.

Mandarin Sweet and Sour Pork

Preparation time: 20 minutes
Cooking time: 30 minutes
Degree of difficulty: moderate
Servings: 4-6
Calories per serving: 568 (1/4)
378 (1/6)

This is one of the dishes taught to students of Winnipeg's Mandarin Restaurant cooking classes. Serve with steamed rice and Chinese tea.

1 pound pork tenderloin
4-6 cups cooking oil
1 cup cornstarch (for coating)

MARINADE

½ teaspoon salt
½ teaspoon soya sauce
1 tablespoon cornstarch
1 tablespoon cold water
1 egg yolk

SEASONING SAUCE

3 tablespoons vinegar
4 tablespoons sugar
4 tablespoons catsup
1 tablespoon cornstarch
1 teaspoon sesame oil
1 tablespoon salt
2 tablespoons oil
1 green pepper, cut in ½-inch pieces
1 onion, peeled and cut in ½-inch pieces
½ cup pineapple chunks, drained
½ cup fresh peas and diced carrots

Flatten the pork with the back of a cleaver or tenderizer and cut into ½-inch squares. Combine the ingredients for the marinade and marinate the pork for ½ hour. Drain. Heat enough oil for deep frying to about 350°F. Coat each piece of pork with cornstarch. Deep-fry pork until just brown (about 2 minutes), and drain on paper towels. Combine seasoning sauce ingredients. Just before serving, reheat the oil and fry the pork once more until crisp. Remove pork from deep fryer and drain.

In a wok or large frying pan, heat 2 tablespoons oil and stir-fry the green pepper, onion, pineapple, and peas and carrots for 1 minute. Add the seasoning sauce and continue to stir-fry until the sauce has thickened. Turn off heat, add pork, mix well and serve immediately.

Beer Stew and Dumplings

Preparation time: 20 minutes
Cooking time: 2-2½ hours
Degree of difficulty: simple
Amount: makes 16 small dumplings
Calories per serving: 415 (stew)
53 (per dumpling)

Serve this tasty stew with salad or green beans.

3 pounds stewing beef or bottom round, cut into small cubes
8 slices of bacon cut in 1-inch pieces
4-5 large onions, finely sliced
2-3 cloves garlic, crushed
4 sprigs fresh or 2-teaspoons dry parsley
Leaves from 2 stalks of celery
1 teaspoon thyme
4 peppercorns
1½ cups beef broth
1 bottle beer
1 tablespoon brown sugar
1 tablespoon vinegar

DUMPLINGS

2 cups Bisquick or Tea Bisk
½ cup water

Preheat oven to 325°F. To save preparation time, we skip the customary flour-dredging and browning of the meat, and simply place meat, bacon, onions, and garlic in a large ovenproof casserole. Tie herbs and spices in cheesecloth and place bouquet garni in centre of casserole. Mix brown sugar and vinegar together in the broth and pour over meat. Add the beer. Cook in oven for 2-2½ hours, until meat is tender.

Twenty minutes before stew is done, remove from oven and place on heated burner on top of stove. (Be sure your container can be used in this manner.) Mix together Bisquick or Tea Bisk and water. Drop mixture by tablespoon onto slowly bubbling stew. Cook first 10 minutes uncovered, second 10 minutes covered.

Veal Chops with Red and Green Peppers

Preparation time: 15 minutes
Cooking time: 1 hour (total)
Degree of difficulty: simple
Servings: 8
Calories per serving: 365

The peppers lend this dish color and the olives give it zing. Serve with rice and dry red wine.

8 loin veal chops
6 tablespoons olive oil
8 large peppers (green and red), seeded and sliced
2 medium onions, chopped
3 cloves garlic, minced
10 green olives, chopped
Salt and freshly ground black pepper to taste
All-purpose flour
2 tablespoons butter

Preheat oven to 350°F. Heat the oil in a frying pan and sauté the peppers, onion, and garlic until tender, stirring often. Transfer to a bowl and add the olives, salt, and pepper.

Dust the chops lightly with flour. Heat the butter in the same skillet, add the chops, and brown on both sides. Place the chops in a covered casserole and cover with pepper mixture. Bake for 40 minutes, or until chops are tender.

Cilantro, or coriander, is an ancient herb, newly popular in California-style cooking. It's fresh, pungent, and not overwhelming in taste, and is used in soups, stews, salads, and grains (especially rice and lentils) as well as in fish and poultry dishes. It's sometimes called Chinese parsley, and is combined with onion and lemon juice for a Thai salad: in Thailand the roots are often used as well as the leaves. In India it's used in curries and chutneys, and a legume dish called dal.

Rosemary Lamb Chops and Spinach Salad with Strawberries (see recipe page 159)

Rosemary Lamb Chops

Preparation time: 5 minutes
Cooking time: less than 30 minutes
Degree of difficulty: simple
Servings: 6
Calories per serving: 325

In this simple recipe branches of fresh rosemary add a wonderful aroma and flavor to barbecued lamb.

6 rib or loin lamb chops, cut 1½ inches thick

6 large sprigs of fresh or dried rosemary

Olive oil

Salt and freshly ground pepper to taste

Place chops on a barbecue rack 3-4 inches above hot coals and place a sprig of rosemary on each, or sprinkle chops with dried rosemary. Brush with oil and grill until browned. Turn, moving the sprig of rosemary to rest on the grill underneath each chop, and brown other side of chops (dried rosemary will cling when chops are turned). Cook and turn, basting with oil as needed, until done as desired, 15-18 minutes for medium-rare and up to 25 minutes for well done. Add salt and pepper to taste.

Pork Cutlets with Tomato Sauce

Preparation time: 15 minutes
Cooking time: 1½ hours (total)
Degree of difficulty: simple
Servings: 6
Calories per serving: 465

Pork chops and cutlets were often served in Victorian and Edwardian times either fried or grilled in a crisp jacket of breadcrumbs. This coating prevents chops from drying out, and adds crispness to meat.

SAUCE

1 28-ounce can tomatoes

4 tablespoons butter

Salt and freshly ground pepper to taste

Dash of lemon juice

PORK

6 thin pork chops, boned and trimmed of fat, or thin pork cutlets

½ cup butter

1½ cups dried breadcrumbs

¼-½ teaspoon dried sage

Salt and freshly ground black pepper to taste

Place the tomatoes and butter in a medium uncovered saucepan over low heat. Season lightly with salt and pepper, and simmer down to a moist purée, stirring occasionally. This will take about 1 hour and 10 minutes.

Meanwhile prepare the pork: melt butter in a small saucepan and pour half into a warm soup plate. Dip chops in the butter, coating on all sides, then in the breadcrumbs mixed with sage, salt, and pepper. Press meat to encrust it with an even layer of crumbs.

Pour the remaining melted butter into a large frying pan and heat through. When the butter is light brown, add chops and fry over medium heat, turning once or twice until they're crisp and brown, about 20 minutes. Drain the chops on paper towels for a minute, add a squeeze of lemon juice to the tomato sauce, and serve in a heated sauceboat along with the chops.

**Sweetbreads in
Puff Pastry**

Sweetbreads in Puff Pastry

Preparation time: 15 minutes
Soaking time: overnight
Cooking time: 1 hour (total)
Degree of difficulty: moderate
Servings: 8-10
Calories per serving: 628 (1/8)
502 (1/10)

Superchef Jacques Pépin designed this recipe, as lovely to look at as it is to eat.

3½-4 pounds calves' sweetbreads

1 package frozen puff pastry, cut into various shapes and baked according to directions

3 tablespoons unsalted butter

3 cups mirepoix (finely diced carrot, onion, and leek)

1½-2 cups dry white wine

2½ cups seeded and finely chopped fresh tomatoes

2 tablespoons chopped fresh or 1 tablespoon dried rosemary

1½ cups demiglace or 3 cups canned beef bouillon, boiled and reduced by half

Soak sweetbreads overnight in cold water. (This whitens the meat. Change water once during soaking.) Put sweetbreads in a large saucepan; cover with change of cold water; bring to boil and cook for 12-15 minutes. Drain and plunge into cold water for 5 minutes (change water once). Trim and peel away as much of the covering membrane as you can. Plunge sweetbreads in clean change of cold water, then place on a cookie sheet covered with a paper towel. Cover with more paper towels, place another cookie sheet on top, and weight down with cans. Leave for 1-2 hours, then slice sweetbreads. In a large frying pan, melt butter until foaming. Add *mirepoix* and sauté for 10 minutes. Meanwhile, preheat oven to 250°F. Add sweetbreads and wine to the *mirepoix*,

cover, and cook over medium heat for 8 minutes. Remove sweetbreads and keep warm in oven. Add tomatoes and rosemary to pan; cook 3 minutes over medium heat. Stir in demiglace and reduce sauce to desired consistency (alternatively, thicken with a little potato starch or arrowroot). Spoon sauce over sweetbreads and decorate with pastry shapes.

Maple syrup, one of Canada's best-known exports, can be kept unopened on a cool, dry shelf for up to two years, but once opened, it can spoil easily at room temperature. Keep it in the refrigerator, tightly capped, for up to a year, bringing it to room temperature before using. It will keep indefinitely in the freezer, of course. If mold forms on the refrigerated syrup, bring to a boil, skim the surface until clear, and pour the new syrup into sterilized jars before sealing, cooling, and putting in the refrigerator or freezer.

Meat Balls Stroganoff

Preparation time: 15 minutes
Cooking time: 20 minutes
Degree of difficulty: simple
Servings: 4
Calories per serving: 520

The real Beef Stroganoff is a deluxe dish prepared with beef tenderloin, white wine, butter, and sour cream. The following economical version tastes surprisingly like the original.

1 pound ground beef
½ cup milk
½ cup dry, fine breadcrumbs
1 teaspoon salt
⅛ teaspoon freshly ground pepper
1 tablespoon chopped parsley
3 tablespoons butter
1 medium onion, diced fine
¼-½ pound fresh mushrooms, sliced
½ teaspoon paprika
2 tablespoons all-purpose flour
1 cup consommé, beef stock, or beef broth
½ cup sour cream
1 teaspoon Worcestershire sauce
Salt and freshly ground pepper to taste
Buttered noodles or rice

Combine ground beef, milk, bread crumbs, salt, pepper, and parsley. Blend well and shape into 1-inch balls.

Melt butter to sizzling in a large frying pan and brown beef balls well on all sides. Remove meat; add onion and mushrooms, and sauté quickly. Sprinkle paprika and flour over contents of frying pan. Pour in consommé, stirring constantly, and cook until mixture thickens. Blend in the sour cream. Return beef balls to pan, add Worcestershire sauce and salt and pepper to taste, and heat thoroughly but gently, without boiling. Serve with buttered noodles or rice.

Navarin d'Agneau

Preparation time: 20 minutes
Cooking time: 2 hours (total)
Degree of difficulty: moderate
Servings: 8
Calories per serving: 495

Serve this with something light for dessert like poached pears with a little scoop of frozen almond cream.

4½ pounds fresh, lean lamb (shoulder or stewing cuts)
3 tablespoons all-purpose flour
Salt and freshly ground pepper to taste
2 tablespoons butter
2 tablespoons cooking oil
2 carrots, coarsely chopped (for meat)
1 large onion, coarsely chopped (for meat)
1½ tablespoons all-purpose flour
½ cup white wine
2 cups bouillon
1 large tomato, peeled, seeded, and coarsely chopped
1 bouquet garni
12-15 carrots
1 large turnip
6 medium potatoes
2 dozen small onions, peeled
¼ pound mushroom caps

Cut the lamb into 2-inch pieces and dust lightly with salt, pepper, and flour. Heat butter and oil in a large, heavy frying pan. Brown the meat well and set aside. Cut 2 of the carrots and 1 large onion in large pieces and brown them in the hot fat. Reserve the carrots and onion with the meat, and pour off most of the fat from the pan. Add the flour to remaining hot fat. Stir till brown. Add the wine and bouillon. (If you think you need more liquid for the amount of meat add more bouillon.) Add the tomato, bouquet garni, salt and pepper. Return meat, onion, and carrots. Simmer, loosely covered, for 1½ hours.

Peel and trim the carrots, turnip, and potatoes into 1½-inch ovals, and cook them separately until just tender. Simmer the onions for about 12 minutes. Simmer the mushrooms for 5 minutes in a little water, lemon juice, and butter. Drain the mushrooms and add this liquid to the meat sauce.

Remove the meat from pan with a slotted spoon when it is tender. Discard the bouquet garni. Strain the sauce, taste, and adjust seasonings.

To serve, place the meat in the middle of a heated serving platter. Alternate the cooked vegetables around the lamb. Sprinkle the potatoes with some finely chopped parsley. Spoon some sauce over the meat. The remaining sauce may be passed in a warmed sauceboat.

Maple-Baked Spareribs

Preparation time: 10 minutes
Cooking time: about 1 hour (total)
Degree of difficulty: simple
Servings: 4-5
Calories per serving: 888 (1/4)
710 (1/5)

Baking spareribs keeps them juicy and moist; this sauce makes them taste barbecued.

3 pounds spareribs
¾ cup maple syrup
1 tablespoon catsup
1 tablespoon cider vinegar
1 tablespoon finely chopped onion
1 teaspoon Worcestershire sauce
Salt and freshly ground pepper to taste
¼ teaspoon dry mustard

Cut spareribs into serving-size pieces and simmer in water just to cover for about 30 minutes. Drain.

Preheat oven to 350°F. Mix remaining ingredients together. Put spareribs in shallow baking pan and pour half the sauce over. Bake for about 30 minutes, turning and basting with remaining sauce. If not brown enough, coat with sauce and place under the broiler for a few minutes.

Braised Shoulder of Lamb with White Beans

Preparation time: 30 minutes
Cooking time: 4 hours (total)
Degree of difficulty: moderate
Servings: 8-10
Calories per serving: 1120 (1/8)
896 (1/10)

Lamb and white beans are a traditional combination that is an adventure to taste. This is a particularly good recipe. Serve it with a lightly steamed green vegetable and a robust red wine.

7-pound shoulder of lamb, boned and tied (about 5 pounds after boning)

3 cloves garlic, slivered

4 tablespoons vegetable oil

4 tablespoons butter

4 medium onions, thinly sliced

3 large carrots, cut in 1-inch pieces

3 large stalks celery, cut in 1-inch pieces

2 cups beef stock, fresh or canned

1 cup dry white wine

1 teaspoon dried thyme

2 medium tomatoes, peeled, seeded, and coarsely chopped

Bouquet of 4 sprigs parsley and 1 bay leaf

Salt and freshly ground pepper to taste

1 pound pea beans, marrow beans or Great Northern beans

2 tablespoons finely chopped parsley for garnish

Make deep incisions along the length of the lamb with a knife and insert slivers of garlic in them. Heat the vegetable oil in a large, heavy frying pan. Add the lamb and brown on all sides, about 20 minutes.

Preheat the oven to 325°F. Melt the butter in a casserole just big enough to hold the lamb shoulder. Add the onion, carrot, and celery. Cook the vegetables over moderate heat for about 15 minutes. Place the browned lamb, fat side up, on the vegetables in the casserole. Add the stock, wine, thyme, tomatoes, and bouquet. Sprinkle the lamb generously with salt and pepper. Cover the casserole and bring to a boil on top of the stove. Transfer to oven and cook for about 3 hours.

Meanwhile, place the beans in a large saucepan, cover with cold water, and bring to a boil. Remove from heat and let stand for 1 hour. Then bring the water to the boil again, reduce heat, and simmer, uncovered, for 1 hour or until beans are tender but not falling apart. Add boiling water if necessary to keep beans covered with liquid. Drain the beans thoroughly and set aside.

Remove the cooked lamb from the casserole and strain the braising juices into a saucepan. Force the vegetables through a sieve into the sauce and boil until the amount of sauce is reduced by half. Return the lamb to the casserole and pour the sauce over it. Add the beans, then reheat meat, beans, and sauce on top of the stove just before serving.

Slice the lamb and arrange the slices down the middle of a heated platter; arrange the beans on either side. Moisten lamb and beans with a few tablespoons of the sauce and sprinkle with chopped parsley. Pour remaining sauce into a heated sauceboat and pass separately.

Leftover Lamb with Onions

Preparation time: 15 minutes
Cooking time: about 2 hours
Degree of difficulty: simple
Servings: 2-4
Calories per serving: 540 (1/2)
270 (1/4)

From actor/director Jean Gascon, this dish is sometimes preferred to fresh leg of lamb.

2-3 cups cooked leftover lamb (from roast leg of lamb)

2 onions per person

1 clove garlic, crushed

2-3 tablespoons butter

3/4 cup dry white wine

1/4 teaspoon thyme

1 bay leaf

1 teaspoon minced parsley

Salt and freshly ground pepper to taste

Remove lamb from bone and cut into bite-size pieces, cutting off most of fat. Reserve bone. Slice onions and sauté with garlic in butter until golden. Add meat, bone, wine, and seasonings. Cover and cook over very low heat for 1½ hours, stirring from time to time. Discard bone, serve with rice, noodles or small potatoes.

When you put together the makings for hamburgers, blend any leftover vegetables and mix with the raw meat before you make the patties. This will add juice, flavor, and often fibre.

Kitty Pope's Orange and Ginger Pork Roast

Preparation time: about 1 hour
Cooking time: about 2½ hours
Degree of difficulty: simple
Calories per serving: 630
Servings: 4-6
(with delicious leftovers)

Cuisine '85 Grand Winner

Yellowknife's talented Kitty Pope has created a wonderful recipe that is flavorful and easy to prepare.

1 4-6 pound boneless pork roast, prepared for stuffing
2 tablespoons butter
1 small onion, finely chopped
1 cup pecans
2 tablespoons candied ginger, chopped
1 teaspoon salt (optional)
1 teaspoon freshly ground pepper
1 teaspoon grated orange peel
3 cups crumbled corn bread (recipe follows)
1 cup fresh orange juice
1 cup orange marmalade
¼ cup chopped candied ginger
Watercress sprigs and orange sections for garnish

To prepare the stuffing, heat the 2 tablespoons of butter until bubbly in a large skillet. Add the onion and sauté until tender. Stir in the pecans, candied ginger, salt, pepper, orange peel, and crumbled corn bread; combine the ingredients well. Remove from heat and cool to room temperature. Spread stuffing over unrolled pork roast; roll up and tie securely. Roast on a rack for 2½-2¾ hours (or according to meat thermometer).

To prepare basting sauce, combine orange juice, orange marmalade, and ¼ cup candied ginger in a blender or food processor and blend until smooth. During the final

PHOTO BY SKIP DEAN

90 minutes of cooking, baste the roast often with basting sauce. Let roast stand at room temperature for 10 minutes before carving. Garnish with watercress and orange sections.

CORN BREAD

¾ cup all-purpose flour
2½ teaspoons baking powder
1 tablespoon sugar
½ teaspoon salt
1¼ cups corn meal
1 egg
2 tablespoons melted butter
1 cup milk

Preheat oven to 425°F. Combine the flour, baking powder, sugar, salt, and corn meal in a bowl. Beat together the egg, melted butter, and milk. Pour the milk mixture into the flour mixture and stir only until combined; do not overmix. Pour into a greased 9-x-9-inch cake pan and bake for 20-25 minutes, or until cake tester inserted into the centre comes out clean. Set aside several hours or overnight before combining with stuffing ingredients.

Stuffed Pork Tenderloin

Preparation time: 20 minutes
Cooking time: 1 hour
Degree of difficulty: moderate
Servings: 6
Calories per serving: 350

Serve this hot for family or company — and hope for enough left over for sandwiches the next day.

2 pork tenderloins, at least ¾ pound each
1 lemon, halved
2 tablespoons butter
1 onion, finely chopped
1 cup well-packed fresh breadcrumbs
1 teaspoon crumbled sage leaves
Grated peel of ½ lemon
½ teaspoon salt
¼ teaspoon freshly ground pepper
1 egg
All-purpose flour
2 bacon slices, diced
1 tablespoon butter
1½-2 cups beef stock or consommé

Split each tenderloin lengthwise, being careful not to separate completely. Open and rub each with lemon. Melt butter in a skillet and add the onion. Cook over medium heat until transparent, but do not brown. Remove from heat and add breadcrumbs, sage, lemon peel, salt, and pepper. Mix well, then break the egg on top and stir well into the breadcrumbs.

Preheat oven to 350°F. Place the stuffing on the split surface of one tenderloin and turn up the tip. Put the second tenderloin on top. Sew together all around, or tie with string, then roll lightly in flour. In a heavy casserole with a tightly fitting lid, melt the diced bacon and add 1 tablespoon of butter. Add the prepared tenderloin and sauté until light brown on both sides. Cover and cook for 45-50 minutes. Transfer the tenderloin to a hot platter. To make gravy, add 1 tablespoon of flour to the drippings and stir until browned. Add beef stock or consommé and stir until gravy is smooth and slightly thickened. Serve separately.

PHOTO BY GARY WHITE

Stuffed Pork Tenderloin with Sautéed Parsnips, Carrots, and Zucchini (see recipe page 187)

Brisket and Cola

Preparation time: 5 minutes
Cooking time: 3 hours
Degree of difficulty: simple
Servings: 10-12
Calories per serving: 732 (1/10)
610 (1/12)

This makes an excellent one-dish meal if you add potatoes, carrots, and onions (they should be parboiled first) for the final 30 minutes of cooking time.

1 5-pound brisket
4 tablespoons all-purpose flour
24 ounces cola
½ cup prepared mustard
½ cup catsup
2 teaspoons soya sauce
½ teaspoon finely chopped garlic
1 teaspoon Italian seasoning
Salt and freshly ground pepper to taste

Preheat oven to 300°F. Place the roast in a roasting pan and season it generously with salt and pepper. Mix together the rest of the ingredients to form a smooth sauce. Pour the sauce over the roast. Bake for 30 minutes a pound, plus an additional ½ hour at the end, basting every ½ hour. Cover the roast for the last ½ hour.

Today's Canadian pork is leaner and more tender than ever before because it's grain-fed. The pork producers are talking up barbecued pork steaks, or sautéed pork steaks, even for company, and point to a low 196 calories for each 3-ounce serving.

Stuffed Pork Chops

Preparation time: 15 minutes
Cooking time: 1 hour (total)
Degree of difficulty: simple
Servings: 6
Calories per serving: 835

This recipe was planned for the demanding workers at a British Columbia construction camp.

12 pork chops ¼-½ inch thick

4 strips bacon, diced

1 onion, peeled and chopped

2 stalks celery, finely sliced

2 cloves garlic, peeled and chopped

3 tablespoons butter

¾ cup breadcrumbs

¼ cup cooked rice

¼ cup applesauce

1 egg, slightly beaten

½ teaspoon sage

Salt and freshly ground pepper to taste

Preheat oven to 350°F. Sauté the bacon, onion, celery, and garlic in the butter until the onion is soft and the bacon crisp. Add the breadcrumbs, rice, applesauce, egg, and seasonings. Mix. Quickly brown the pork chops and place 2 tablespoons of stuffing on 6 of the chops. Cover each with another chop as if to make pork chop sandwiches. Salt and pepper the top chops. Bake for 45 minutes.

Steak with Raisins and Pine Nuts

Preparation time: 15 minutes (including sauce)
Cooking time: 5-10 minutes
Degree of difficulty: simple
Servings: 2
Calories per serving: 775

A festive dish with the added interest of wine-soaked raisins and toasted pine nuts. Serve with buttered noodles and a green salad.

2 boned sirloin steaks, ½ inch thick

2 tablespoons butter

Salt to taste

2 tablespoons raisins soaked in port

4 tablespoons pine nuts

2 tablespoons sherry

Cognac

4 tablespoons chopped fresh tomato

Chopped parsley

SAUCE

2 tablespoons butter

2 tablespoons chopped green onion

1 tablespoon finely chopped parsley

1 tablespoon Worcestershire sauce

2 tablespoons sherry

¼ teaspoon cinnamon

Combine all the sauce ingredients, heat gently for 1 minute and set aside. Flatten the steaks to about ⅓ inch. Melt the butter in a frying pan, add steaks, and salt lightly. Add the nuts and raisins. Turn the steaks and cook for about 1 minute. Add the sherry and a little cognac and flame briefly. Stir in the tomato. Cook for 1 minute for rare steaks, or to taste. Add sauce. Garnish with chopped parsley.

Veal Scallops with Fresh Orange Sauce

Preparation time: 15 minutes
Cooking time: 1 hour (total)
Degree of difficulty: moderate
Servings: 4
Calories per serving: 540

Tender veal is cooked in butter and napped with a sauce of vermouth, rum and fresh orange juice. This recipe is from Au Tournant de la Rivière, an excellent restaurant in Carignan, 20 kilometres from Montreal.

4 veal scallops

Peel of 4 oranges (all white removed), cut into thin strips (julienned)

2 tablespoons sugar

2 tablespoons butter

2 tablespoons dark rum

1 cup dry vermouth

Juice of 4 oranges

1 teaspoon green peppercorns

2 tablespoons very cold butter

To prepare the orange julienne, slice the orange peel into very thin strips. Bring to a boil 3 times in 3 changes of water. (Each time the water comes to a boil, remove the orange peel, discard the water, and add fresh water to the pot.) The fourth time, barely cover the julienne with fresh water and add 2 tablespoons of sugar to the water. Cook slowly over low heat for about 20 minutes, or until water has evaporated. Drain and set aside.

Sauté the veal scallops in 2 tablespoons butter for 2-3 minutes on each side. As each scallop is cooked, place it on a warm platter. When all are cooked, drain the pan of excess butter. Add the rum and vermouth to the frying pan. Scrape up any bits stuck to the bottom of the pan and include them in the sauce. Ignite the sauce and let the flame die out. Add the orange juice. Reduce the sauce to half by simmering rapidly. Add the peppercorns and the julienne and quickly whip in the cold butter with a wire whisk. Pour the sauce over the scallops and serve immediately.

Veal with Cherries

Preparation time: 20 minutes
Cooking time: 2¼-2½ hours
Degree of difficulty: simple
Servings: 6-8
Calories per serving: 360 (1/6)
270 (1/8)

This dish appears in so many Russian cookbooks it's surprising it isn't as ubiquitous as Chicken Kiev or Beef Stroganoff. It's a delicious example of the Russian predilection for combinations of fruit and meat.

3 pounds veal shank, cut in ½-inch slices
3 tablespoons butter
2 medium onions, chopped
2 14-ounce cans cherries
1 cup seedless raisins
1 cup beef, chicken, or veal stock
½ cup dry red wine
12 cardamom buds or 1 teaspoon powdered cardamom
1 teaspoon salt
Freshly ground pepper to taste
Rice or noodles

Brown meat gently in butter in a heavy 2-quart casserole. Add chopped onion and sauté until tender, but not brown. Drain cherries, reserving liquid. Add pitted cherries, raisins, stock, wine, cardamom, and ¼ of cherry juice. Season with salt and pepper. Cover with a tightly fitting lid and simmer on top of the stove until meat is tender, about 2 hours. Remove to a serving platter and keep warm. Thicken sauce if necessary by adding a roux made by heating together 2 tablespoons flour and 1 tablespoon butter in a small skillet. Stir into sauce and bring to a boil. Pour over meat. Serve with rice or buttered noodles.

Veal Mozzarella

Preparation time: 20 minutes
Cooking time: about 1 hour
Degree of difficulty: simple
Servings: 6
Calories per serving: 385

Good with rice or pasta to soak up the sauce.

1½ pounds veal cutlets, sliced ¼-inch thick
1 large onion, chopped
2 cloves garlic, minced
3 tablespoons chopped green pepper
¼ pound fresh mushrooms, sliced
¼ cup olive or vegetable oil
3 8-ounce cans tomato sauce
1 bay leaf
¼ teaspoon oregano
1 egg
½ cup milk
1 teaspoon salt (or to taste)
⅛ teaspoon freshly ground pepper (or to taste)
½ cup fine dry breadcrumbs
6 ounces Mozzarella cheese slices

Sauté onion, garlic, pepper, and mushrooms in oil until just limp. Add tomato sauce, bay leaf, and oregano. Simmer, covered, for 20 minutes. Remove bay leaf. Beat together egg, milk, salt, and pepper. Pound veal very thin and dip into egg mixture, then coat in crumbs. Brown on both sides in a little hot oil. Place veal in a shallow baking dish. Pour sauce over and bake for 30 minutes. Arrange cheese slices on top and bake about 5 minutes more, or until cheese is bubbly and golden.

Leg of Lamb, Juniper

Preparation time: 15 minutes
Chilling time: 3 days
Cooking time: 1½-2 hours
Degree of difficulty: simple
Servings: 6-8
Calories per serving: 460

Wonderfully traditional way to serve lamb — add curried rice, mango chutney, and green peas.

1 3-4 pound boned leg of lamb
Salt and freshly ground pepper to taste
10 juniper berries
2 tablespoons soft butter
1 teaspoon dry mustard
¼ cup brandy

Salt and pepper the lamb. Crush 5 juniper berries (they can be purchased at drugstores and gourmet shops), and sprinkle over the lamb. Roll the leg and tie. Wrap in a cloth and refrigerate 3 days.

Preheat oven to 325°F. Cream together the butter and dry mustard, and spread over the lamb. Place in a roasting pan. Add the remaining juniper berries. Roast meat 30-35 minutes per pound or until internal temperature reaches 160°F on meat thermometer.

Remove from oven when cooked, and baste with brandy. Flame, basting with the juices until the flame dies out.

For the most success with your microwave, always undercook, because you can always add more time, but never take it away.

Baked Ham in Maple Syrup

Pork Fillets with Fig Purée

Preparation time: 45 minutes
Cooking time: 45 minutes
Degree of difficulty: simple
Calories per serving: 560

Cuisine '85 Semifinalist
A satisfying, surprising combination.

1½ pounds pork tenderloin
6 dried figs, chopped
3 tablespoons port
Pinch of salt
7 tablespoons butter
2 tablespoons water
Salt and freshly ground pepper to taste
2 tablespoons red wine vinegar
2 tablespoons minced shallots
1 cup whipping cream

Marinate the figs in the port for 45 minutes. Add salt, 1 tablespoon of butter, and 2 tablespoons water. Cover and simmer 20 minutes until the figs are very soft. Transfer to a blender or food processor; add 2 more tablespoons of butter, and purée until smooth; set aside. Slice the pork against the grain in 1-inch slices. Flatten by pounding it between sheets of wax paper. Season with salt and pepper. Melt 3 tablespoons of the butter in a frying pan and sauté the pork in batches. Transfer to a serving platter, cover, and keep warm in the oven. Deglaze the pan with the vinegar. Add 1 more tablespoon of butter and the minced shallots and cook until shallots are soft. Add the cream and any juices that have accumulated from the meat. Simmer sauce until slightly reduced, whisk in fig purée, strain, taste for seasoning, and serve pork napped with sauce.

Baked Ham in Maple Syrup

Preparation time: 10 minutes
Cooking time: 90 minutes
Degree of difficulty: simple
Servings: 12-15
Calories per serving: 670 (1/12)
536 (1/15)

A recipe adapted from one by Marcel Kretz, chef at Val-David's La Sapinière, that's perfect for summer Sunday brunches or dinner parties.

1 ready-to-eat, 7-11-pound ham
1 tablespoon cinnamon
1 tablespoon ground cloves
½ cup brown sugar
1 cup maple syrup
1 cup water

Preheat oven to 350°F. Remove skin from ham and score the fat in a diamond pattern. Rub with cinnamon and cloves and cover evenly with brown sugar. Place in a roasting pan. Combine maple syrup and water and pour around the ham. Bake 90 minutes, basting frequently. A ready-to-eat ham is done when its internal temperature registers 130°F, Agriculture Canada reports. (Add water if necessary to prevent syrup from caramelizing.)

Steak, Kidney, and Oyster Pie

Preparation time: 30 minutes
Soaking time: 1 hour
Cooking time: 1½ hours
Degree of difficulty: moderate
Servings: 8
Calories per serving: 430

This adaptation of a medieval recipe is from Fenton's restaurant in Toronto.

¼ cup chopped onion
1 cup fresh oysters
½ cup white wine
1½ pounds veal kidneys, washed and trimmed
1 tablespoon vinegar
2 tablespoons clarified butter or oil
2 pounds lean diced beef (blade, bottom butt, top sirloin)
Vegetable oil
1 large onion, sliced
1 clove garlic, crushed
2 tablespoons tomato paste
½ cup red wine
1 bay leaf
2 teaspoons thyme
2 cups beef bouillon
1 tablespoon each softened butter and all-purpose flour, mixed well
Salt and freshly ground black pepper to taste
Puff pastry or short crust

Sauté chopped onion in butter. Add oysters with their liquid and the white wine. Bring to a boil and remove oysters immediately; they should be only partially cooked. Reserve.

Soak the diced, cleaned kidneys in enough water to cover plus 1 tablespoon vinegar for 1 hour. Drain well. Sauté in clarified butter or oil for 4-5 minutes. Drain and reserve.

Thoroughly brown the meat in hot oil, stirring constantly. Remove from the pan, leaving the drippings.

Sauté onion and garlic in the drippings. Add tomato paste, stir, and cook until brown. Add the red wine, stir, and let simmer until reduced by half. Add meat, bay leaf, and thyme. Stir. Add beef stock to cover and simmer until the meat is tender. Thicken the sauce with the butter-flour mixture. Season to taste with salt and pepper.

Preheat oven to 350°F. Arrange the oysters and kidneys in the bottom of an earthenware or ceramic pot. Cover with the steak mixture. Top with pastry, cutting small steam vents. Bake until pastry is brown.

Lamb Noisettes with Candied Lemon Peel

Preparation time: 10 minutes
Cooking time: 20-25 minutes
Degree of difficulty: simple
Servings: 6-8
Calories per serving: 267 (1/6)
200 (1/8)

The recipe for this exquisite dish was prepared for *Homemaker's* by the New Zealand Lamb Information Centre.

8 lamb noisettes (sliced loin fillets, or substitute boned loin chops)
2 teaspoons crushed cumin seeds
1 large lemon
½ cup sugar
½ cup water
1 tablespoon butter
1 teaspoon finely chopped shallots
¼ cup white vermouth
1 teaspoon grated lemon peel
½ cup whipping cream

Rub lamb with 1 teaspoon cumin and set aside. To prepare a candied lemon-peel garnish, cut the peel from the lemon, making sure all the pith is removed, and slice into thin strips. Bring sugar and water to a boil in a small saucepan. Add peel and cook until coated with sugar syrup. Remove from syrup and drain on a rack.

Melt butter in a large frying pan. Add noisettes and sauté lightly on both sides until nicely browned outside and just pink inside. Remove and set aside. Add shallots to pan and cook gently, adding more butter if necessary. Deglaze pan with vermouth. Add remaining cumin and the grated lemon peel. Reduce by half. Stir in cream and boil until thickened. Return lamb to pan. Heat through. Serve immediately, garnished with candied lemon peel.

Lamb Noisettes with Candied Lemon Peel

Veal Scallops with Fontina Cheese

Preparation time: 5 minutes
Cooking time: 10 minutes
Degree of difficulty: simple
Servings: 4-6
Calories per serving: 580 (1/4)
385 (1/6)

Fontina cheese can be purchased at most specialty stores. This dish is quickly and easily prepared just before serving.

6 veal scallops, pounded thin between pieces of wax paper
3 tablespoons butter
Salt and greshly ground pepper to taste
6 slices Fontina cheese

Heat the butter in a frying pan and sauté veal for 2 minutes on each side. Sprinkle with salt and pepper. Place the cheese on top, place under broiler a few minutes, and serve as soon as cheese has melted.

MEAT

Taste is a matter of personal choice, but quality is a matter of fact. The two may be difficult to dissociate when it comes to classical music and painting, but it's fairly easy where food is concerned. (*André Simon*)

Festive Ham with Kiwi Orange Glaze

Preparation time: 15 minutes
Cooking time: 1-1½ hours
Degree of difficulty: simple
Servings: 20-24
Calories per serving: 682 (1/20)
569 (1/24)

When New Zealand's kiwi fruit are peeled and sliced, their beautiful, clear green makes them an attractive garnish.

10-14-pound ham
1½ cups orange marmalade
½ cup orange juice
1 teaspoon rum or brandy flavoring
2 kiwis, peeled and sliced
2 oranges, peeled and sliced

Bake ham according to directions on wrapper (10-15 minutes per pound if it's a fully cooked ham). Combine marmalade and orange juice and simmer for 2-3 minutes. Add flavoring. Cool. Half an hour before ham is done, arrange kiwi and orange slices over ham and secure with toothpicks. Spoon orange glaze over ham and continue baking, basting with glaze a couple of times.

Roast Veal with Spinach Stuffing

Preparation time: 20 minutes (including cooking spinach)
Cooking time: 2½ hours
Degree of difficulty: simple
Servings: 6-8
Calories per serving: 630 (1/6)
472 (1/8)

A delicious roast, meant for festive sharing. Serve it with baked tomatoes, steamed peas, and a good dry red wine.

1 3-pound boned veal leg
3 tablespoons butter
1 medium onion, chopped
½ pound mushrooms, chopped
1 pound fresh spinach, cooked just until leaves are wilted
1 egg, slightly beaten
½ teaspoon rosemary
½ teaspoon salt
Freshly ground black pepper
1 cup cooked brown rice
4 slices bacon
1 cup beef stock
All-purpose flour

Preheat oven to 325°F. Cook the onion in the butter until translucent. Add the mushrooms and cook 3 minutes. Drain the cooked spinach and chop. Mix the vegetables with the egg, seasonings, and rice. Stuff the veal leg and close with skewers. Place on a rack in a shallow baking pan. Arrange the bacon over the meat and add the stock to the pan. Cover with aluminum foil and cook for 1 hour. Uncover and bake 30 minutes longer. Thicken the pan juices with a little flour mixed with water (if desired), and serve with the hot meat.

Marilyn's Chili

Preparation time: 15 minutes
Cooking time: 1¼-1½ hours (total)
Degree of difficulty: moderate
Servings: 8-10
Calories per serving: 500 (1/8)
400 (1/10)

Some people say the authentic Texan chili is beanless, but this is a beanful chili sleeper come to life with the addition of — you might say — everything but the kitchen sink.

2 hot Italian sausages
2 14-ounce cans kidney beans
4 slices bacon
1 medium onion, coarsely chopped
2 pounds lean ground beef
4 cloves garlic, crushed
1 teaspoon anise seeds
½ teaspoon coriander seeds, crushed
½ teaspoon fennel seeds, crushed
½ teaspoon ground cloves
1 1-inch stick cinnamon
1 teaspoon freshly ground pepper
1 teaspoon paprika
½ teaspoon ground nutmeg
1 teaspoon ground cumin
2 teaspoons ground oregano
4 teaspoons sesame seeds
¼ pound ground almonds
1 10-ounce can chicken broth
5-6 tablespoons chili powder
1½ ounces milk chocolate, broken into pieces
¾ cup tomato sauce
2 tablespoons vinegar
3 tablespoons lemon juice

Preheat oven to 350°F. Place the sausages in a baking dish and cook until done, about 20 minutes; slice and set aside. Place the kidney beans in a large pot. Fry the bacon in a saucepan. Add the onion and sauté until browned. Add the ground beef and sauté until cooked through. Mix in the sausage. Stirring continuously, add the other ingredients in order. Pour the mixture over the beans and bring to a boil, then lower heat and simmer about 45 minutes. Check occasionally and add water if necessary to maintain the consistency of a chunky soup. Adjust seasonings.

Scottish Beef and Kidney Pie

Preparation time: about 45 minutes
Cooking time: about 2 hours (total)
Standing time: overnight
Degree of difficulty: moderate
Servings: 6
Calories per serving: 295

Quite different from the English type, with the beef kidney often replaced by 3-4 lamb kidneys or 2 veal kidneys.

Pie crust of your choice

1 ½ pounds bottom round steak

1 small beef kidney

All-purpose flour

1 large onion, chopped

1 tablespoon butter

1 ¼ cups boiling water

1 teaspoon salt

¼ teaspoon freshly ground pepper

1 tablespoon Worcestershire sauce

1 tablespoon strong prepared mustard

2 tablespoons all-purpose flour

Remove and reserve all fat from the steak and cut meat into ¾-inch cubes. Cut kidney into ¼-inch cubes and roll both meats in flour. Melt fat from meat in a large frying pan, add butter, and fry onion until golden brown. Gradually add beef and kidney, stirring over high heat until all rawness disappears; then remove to a heavy metal saucepan. Add remaining ingredients to fat in frying pan, bring to a boil while stirring, and pour over meat. Cover and simmer 1 hour, or until meat is tender. Let cool and, if you wish to de-fat the sauce, refrigerate overnight.

The next day, remove fat on top and proceed. Preheat oven to 425°F. Place a small funnel or a pie bird in the centre of a deep, 10-inch-round baking dish, preferably one with a ½-inch rim. Pour in meat and about half the gravy. Roll enough pastry to cover the top, making a hole in the middle to pass over the funnel or bird, and brush with milk. Bake for 30-35 minutes, or until golden brown. Reheat leftover gravy and serve in sauceboat.

Roast Pork with Prunes

Preparation time: 20 minutes
Cooking time: about 1 ½ hours (total)
Degree of difficulty: simple
Servings: 6-8
Calories per serving: 869 (1/6)
645 (1/8)

This hearty, succulent pork roast is cooked with sage, thyme, and parsley. The prunes are plumped in port.

3 pounds pork loin, in one piece, boned and tied

12 prunes

½ cup port

¼ pound beef tongue, thinly sliced, or prosciutto ham

½ cup Dijon mustard

½ teaspoon crushed sage

½ teaspoon crushed thyme

½ teaspoon chopped parsley

½ cup brown sugar

2 cups beef bouillon (approximately)

Preheat oven to 375°F. Wipe the meat. Put the prunes in the port to steep. Push the tongue slices into the pork in several spots, using a thin sharp knife. Combine mustard with herbs and paint on meat; then roll meat in brown sugar. Place in a roasting pan or large casserole and pour the bouillon around. Roast for 30 minutes, then reduce temperature to 350°F and cook an additional hour, adding more bouillon if necessary. Add prunes and their liquid and cook another 20 minutes. Transfer meat and prunes to a warm platter. Strain the cooking liquid and serve with the roast.

NOTES

PASTA, RICE, AND GRAINS

ust a few short years ago Canadians were confined to eating their pasta in the shape of macaroni and cheese or spaghetti and meatballs — indeed, we hardly knew that the word for these homey foods *was* pasta. But there are more than 500 different shapes, sizes, and varieties of this nutritious, inexpensive, and easy-to-cook food to choose from, including those shaped like seashells, bow ties and corkscrews. A relatively inexpensive hand-operated machine allows us to make the less complicated kinds at home, while numerous delicatessens and stores specializing in pasta can provide freshly made dough cut in many shapes, as well as sauces of infinite variety (Pastissima, a Toronto store, sells black pasta, made with squid ink; with a smoked salmon sauce, it's a sublime combination even for people who don't like smoked salmon).

Rice, of course, has been around for centuries, and the best rule of thumb for simple boiled rice is to cook it in twice its quantity of water for about 25 minutes — brown rice will require more like 45 minutes. Short-grain rice is best for puddings and stuffings for vegetables, long-grain for casseroles and for stuffing chicken and poultry. Don't overlook some of the more exotic varieties available to us, like the purple rice used in sweet puddings, scented Thai rice, or pecan rice, all of which are fun to experiment with. Wild rice isn't really rice at all, but the seed of an aquatic grass native to America. It's expensive, but expands to about four times its original volume, so a little goes a long way, and its nutty flavor can provide a treat for special occasions.

Cold Pasta with Asiago Cheese, Pine Nuts, and Sun-Dried Tomatoes
(see recipe page 110)

Generally, dried fruits and vegetables, including dried mushrooms, can be kept from only 6 months to a year since, after that, flavors will dim and textures can change. Even before that, to ensure good quality, store dried foods in airtight, moisture-resistant containers in a cool, dark, dry place.

Company Macaroni and Cheese

Preparation time: 15 minutes
Cooking time: about 1 hour
Degree of difficulty: simple
Servings: 6-8
Calories per serving: 450 (1/6)
338 (1/8)

Breathes there a soul who doesn't secretly love homey macaroni and cheese?

1¾ cups elbow macaroni

¾ cup coarsely chopped onion

½ cup chopped green pepper

1 cup sliced fresh mushrooms or
1 10-ounce can sliced mushrooms, drained

3 tablespoons butter

1½ tablespoons all-purpose flour

1 teaspoon dry mustard

¾ teaspoon salt

¼ teaspoon oregano

2½ cups milk

2½ cups shredded Canadian Cheddar cheese

½ cup fine, dry breadcrumbs

Cook macaroni and drain. Turn into a buttered, 2-2½-quart casserole. Preheat oven to 350°F. Sauté onion, green pepper, and mushrooms in butter until tender. Blend in flour, mustard, salt, and oregano. Gradually stir in milk and cook over medium heat until slightly thickened. Add 2 cups cheese and stir until melted. Pour over macaroni and stir gently. Combine remaining cheese and breadcrumbs and sprinkle on top. Bake for 30-40 minutes.

Great Wild Rice Casserole

Soaking time (for rice): overnight
Preparation time: 15 minutes
Cooking time: about 1 hour (total)
Degree of difficulty: simple
Servings: 6
Calories per serving: 395

Wild rice is expensive but a little goes a long way, and the fine, nut-like taste is a brilliant complement to game or meat.

1 cup wild rice

4 cups water

8 slices of bacon

1 large onion, finely chopped

3 stalks celery, finely chopped

½ pound fresh mushrooms, finely sliced

½ cup blanched almonds

1 teaspoon oregano

Salt and freshly ground pepper to taste

½ cup consommé

Soak rice overnight. Drain and boil for about 25 minutes in 4 cups of water. (Some people suggest that the rice be drained in mid-boiling, but the water is rich in nutrients and taste.) Stir gently with a fork, if and as required. Preheat oven to 325°F. Crisp the bacon, cut in small pieces, remove from pan and sauté onion until transparent. Add the celery and mushrooms. Cook for about 2 minutes. Mix this mixture with the cooked wild rice, add the almonds, oregano rubbed in the palm of one's hand, salt and pepper to taste, and moisten as required with the consommé. Heat in oven for about 30 minutes. This casserole can be made well ahead of time and heated 30 minutes before serving.

Cold Pasta with Asiago Cheese, Pine Nuts, and Sun-Dried Tomatoes

Preparation time: 20 minutes
Degree of difficulty: simple
Servings: 6-8
Calories per serving: 316 (1/6)
237 (1/8)

This recipe, from Fenton's restaurant in Toronto, is a toast to the great Italian Renaissance painters, and is representative of pasta's renaissance.

8 ounces linguine, cooked al dente

½ cup Asiago or
Parmesan cheese, grated

2 ounces toasted pine nuts

2 ounces sun-dried tomatoes (available in gourmet shops or Italian grocery stores; if unavailable, substitute 1 tomato, peeled, seeded and finely diced)

1 teaspoon finely chopped garlic

¼ cup chopped fresh basil (optional)

¼ cup chopped Italian parsley

1 teaspoon Dijon mustard

1 egg yolk

3 tablespoons walnut or olive oil

2 tablespoons fresh lemon juice

2 tablespoons dry white wine

Salt and freshly ground white pepper to taste

Combine the cheese, pine nuts, tomatoes, garlic, basil, and parsley; toss with linguine. Whisk the mustard into the egg yolk. Slowly whisk in the walnut oil, a few drops at a time. Add the lemon juice and wine, and season to taste with salt and pepper. Toss dressing with linguine mixture and serve at room temperature.

Homemade Noodles with Poppyseeds

Preparation time: 30-45 minutes
Standing time: 45 minutes
Cooking time: 60-90 minutes
Degree of difficulty: challenging
Servings: 6
Calories per serving: 217

2 cups all-purpose flour
Pinch of salt
2 eggs, beaten
Flour for rolling and cutting dough
2 tablespoons poppyseeds
3 tablespoons butter
1 tablespoon parsley, chopped

Place flour and salt in a bowl and make a well in the centre. Put beaten eggs into the well. Using a fork, gradually blend the flour and egg from the centre out, until all the flour is incorporated into the egg. (If egg-flour mixture is too dry, add water; if too wet, add a little more flour.) Transfer mixture to a lightly floured surface and knead well for about 10 minutes, or until the dough is firm and smooth. (Extra water or flour may also be added at the beginning of kneading if necessary.) Cover dough with a towel and allow to stand 45 minutes.

Divide the dough into two portions; on a floured surface, roll out each into sheets as thin as possible. Flour sheets and, using a sharp knife or wheel cutter, cut the pasta cross-wise into noodles about ½ inch wide. (Rolling and cutting may also be done with a pasta machine.) Separate noodles on a large tray and set aside until cooking time. Bring a large pot of salted water to a rapid boil. Add noodles and cook to desired tenderness (1 minute for *al dente*; 1½ minutes for well done). Drain noodles. Toss with poppyseeds, butter, and parsley.

Pasta Partouz

Standing time: (zucchini) 1 hour
Preparation time: 15 minutes
Cooking time: 15-20 minutes
Degree of difficulty: simple
Servings: 6-8
Calories per serving: 765 (1/6)
540 (1/8)

This colorful mixture makes good use of tomatoes and zucchini.

6 ripe tomatoes, chopped
3 zucchini, unpeeled, chopped
1 tablespoon salt
1 medium onion, coarsely chopped
4 cloves garlic, chopped
½ pound fresh mushrooms, sliced
⅓ cup olive oil
4 slices good quality ham,
cut in strips
1 tablespoon dried oregano or
2 tablespoons fresh
1½ pounds spaghetti
1 tablespoon salt
3 tablespoons butter
Freshly ground black pepper
1 cup freshly grated
Parmesan cheese

Salt the tomatoes and zucchini and let drain in a collander for about 1 hour. Sauté the onion, garlic, and mushrooms in some of the olive oil until the onion begins to brown. Drain and reserve. Using the same frying pan, add a little more olive oil and sauté the ham strips for 1 minute. Add the tomatoes and zucchini, the mushroom mixture, and the oregano. Cook slowly while you boil the spaghetti in a large pot with 1 tablespoon of salt and a little olive oil. When cooked *al dente*, drain and toss with the butter. Place the spaghetti on a serving platter and cover with the vegetable mixture. Grind some fresh pepper over and serve immediately with a bowl of freshly grated Parmesan cheese.

Lemon Rice

Preparation time: 6 minutes
Cooking time: 30-40 minutes
Degree of difficulty: simple
Servings: 4-6
Calories per serving: 357 (1/4)
238 (1/6)

A nice fresh accompaniment to any meat dish. This can also stand on its own — nuts supply the protein.

1 cup long-grain rice
2 tablespoons cooking oil
2 cups water
½ teaspoon mustard seeds
1 teaspoon urad dal (a lentil with
a black husk)
½ teaspoon chickpeas, split
1 dried red chili pepper
½ teaspoon turmeric
¼ cup cashew nuts,
halved or broken
¼ cup peanuts
½ teaspoon salt
Juice of 1 lemon or lime
1-2 tablespoons chopped fresh
coriander or parsley leaves

Wash and drain rice. In a heavy saucepan, heat oil until a drop of water flicked into it splutters; add mustard seeds, urad dal, chickpeas, broken chili pepper, and turmeric. Fry for a couple of minutes. Add rice and stir to coat with oil. Add water and bring to a boil; turn heat down and simmer until rice granules are soft but still not sticking together. Add cashews and peanuts and juice of lemon or lime. Heat through. Sprinkle with coriander or parsley leaves before serving.

Noodles, spaghetti, and all similar Italian specialties aren't originally Italian, but Chinese (some say Japanese). Marco Polo is said to have brought back a recipe for pasta from China to Venice, but other experts say the Germans learned first about pasta, and the Italians were simply the first to appreciate it.

Saffron Pasta with Veal Sauce

*Preparation time: about 1 hour,
including pasta*
Cooking time: about 40 minutes
Degree of difficulty: challenging
Servings: 6
Calories per serving: 500

For a very special dinner, making saffron noodles is worth the time, trouble, and expense. The color is wonderful and the veal sauce (not unlike an osso buco) fabulous.

3 leeks, ends trimmed, white and light green parts thinly sliced and soaked in cold water for ½ hour
¼ cup olive oil
2 tablespoons unsalted butter
¾ pound stewing veal, cut in bite-size chunks
1 tablespoon all-purpose flour
1 small celery stalk, chopped
1 small carrot, chopped
1 small piece lemon peel
1 cup dry white wine
1 cup canned Italian tomatoes, drained
1 teaspoon tomato paste
Salt and freshly ground pepper to taste
1 large clove garlic, peeled and minced
10 leaves Italian parsley, minced
4 sage leaves, minced
Grated peel of 1 lemon

SAFFRON PASTA

3 large eggs
1 teaspoon olive oil
½ teaspoon salt
½–1 teaspoon powdered saffron
2 cups all-purpose flour

To prepare the sauce, drain the leeks and pat dry. Heat the olive oil and butter in a large saucepan and sauté leeks for about 5 minutes. Dredge the veal in flour and add to the pan; brown on all sides. Add the chopped celery and carrot and sauté 2 minutes more. Add the lemon peel and wine and cook over low heat for 20 minutes. Add the tomatoes and tomato paste, cover and cook over low heat 40 minutes, stirring occasionally. Salt and pepper to taste. Put the sauce through a food mill (reserving veal chunks if desired), using the disk with medium-size holes; transfer back to saucepan and keep warm over low heat. Combine the garlic, parsley, sage leaves, lemon peel and set aside.

To prepare the pasta, place eggs, oil, salt, and saffron in the bowl of a food processor fitted with a metal blade. Blend for 4 seconds. Add 1½ cups of the flour and process, using on-off motion, until dough comes away from the sides (if dough is sticky, add flour by the tablespoon until dough comes together). Process dough 40 seconds until well kneaded. Cut dough in half; dust a pastry board with remaining flour and roll and cut the pasta into fettuccine or spaghetti. (Follow the instructions for your pasta machine. If making by hand, roll as thin as possible, then cut with a sharp knife into long strips.) Cook the pasta *al dente*, about 2 minutes, in plenty of boiling salted water. Drain and serve with the veal sauce; garnish with garlic and herb mixture.

Rice Pilaf Mold

Preparation time: 10 minutes
Cooking time: 1 hour
Degree of difficulty: simple
Servings: 6
Calories per serving: 325

1 small onion, chopped
2 tablespoons butter
2 tablespoons oil
1 cup long-grain brown rice, well rinsed and drained
½ cup wild rice, well rinsed and drained
4–5 cups chicken stock
¼ cup butter, softened and sliced
2 tablespoons freshly grated Parmesan cheese

Preheat oven to 350°F. In an ovenproof 7-inch saucepan, gently sauté onion in butter and oil until soft but not browned. Add brown and wild rice and stir until coated. Pour in enough chicken stock to cover the rice by 1 inch, bring to a boil and place in oven. Bake for 45 minutes or until rice is tender. Drain any excess liquid. Fluff the rice with a fork and add the butter and cheese, stirring to mix. Pack firmly into a buttered 4-cup smooth-sided mold, place a heated platter over the mold, and invert it onto the platter, rapping to remove the rice.

PHOTO BY PAT LACROIX/THE BRANT GROUP

Rigatoni with Sausages and Mushrooms

Preparation time: 15 minutes
Cooking time: 15 minutes
Degree of difficulty: simple
Servings: 2-3
Calories per serving: 780 (1/2)
520 (1/3)

Buy fresh pasta from one of Canada's many specialty shops or make it yourself. The finished dish will rival any found in restaurants.

6 ounces rigatoni (about 3½ cups)

1 clove garlic, peeled

3 tablespoons olive oil

2 cups fresh mushrooms, coarsely chopped

2 Italian sweet sausages

1 tablespoon chopped Italian parsley

Salt and freshly ground pepper to taste

2 tablespoons unsalted butter

Grated Parmesan cheese to taste

Cook pasta in at least 4 quarts of boiling salted water. In a frying pan large enough to hold the cooked pasta, sauté the garlic in the oil. When the garlic is golden, press it with a fork to release its flavor and then discard. Add the mushrooms to the pan, and stir. Skin the sausages and shred them directly into the frying pan. Add the parsley, salt, and freshly ground pepper to taste. Cook and stir over medium heat until mushrooms and sausages are cooked, about 10 minutes. When the pasta is cooked, drain and add to the frying pan. Toss thoroughly, dot with butter, and cook over low heat for 2 minutes. Serve with grated Parmesan cheese.

Rigatoni with Sausages and Mushrooms (below)

PHOTO BY TIM SAUNDERS

Wild Rice with Pine Nuts

Preparation time: 5 minutes
Cooking time: 1½ hours
Degree of difficulty: simple
Servings: 6
Calories per serving: 185

2 cups beef broth

1½ cups water (approximate)

1 cup wild rice, rinsed

½ cup currants

Freshly ground black pepper to taste

½ cup pine nuts

1 tablespoon butter or margarine

1 medium onion, finely chopped

Bring broth and water to a boil in a large saucepan; add wild rice, currants, and pepper. Reduce heat to low, cover and simmer for 1 hour, or until liquid is absorbed and rice is tender. Add more water, if needed, to cook the rice fully.

Meanwhile, place nuts in a small frying pan and toast, tossing constantly, until golden. Remove from pan and set aside. In the same frying pan, melt the butter or margarine and sauté the onion for about 3 minutes, or until soft. When rice is done, toss with the onion and nuts and serve at once.

Some people's food always tastes better than others, even if they're cooking the same dish at the same dinner. One person has much more life in them — more fire, vitality, guts — than others. A person without those things can never make food taste right, no matter what material you give him. You have got to throw feeling into your cooking. *(Rosa Lewis, the Duchess of Duke Street)*

Umberto Menghi's Fettuccine with Prosciutto and Peas

Preparation time: 10 minutes
Cooking time: 10-15 minutes
Degree of difficulty: simple
Servings: 6
Calories per serving: 670

This recipe is from Umberto Menghi's popular Il Giardino di Umberto Italian restaurant in Vancouver. This dish, a bottle of dry red wine, and a salad make a meal.

1 pound fettuccine noodles
6 slices prosciutto ham, cut in slivers
2 tablespoons butter
1 1/2 cups peas, thawed if frozen, drained if canned
1 teaspoon white pepper
3/4 cup light cream
1 cup freshly grated Parmesan cheese

Boil the fettuccine in rapidly boiling salted water. While it's cooking, sauté the prosciutto in the butter until soft but not crisp. Add the peas and sauté until cooked through. Add the white pepper. Avoid the temptation to add salt — the prosciutto and cheese are salty enough. Drain the fettuccine and add, mixing quickly with the peas and ham. Add the fresh cream to moisten. Cook for 1 minute until the cream thickens. Add the freshly grated Parmesan and serve immediately, passing extra cheese.

Bow-Tied Escargots in Pasta

Preparation time: 30 minutes
Cooking time: 30 minutes (total)
Degree of difficulty: moderate
Servings: 4-6
Calories per serving: 604 (1/4)
402 (1/6)

This is a favorite recipe of Barbara Gordon, owner-chef of Toronto's Beaujolais restaurant. Deft handwork makes this creative recipe look special.

36 large pasta shells, cooked according to package directions
6 green onions
36 small snails (tinned)
2 tablespoons peanut oil

SAUCE
1/2 cup unsalted butter
2 tablespoons plus 1 teaspoon finely chopped garlic
2 tablespoons plus 1 teaspoon finely chopped ginger root
2 tablespoons plus 1 teaspoon finely chopped shallots
2 tablespoons plus 1 teaspoon finely chopped cashews
2 tablespoons plus 1 teaspoon finely chopped parsley
4 tablespoons tomato paste
2 tablespoons lime juice
1 1/2 cups dry white wine
1 teaspoon Dijon mustard
1 teaspoon nutmeg
1 teaspoon sugar
Salt and freshly ground pepper to taste

To prepare the escargots, blanch the green tops of the onions by immersing them in boiling water for 1 minute, then plunging them immediately into cold water. Cut the blanched onion into long strips.

Reserve. Drain the snails and sauté them in the peanut oil for 5 seconds. Drain. Carefully tie the long strips of green onion in a bow tie around each snail.

Preheat oven to 450°F. To make the sauce, heat the butter and add the spices. Cook gently for 2 minutes without browning. Add remaining ingredients and bring to a boil.

To assemble, stuff the shells with the bow-tied escargots and place in a baking dish. Pour sauce over. Bake for 15 minutes.

Crunchy Casserole

Preparation time: 15 minutes
Cooking time: 50 minutes
Degree of difficulty: simple
Servings: 6
Calories per serving: 195

This has a nutty flavor that's hard to resist.

4 tablespoons butter
1 medium onion, finely sliced
1/2 cup finely sliced mushrooms
1/2 cup diced green pepper
1 cup cooked brown rice or lentils
1 cup chopped tomatoes
1 cup granola
1/4 cup cashews, pine nuts, or pumpkin seeds
1 egg
1 teaspoon thyme
1 tablespoon parsley
Salt and freshly ground black pepper to taste
1/4 cup breadcrumbs

Preheat oven to 350°F. Sauté the onion, green pepper, and mushrooms in the butter. In a large bowl, blend all the ingredients except the breadcrumbs. Grease a 1 1/2-quart ovenproof casserole and pour in the ingredients. Top with the breadcrumbs, dot with butter. Bake for 45 minutes. Brown top under broiler before serving.

Paella

Preparation time: 30 minutes
Cooking time: 45 minutes-1 hour (total)
Degree of difficulty: moderate
Servings: 4-8
Calories per serving: 715 (1/4)
358 (1/8)

Gather some friends and spend the afternoon sipping Spanish wine and preparing this attractive and delicious dish. Serve with a green salad, with fresh fruit for dessert.

4 small hot or sweet Italian sausages, or chorizos
3 tablespoons olive oil
2 tablespoons butter
¾ cup finely chopped onion
1 teaspoon finely chopped garlic
1 green pepper, seeded and cut in strips
1 red pepper, seeded and cut in strips
1 cup raw long-grain rice
¾ pound fresh ripe tomatoes, peeled, seeded, and coarsely chopped
1-1½ cups chicken stock
¼ teaspoon powdered saffron
2½ cups cubed cold roast chicken
8-12 large uncooked shrimp, shelled and deveined
1 dozen clams, scrubbed
1 dozen mussels, scrubbed and bearded
Salt and freshly ground pepper to taste
2 tablespoons finely chopped parsley

In a small frying pan cover the sausages with cold water and bring to a rapid boil. Cook briskly, uncovered, piercing them with a fork to allow the fat to escape. When all the water has evaporated, reduce heat and brown the sausages in the fat that has settled to the bottom. Drain and cut into 2-inch lengths.

Preheat oven to 350°F. Heat the oil and butter in a *paellero* or heavy 3-quart casserole and slowly cook the onion and garlic for 5 minutes. Add the strips of red and green pepper and cook for about 5 minutes longer. Add the rice and cook until the grains turn slightly opaque. Add the tomatoes. Heat the chicken stock, dissolve saffron in 1 cup of it, and add this mixture to the casserole. Bring to a boil on top of the stove, then transfer to oven and bake for 15 minutes, or until the rice is almost done. Remove the casserole from the oven and if the rice seems dry add the remaining ½ cup of hot chicken stock. Bury the chicken, shrimp, clams, and mussels in the rice. Cover and return to the oven. Bake until the clams and mussels open and the shrimp is cooked, about 5-10 minutes. Season lightly with salt and freshly ground pepper and garnish with chopped parsley.

Penne Aglio E Olio

Preparation time: 5 minutes
Cooking time: 9 minutes
Degree of difficulty: simple
Servings: 4-6
Calories per serving: 607 (1/4)
405 (1/6)

This deceptively simple recipe is subtle and well mannered.

1 pound penne pasta
3 tablespoons virgin olive oil
2 medium cloves garlic, finely chopped
1 tablespoon unsalted butter
Salt and freshly ground pepper to taste
4 to 6 tablespoons freshly grated Parmesan cheese
2 tablespoons finely chopped fresh parsley

Cook the penne until *al dente* (3 to 5 minutes for fresh, 7 to 9 for dried). Drain, rinse, and place on warm plates. Drizzle olive oil over penne, add garlic and butter and toss. Season with salt and pepper. Sprinkle with Parmesan cheese and parsley.

Spaghetti Alla Joso

Preparation time: 30 minutes
Cooking time: 1½ hours
Degree of difficulty: moderate
Servings: 6
Calories per serving: 825

This is a spectacular dish from Joso's, an Adriatic fish restaurant in midtown Toronto.

1 pound octopus, thawed if frozen
2 onions, chopped
2 cloves garlic, crushed
2 tablespoons olive oil
10 whole black peppercorns
1 tablespoon Italian tomato paste
2 bay leaves
Thyme
1 teaspoon rosemary, fresh if possible
2 14-ounce tins Italian plum tomatoes, chopped, or 10 ripe, fresh tomatoes peeled and chopped
1 pound squid, thawed if frozen, cleaned and cut into 1-inch pieces
Salt to taste
2 pounds spaghetti
6 fresh clams

Cut the octopus into 1-inch pieces. Boil for 30-45 minutes (depending on the thickness) until tender. Meanwhile, prepare the sauce: sauté the onion and garlic in olive oil until onion is translucent. Add peppercorns, tomato paste, bay leaves, thyme, and rosemary. Add the chopped tomatoes. Stir and simmer until ingredients are blended. Add the boiled octopus and the squid. Mix and bring to the boil. Reduce heat and simmer for 30 minutes. Add salt to taste. Meanwhile, boil the spaghetti *al dente*. Drain. To assemble, toss the spaghetti with the octopus-squid sauce, place on a serving platter and arrange the clams on top, one per person.

Apicius of Rome used practically all the cooking utensils that are in use today. There is only one difference between his cooking utensils and ours: the old ones are handmade, more individualistic, more beautiful and more artistic than our machine-made varieties. (*Apicius: Cooking and Dining in Imperial Rome* by Joseph Vehling)

Fettuccine with
Smoked Salmon
(right); Wild
Rice with Apples,
Apricots, and
Walnuts (below)

Fettuccine with Smoked Salmon

Preparation time: 10 minutes
Cooking time: 20-25 minutes (total)
Degree of difficulty: simple
Servings: 6
Calories per serving: 950

Bonnie Stern, director of the Bonnie Stern Cooking Schools in Toronto, has passed on this delicious recipe for pasta tossed with smoked salmon, green onions, and Parmesan cheese. You could add a spoonful of red or black caviar to each serving.

3 tablespoons unsalted butter

2 shallots, finely chopped, or 1 onion plus ½ clove garlic

½ pound smoked salmon, diced

1 cup whipping cream

½ cup unsalted butter, cut into cubes

4 green onions, thinly sliced

¾ cup grated Parmesan cheese (preferably Parmigiano Reggiano)

1½ pounds green or white fettuccine

Salt and freshly ground pepper to taste

Melt 3 tablespoons butter in a frying pan and cook shallots until fragrant and tender but not brown. Add salmon and cook 2 minutes. Add cream and heat thoroughly. Either remove from heat at this point and reheat 1 minute before tossing with pasta, or prepare this when you put the pasta on to boil. Place cubes of butter in a large flat serving dish. Have onion and cheese close at hand. Bring a large pot of water to the boil, add a little salt, then cook the pasta *al dente*. Fresh homemade pasta will require only 1-1½ minutes of cooking, fresh pasta from Italian specialty shops will require 4-5 minutes, and commercial pasta will take 10-12 minutes. Drain noodles well and shake off any excess water. Place immediately in the serving dish. Pour hot sauce over and sprinkle with cheese and onion. Toss well until sauce thickens and the noodles are coated. Season with salt and pepper.

PHOTOS BY TIM SAUNDERS

Wild Rice with Apples, Apricots, and Walnuts

Preparation time: less than 1 hour
Cooking time: about 30 minutes
Marinating time: about 1 hour
Degree of difficulty: simple
Servings: 8-10
Calories per serving: 400 (1/8)
320 (1/10)

SALAD

2 cups wild rice

⅓ cup white long-grain rice

½ cup dried apricots, diced

3 tablespoons Calvados or other brandy

¼ cup raisins

½ cup broken or halved walnuts

1 Granny Smith apple, cut into 8 wedges, each wedge cut into eights

Boil wild rice in about 6 cups salted water for 35-40 minutes or until tender. Refresh under cold running water and drain well. Boil the white rice in about 2 cups salted water for 15-20 minutes, or until tender but not mushy. Refresh with water, drain, and set aside with wild rice. Soak the dried apricots in the Calvados for 1 hour. Toss together the wild rice, white rice, marinated apricots, raisins, walnuts, and apple wedges.

DRESSING

2 egg yolks

2 tablespoons red wine vinegar

1 tablespoon Dijon mustard

¾ cup vegetable oil

2 teaspoons walnut oil (optional)

1 teaspoon demerara sugar

2 tablespoons warm water

Salt to taste

Pinch of nutmeg

¼ cup light cream

To prepare dressing, whisk together the egg yolks, red wine vinegar, and Dijon mustard. Begin adding oil slowly, whisking continuously until thickened slightly. Blend in sugar. Add ½ the warm water to smooth the dressing, then continue adding oil; finish with the remaining warm water and whisk until smooth. Season with salt, pepper, and nutmeg; mix in cream. Pour dressing over salad and toss with a fork.

Spaghetti Nuovi

Preparation time: 15 minutes
Cooking time: 10-15 minutes
Degree of difficulty: simple
Servings: 4-6
Calories per serving: 850 (1/4)
566 (1/6)

From Toronto's Pronto Ristorante comes this unusual spaghetti.

2 tablespoons unsalted butter

2 cloves garlic, minced

1 tablespoon minced shallots

1 leek, julienned

1 tablespoon chopped fresh basil (or 1 teaspoon dried)

4 sliced shiitake mushrooms

½ cup green seedless grapes, halved

2 ripe tomatoes, seeded and diced

2 tablespoons Pernod

1 cup whipping cream

1 cup tomato sauce

1 pound fresh or dried spaghetti

Fresh Parmesan cheese

Fresh parsley sprigs

In a large frying pan over medium high heat, sauté garlic and shallots in butter. Add leeks, basil, mushrooms, grapes, and tomatoes. When hot, flambé mixture with Pernod. Add cream and tomato sauce and reduce until thickened. Meanwhile, in a large pot bring plenty of water to a rolling boil and cook the pasta *al dente*. Drain pasta and add to the mixture in the saucepan; mix well. Sprinkle with freshly grated Parmesan cheese and garnish with parsley sprigs.

Fettuccine Alfredo

Preparation time: 15 minutes
Cooking time: 10 minutes
Degree of difficulty: simple
Servings: 4
Calories per serving: 765

Wonderful with grilled lamb chops and sliced tomatoes — or add slivered ham and cooked peas for a complete meal with a tossed salad.

3/4 pound fettuccine noodles
1/2 cup butter, at room temperature
1 cup table cream
1 cup grated Parmesan cheese
Freshly ground pepper
1 tablespoon finely chopped parsley

Cook fettuccine in plenty of boiling water and drain; return to pot and set over low heat. Add 2 tablespoons of the butter and a little cream and stir well. Stir in a few tablespoons of cheese. Continue to stir in remaining butter, cream, and cheese for a thick, creamy, rich sauce. Sprinkle with pepper and parsley.

Rio Rice with Chilis

Preparation time: 15 minutes
Cooking time: about 1 hour
Degree of difficulty: simple
Servings: 8-10
Calories per serving: 348 (1/8)
278 (1/10)

You can add more chili peppers to this recipe — but first make sure your guests' mouths are lined with asbestos.

1/4 cup olive oil
1 large onion, thinly sliced
3 cups long-grain rice
3 cups boiling chicken stock, fresh or from bouillon cubes
3 cups boiling water
3 tomatoes, seeded and chopped, or 1 cup canned tomatoes
1 teaspoon salt
2 dried chili peppers, finely chopped

Preheat oven to 350°F. Heat the oil in a 4-quart Dutch oven, or a saucepan that can go in the oven, making sure the bottom is evenly coated. Add onion and cook until transparent. Add rice and cook, stirring constantly, until all the grains are coated with oil. Do not let the rice brown. Add the stock, water, tomatoes, and salt. Stir. Add chilis and stir again. Bring the mixture to just under a boil, stirring constantly. Cover and bake for 45 minutes or until the rice has absorbed all the liquid.

Fettuccine with Mushrooms

Preparation time: 5 minutes
Cooking time: 10-15 minutes
Degree of difficulty: simple
Servings: 4-6
Calories per serving: 772 (1/4)
515 (1/6)

Although the recipe calls for Italian porcini, you may use any combination of fresh and imported mushrooms you like. During the spring, chanterelles and other exotic species may be gleaned from Canadian woods and marketplaces. *Warning*: Do not pick mushrooms unless you know a great deal about them. Suggested reading: *Mushrooms of North America* by Orson Miller Jr. This recipe is from Bersani & Carlevale, Toronto's successful proponents of pasta chic.

1 pound fettuccine
1 1/3-ounce package imported dried mushrooms (porcini), soaked in water according to directions
1 pound fresh mushrooms, sliced
1/2 cup chopped onion
1/2 cup butter
3 tablespoons freshly grated Parmesan cheese

Cook the fettuccine in boiling water until *al dente*. Meanwhile, sauté the dried and fresh mushrooms and the onion in the butter until limp. Drain the pasta and combine with the mushrooms and butter. Toss with Parmesan cheese. Serve immediately.

Pasta with Artichokes

Preparation time: 30 minutes
Cooking time: 10-15 minutes
Degree of difficulty: moderate
Servings: 4
Calories per serving: 615

In this adventuresome recipe, fresh artichokes are prepared in small wedges, tossed with pasta, and sprinkled with Parmesan cheese.

2 large artichokes

Juice of 1 lemon

5 tablespoons olive oil

10-12 sprigs parsley, minced

1 clove garlic, minced

1 medium onion, minced

¼ teaspoon dried marjoram

1 beef bouillon cube, crushed

¾ teaspoon salt

Freshly ground pepper to taste

1 teaspoon all-purpose flour

⅔ cup light cream

¾ pound spaghetti or homemade pasta

Grated Parmesan cheese

To prepare the artichokes, snap off the outside green leaves until you reach a layer of leaves that range in color from pale yellow at the base to green at the top. With a sharp knife cut off the tops of the leaves to ¾ of their height. Rinse in cold water. Peel the stems by removing the dark outer skin, leaving only the inner, almost white flesh. Cut off and discard about ⅛ inch from the bottom of the stem, then cut off the stems themselves and slice in rounds. Cut the artichokes in thin wedges and remove the choke (a light-colored cone of leaves) and the fuzzy centre. Put the wedges and the rounds together with the lemon juice in a bowl of cold water. Heat the oil in a large saucepan over moderate heat. Add the parsley, garlic, and onion and cook until limp. Drain and add the artichoke. Stir gently and add the marjoram, bouillon cube, salt, pepper, and flour. Cook 4 minutes or until the artichoke is tender but still crisp. Add ½ cup of the cream and cook over very low heat for 3 minutes. Adjust seasoning. Add remaining cream if the sauce is too thick.

Bring 4 quarts of water to a boil, add 4 teaspoons salt and the pasta. Cook the pasta *al dente*. Drain, place in a serving dish, and dress with the artichoke sauce. Serve with Parmesan cheese on the side.

NOTES

PASTRIES

Jimmy Stewart wasn't the only one who liked mom's apple pie. It's far and away the favorite of most North Americans, followed by pumpkin pies in the fall and mince pies at Christmas time.

Everyone likes pastry, if it comes to that: the French have chocolate éclairs and cream puffs, Italians like cheesecakes, Middle Easterners adore honey-drenched layers of nut-filled phyllo, and the lattice-weave crust of cherry pie is intrinsically American, particularly available around George Washington's birthday — and that's no lie.

Although many 30-year-olds have never tasted a custard pie, those of us who have eaten this old-fashioned dessert tend to grow nostalgic when it's mentioned. Flapper pie, a lovely ending for dinner with its graham-wafer crumbs, smooth custard filling, and meringue topping, is another walk down memory lane, as is a real lemon meringue, with its tart filling high and quivering, its meringue topping even higher, browned to a golden caramel.

Pastry flour is often used by experts for pie crusts because it makes them exceptionally tender; it's found at specialty food shops and occasionally in bakery outlets; its texture is between all-purpose and cake flour. Whatever fat is used in making pie crust (shortening, lard, or a mixture of both), it should be chilled before using. To bake a pie "blind" means to place a round of wax paper in a pie shell and fill it with dried beans or ceramic pie weights: this keeps the shell from shrinking or buckling.

Nicely browned pie crusts result from the use of glass, dark metal, or Teflon-lined pans. Shiny pans deflect heat and produce pale crusts. Roll pastry from the centre outward, using short strokes and changing the direction of the rolling pin to make the proper shape. Preheat your oven 15-20 minutes before baking. By all means, buy a saucy china pie bird to put in the centre of fruit pies: it will suck up the juices and leave the crust crisp.

Lemon Meringue Pie (see recipe page 122)

Lemon Meringue Pie

Preparation time: 15 to 20 minutes
Chilling time: 30 minutes
Cooking time: about 1 hour
Degree of difficulty: simple
Servings: 8-10
Calories per serving: 668 (1/8)
535 (1/10)

More like a French *tarte au citron* than a North American "mile-high" lemon pie.

PASTRY

2 cups all-purpose flour
½ teaspoon salt
¾ cup unsalted butter
Grated peel of 1 lemon
3 tablespoons sugar
3 tablespoons lemon juice
3 tablespoons water
Melted butter

CRUMB LAYER

¼ cup sugar
3 tablespoons dry white breadcrumbs
½ teaspoon ground cardamom

LEMON LAYER

Peel and strained juice of 2 lemons
1 cup sugar
3 eggs, well beaten
1 cup unsalted butter

MERINGUE

6 egg whites
1 cup sugar

Preheat oven to 375°F. To make pastry, combine flour and salt in a bowl. Rub in unsalted butter with fingertips, then add lemon peel, sugar, lemon juice, and water and mix lightly with a fork until it comes together. Shape dough in a ball, chill 30 minutes, then roll out and line a 10-inch tart tin with a removable bottom. Prick pastry, brush with melted butter and bake 30 minutes. Mix the crumb layer ingredients and place in the baked pastry shell after it is removed from the oven. Leave oven at 375°F.

Prepare the lemon layer while pastry is cooking. Beat lemon peel, juice, sugar and eggs in a saucepan; stir over low heat, adding the butter in small pieces. When mixture is hot — keep it well below the boiling point — pour it over the crumb-lined pastry. Return to the oven for 10 minutes, until filling is just set but still a little shaky in the middle. Let cool.

Beat egg whites until stiff, adding sugar gradually, beating after each addition. Pipe or pile on top of the pie, completely covering the lemon filling. Bake 10 to 15 minutes until meringue is browned.

Foolproof Pastry

Preparation time: 20 minutes
Standing time: 30 minutes
Degree of difficulty: moderate
Amount: makes enough for 3 or 4 2-crust pies

This pastry is so simple even a child can make it. The dough will keep for about 10 days in the refrigerator, or it can be frozen indefinitely.

5 cups all-purpose flour
1 tablespoon salt
1 pound lard, chilled
1 egg
1½ tablespoons white vinegar
Cold water

Dump the flour and salt into a large mixing bowl. Cut the lard into the flour with two knives or a pastry blender, until the lard lumps are no larger than pea-size and the mixture is rather mealy. (You can even rub it between your fingers at the last, to break up the lumps.) Put the egg into an 8-ounce measuring cup, and beat it with a fork. Add the vinegar, and beat again. Add just enough cold water to fill the 8-ounce cup and beat again with a fork. Pour this over the flour-lard mixture, stirring with a fork until all the flour is moistened and the pastry sticks together. Again, you can use your hands to form one large lump of pastry. Put the whole lump (wrapped in plastic wrap) into the refrigerator for ½ hour or so, and then cut off as much as you need and roll it out on a floured board. Cut tops for individual pies, or one large top for a deep-dish pie. Cut a small hole in the centre of each pie, and insert a small funnel of brown paper to let the steam out. If you're making one large pie, you may want to prop up the pastry in the middle with a small inverted egg cup; even better is one of those fetching ceramic blackbirds that also acts as a funnel. Be sure the pastry is tucked around the outside edges of the pie plate on a large pie, as it will draw toward the centre while cooking.

Flapper Pie

Preparation time: 30 minutes
Cooking time: 40 minutes
Degree of difficulty: moderate
Servings: 6-8
Calories per serving: 490 (1/6)
368 (1/8)

It's nearly impossible to stop at one piece of Flapper Pie.

PASTRY

1½ cups graham wafer crumbs

⅓ cup brown sugar

¼ cup melted butter

FILLING

6 egg yolks

½ cup sugar

4 tablespoons cornstarch

4 cups whole milk, scalded

2 teaspoons vanilla extract

MERINGUE TOPPING

6 egg whites

3 tablespoons sugar

½ teaspoon cornstarch

1 tablespoon graham wafer crumbs

Preheat oven to 350°F. Combine 1½ cups graham wafer crumbs, brown sugar, and melted butter, and press into a 9-inch pie plate. Bake for 10 minutes. Set aside. To prepare the filling, beat the egg yolks lightly with a fork, add ½ cup sugar and 4 tablespoons cornstarch. Slowly add the scalded milk, stirring constantly. Cook over a low flame until thickened. Add the vanilla extract. Cool.

For the meringue, beat egg whites until soft peaks form. Add 3 tablespoons sugar and ½ teaspoon cornstarch and continue beating until the peaks stiffen. Pour the cooled filling into the baked pie crust. Top with meringue. Sprinkle remaining crumbs over the meringue. Bake until golden brown, about 15 minutes.

Butter Tarts

Preparation time: 30 minutes
Cooking time: 18-20 minutes per tart tin
Degree of difficulty: moderate
Amount : makes 2½ dozen
Calories per serving: 380

These exceptional butter tarts from the Dew Drop Inn in Virgil, Alberta, are slightly less sweet than most.

PASTRY

5 cups all-purpose flour

3 tablespoons brown sugar

½ teaspoon baking powder

1 teaspoon salt

1 pound lard, cold

1 egg

3 tablespoons vinegar

FILLING

3 cups brown sugar

1 cup butter, melted

2 teaspoons vanilla extract

3 eggs

¾ cup breadcrumbs

1 cup light cream

1 cup raisins

Combine flour, 3 tablespoons sugar, baking powder, and salt. Cut the lard into tiny bits and mix into the flour mixture with a pastry cutter or two knives; do not overwork the pastry. Mix 1 egg with the vinegar in a 1-cup measuring cup. Fill the cup with ice-cold water and pour the mixture over the flour mixture. Combine carefully, without overworking. Preheat oven to 400°F.

For the filling, combine 3 cups sugar, butter, vanilla, and eggs. Soak the breadcrumbs in the cream and add. Roll out the pastry and line tart tins. Place raisins in each tin. Fill ¾ with the filling. Bake for 18-20 minutes.

Dora's Apple Pie

Preparation time: 20 minutes
Cooking time: 50-55 minutes
Degree of difficulty: simple
Servings: 6-8
Calories per serving: 305 (1/6)
230 (1/8)

An apple pie with a difference.

Pastry for 10-inch pie-shell

4 medium apples

2 eggs

1 cup milk

⅓ cup sugar

Salt to taste

3 tablespoons finely ground pecans or walnuts

¼ teaspoon grated lemon peel

½ teaspoon vanilla extract

Dash nutmeg

Line a deep 10-inch pie pan with pastry, fluting the rim. Peel apples and cut in half *crosswise*. Remove core without breaking through apple. Place apples cut side down in pastry shell, six halves around edge and one in middle (eat the other half).

Preheat oven to 400°F. Beat eggs slightly with fork, then beat in milk, sugar, and salt. Add ground nuts, lemon peel, and vanilla. Carefully pour mixture into pie shell over the apples. Sprinkle with nutmeg. Bake for 15 minutes, then reduce heat to 350°F and bake for 30-40 minutes longer, or until apples are tender. To serve, cut so that each serving has half an apple.

Since 1811, when the MacIntosh apple was first discovered in Dundas County, Ontario, it has been a Canadian success story. More than 3 million bushels a year are produced, to be eaten crisply fresh, combined with cinnamon, cloves and brown sugar for apple sauce, or with a dab of butter in wonderful apple pies. Whether it's grown in Ontario, Nova Scotia's Annapolis Valley or the Okanagan Valley of B.C., the MacIntosh is a favorite.

No Crust Coconut Pie

Preparation time: 5 minutes
Cooking time: 40 minutes
Degree of difficulty: simple
Servings: 6
Calories per serving: 290

This easy dessert pie makes its own crust.

2 eggs
1 cup milk
¼ cup sugar
1 cup flaked coconut
¼ cup all-purpose flour
¼ cup melted butter
¼ teaspoon baking powder
Salt to taste

Preheat oven to 350°F. With an electric or hand beater, beat eggs until light and fluffy. Mix in remaining ingredients. Pour into a 9-inch buttered and floured pie plate. Bake for about 40 minutes, or until firm and golden.

Chocolate Brownie Tart

Preparation time: 30 minutes
Cooking time: 45 minutes (total)
Degree of difficulty: moderate
Servings: 8-10
Calories per serving: 720 (1/8)
555 (1/10)

For chocoholics this will provide a lift.

BROWN SUGAR PASTRY

1 cup all-purpose flour
2 tablespoons cocoa
¼ cup brown sugar
Pinch of salt
½ cup chilled butter, cut into pieces
2 teaspoons milk
1 teaspoon vanilla extract
1 teaspoon cinnamon

To prepare pastry, combine flour, cocoa, brown sugar, and salt in a bowl or in a food processor. Cut in the butter. Mix in the milk, vanilla, and cinnamon. Press dough into the sides and bottom of an 11-inch flan pan (keep crust as thin as possible).

FILLING

3 ounces unsweetened chocolate
3 ounces semisweet chocolate
½ cup butter, cut into pieces
1½ cups sugar
3 eggs, beaten
2 teaspoons vanilla extract
½ cup chopped nuts (optional)
¾ cup all-purpose flour

CHOCOLATE GLAZE

3 ounces semisweet chocolate
2 tablespoons whipping cream or butter
Whipped cream for garnish (optional)

Preheat oven to 350°F. To prepare filling, melt chocolates together in top of double boiler. Remove from heat and stir in butter 1 piece at a time. Transfer mixture to a bowl; add sugar and blend well. Add beaten eggs, stirring to blend. Mix in vanilla. Stir in chopped nuts and flour. Pour into prepared pastry shell and bake for 25-30 minutes. Cool. Prepare chocolate glaze by melting chocolate in a double boiler over simmering water. Stir in whipping cream or butter. Spread over cooled brownie tart. Garnish with whipped cream, if desired.

PHOTO BY SKIP DEAN

Tarte au Riz

Preparation time: 20 minutes
Cooking time: 1²/₃ hours (total)
Degree of difficulty: simple
Servings: 8
Calories per serving: 265

This pie, of Flemish origin, is an old family recipe. Use a good short crust pastry.

1 unbaked 9-inch pie shell
½ cup long-grain white rice
3 cups milk (approximately)
1 egg
¾ cup light brown sugar
¼ teaspoon nutmeg
1¼ teaspoons vanilla extract
Pinch of salt

Put the rice and 2½ cups of the milk in the top of a double boiler and cook, covered, until rice is tender, about 1 hour. You'll probably but not necessarily, have to add another ½ cup of milk. The mixture should not be sloppy, nor should it be too stiff. Meanwhile, preheat oven to 375°F. In a bowl, beat the egg with a fork, add sugar, nutmeg, vanilla and salt and mix well. Pour in cooked rice and mix. Pour into an unbaked pie shell and bake until set, about 40 minutes, or until crust is lightly browned.

French Silk Pie

Preparation time: 20 minutes
Cooking time: 15 minutes
Chilling time: 3-4 hours
Degree of difficulty: simple
Servings: 8
Calories per serving: 570

1½ cups graham wafer crumbs
⅓ cup melted butter
2 ounces unsweetened chocolate
2 tablespoons brandy
2 tablespoons instant coffee
1 cup unsalted butter, softened
1 cup sugar
2 eggs
½ cup ground almonds
½ cup ground hazelnuts
1 cup whipping cream, whipped and sweetened

Preheat oven to 350°F. Mix the graham wafer crumbs with the melted butter and pat into a 9-inch pie plate. Bake for 10 minutes.

In a double boiler, melt the chocolate. Stir in the brandy and the instant coffee. Using a hand mixer or electric mixer, cream the butter and sugar together in a large mixing bowl. Beat in the eggs, 1 at a time. Beat in the chocolate mixture and finally the nuts. Pour the mixture into the pie shell. Chill for 3-4 hours. Serve cold in thin slices with whipped cream.

French Silk Chocolate Pie with Raspberries

Preparation time: less than 1 hour
Chilling time: at least 2 hours
Degree of difficulty: simple
Servings: 6
Calories per serving: 815

Cuisine '85 Semifinalist

GRAHAM CRUST

1¼ cups graham wafer crumbs
¼ cup sugar
⅓ cup melted butter

FILLING

¾ cup sugar
½ cup butter, softened
2 1-ounce squares unsweetened chocolate, melted
1 teaspoon vanilla
2 eggs
2 cups fresh raspberries
½ cup whipping cream, whipped
Semisweet chocolate shavings

RASPBERRY GLAZE

2 cups fresh raspberries
¾ cup sugar
1 tablespoon lemon juice

Preheat oven to 350°F. To prepare the crust, mix the ingredients well, then press the mixture onto the bottom and partly up the sides of a greased 9-inch pie plate. Chill the crust for 10 minutes in the freezer or until set, or bake for 10 minutes (or microwave 1½ to 2 minutes on high); cool. To prepare filling, combine sugar, butter, chocolate, and vanilla in a bowl and blend well. Add the eggs, 1 at a time, beating with an electric mixer at medium speed for 3 to 5 minutes after each egg. Pour mixture into prepared pie shell and refrigerate at least 2 hours. Arrange the raspberries over the chilled pie. To prepare the raspberry glaze, simmer ingredients until reduced to 1 cup. Using a pastry brush, paint berries with warm raspberry glaze. Chill again until ready to serve. At serving time, garnish with whipped cream and chocolate shavings.

PHOTO BY GARY WHITE

When making lemon or other meringue pies, if the meringue is spread over the filling and slightly overlaps the crust, it will not shrink away from the edges and give the impression of ring around the collar.

Glazed Blackberry Pie

Preparation time: 15 minutes
Cooking time: 15 minutes
Chilling time: at least 2 hours
Degree of difficulty: simple
Servings: 6-8
Calories per serving: 460 (1/6)
345 (1/8)

This is surely the ultimate berry dessert. The fruit is left whole and uncooked, its flavor and freshness intact. It is encased in a pie shell and drizzled with a glaze made from cooked berries. Strawberries, blueberries, or raspberries may be substituted for the blackberries.

1 baked 9- or 10-inch pie shell
5 cups blackberries
3 tablespoons cornstarch
1 cup sugar
¾ cup water
1 teaspoon lemon juice
1 cup whipping cream

Crush and sieve 1 cup of the blackberries to remove seeds. Combine cornstarch, sugar, sieved berries, and water. Cook over medium-low heat until thickened and clear, about 10 minutes. Cool slightly, then add the lemon juice and remaining berries. Mix lightly and pile into baked pie shell. Cool and chill about 2 hours. At serving time, whip the cream and pipe or spoon around the pie rim.

Manly Apple Meringue Pie

Preparation time: 30 minutes
Cooking time: 1 hour
Degree of difficulty: simple
Servings: 8-10
Calories per serving: 326 (1/8)
261 (1/10)

1 unbaked 10-inch pie shell
½ cup sugar
1½ tablespoons all-purpose flour
¾ teaspoon each nutmeg and cinnamon
1 tablespoon grated lemon peel
10 cups thinly sliced apples
¼ cup lemon juice
3 tablespoons butter

MERINGUE
5 egg whites
⅔ cup sugar

Preheat oven to 400°F. In a small bowl, combine sugar, flour, nutmeg, cinnamon, and lemon peel. Sprinkle bottom of pie shell with 3 tablespoons of the sugar mixture. Top with a layer of apples. Alternate layers of apple slices and sugar mixture, ending with sugar mixture. Sprinkle lemon juice over all and dot with butter. Bake for 40 minutes, or until apples are tender. Cool to room temperature. Lower oven temperature to 350°F. To prepare meringue, beat egg whites until soft peaks form. Add sugar, 1 tablespoon at a time, beating well after each addition until stiff peaks form. Using the back of a spoon, swirl the meringue on top of the pie, bringing it to a peak in the centre. Be sure the meringue touches all edges of the pie shell. Bake 20 minutes or until the meringue is lightly browned. Cool.

Grand Marnier Strawberry Tart

Preparation time: 30 minutes
Standing time: 30 minutes
Cooking time: 40-45 minutes (total)
Chilling time: 1-2 hours
Degree of difficulty: challenging
Servings: 6
Calories per serving: 340

Delicious, decadent, but fresh-tasting.

⅔ cup all-purpose flour
2 tablespoons sugar
2 tablespoons walnuts
3 tablespoons butter, chilled and cut into small pieces
1-2 tablespoons ice water
3 pints fresh strawberries, washed and hulled
¼ cup Grand Marnier (or kirsh or Cognac)
½ cup apricot jam
Whipped cream for garnish

Place the flour, sugar, and nuts in the bowl of a food processor fitted with a metal blade. Mix, using 1-2 on-off motions. Gradually drop the chilled butter through the feed tube, and process using on-off pulses until the mixture is the texture of coarse meal — about 15 seconds. Add 1-2 tablespoons ice water and process just until dough begins to form a ball. Refrigerate dough for 30 minutes.

Preheat oven to 350°F. Roll dough out to fit the bottom and sides of a 9-inch pie plate or quiche or tart pan; prick dough with a fork. Bake until golden, 15-20 minutes; set aside to cool. Meanwhile, place strawberries in the liqueur to soak; purée the rest in a food processor or blender. Cook the puréed berries with the the apricot jam in a nonaluminum saucepan until reduced by half. Cool. Pour the strawberry sauce into the pie crust; arrange whole berries on top. Refrigerate 1-2 hours. Serve with whipped cream.

Blueberry Chocolate Cheesecake Pie

Preparation time: 30 minutes
Cooking time: 30 minutes (total)
Chilling time: 4 hours
Degree of difficulty: moderately challenging
Servings: 8-10
Calories per serving: 560 (1/8)
450 (1/10)

From Toronto baker Sue Devor of Sweet Sue Pastries, this pie is apropos any time.

PASTRY

1½ cups all-purpose flour
¼ cup sugar
¾ cup butter at room temperature
1½ teaspoons vinegar

Preheat oven to 375°F. To make pastry, combine flour and sugar in the bowl of a food processor. Cut butter into 6 pieces and add. Process for 10 seconds. With machine running, add vinegar through feed tube and let machine run until dough forms a ball, about 10-15 seconds. Press into an 11-inch flan pan with a removable bottom. Chill about 1 hour.

CHEESECAKE

2 ounces semisweet chocolate
1 tablespoon whipping cream
¾ pound cream cheese
2 tablespoons sugar
¼ teaspoon vanilla extract
1-2 tablespoons milk

TOPPING

2 cups blueberries
2 tablespoons red currant jelly
½ cup sugar
¼ teaspoon cinnamon
4 teaspoons cornstarch (or more if berries are juicy)
1 teaspoon lemon juice
2-3 teaspoons water
4 tablespoons toasted almonds

To prepare the cheesecake, melt chocolate over hot water. Stir in cream and mix until well blended. Spread over bottom of cooled crust. Chill until chocolate has hardened. Combine cream cheese, sugar, vanilla, and milk and beat until very smooth. Spread on top of chilled chocolate. Chill for about 3-4 hours.

Meanwhile, make blueberry topping: combine berries, red currant jelly, ¼ cup sugar, and cinnamon in a saucepan. Heat until liquid is released and begins to boil. Meanwhile, combine the rest of the sugar and the cornstarch in a small bowl. Add the lemon juice and enough of the water to make a thin, smooth paste. Add this to the berry mixture and cook, stirring, until thickened. Cool a little; carefully spread over cream cheese. Chill. Garnish with almonds.

Pecan Pie

Preparation time: 10 minutes
Cooking time: 45 minutes
Degree of difficulty: simple
Servings: 8
Calories per serving: 670

Pecan pie was invented for people with a hearty hunger for sweetness. This recipe has a hint of cognac.

1 unbaked 9-inch pie shell
4 eggs
¼ teaspoon salt
1 cup brown sugar (not packed)
1 cup corn syrup
⅓ cup melted butter
2 teaspoons Cognac
1½ cups pecan halves
1 cup whipping cream, whipped and sweetened

Preheat oven to 350°F. Line a pie plate with the pastry and crimp the edges. Beat eggs slightly with the salt. Add sugar, corn syrup, butter, and Cognac. Mix thoroughly with a beater. Sprinkle pecans evenly over the bottom of the pie shell (reserve a few for garnish) and pour in the egg mixture. Bake for about 45 minutes, until filling is just set. Border the pie with whipped cream and decorate with reserved pecans.

Heavenly Pumpkin Pie

Preparation time: 20 minutes
Cooking time: 1½ hours (total, including pumpkin)
Degree of difficulty: simple
Servings: 6-8
Calories per serving: 305 (1/6)
230 (1/8)

This recipe is unusual in that it calls for less pumpkin than other recipes; it makes a lighter, more custardy pie.

1 unbaked 9-inch pie shell
1 cup cooked pumpkin
¾ cup packed brown sugar
2 tablespoons all-purpose flour
1 teaspoon cinnamon
1 teaspoon salt
½ teaspoon ginger
2 eggs, beaten
2 cups whole milk
(If you are making custards add ½ cup more milk and a touch more sugar)
1 cup whipping cream, whipped and sweetened
Nutmeg

Preheat oven to 450°F. Peel a pie pumpkin and cut the meat into small pieces. Steam them until soft, then drain, mash, and put through a sieve, ricer, food mill, or blender. Stir together the brown sugar, flour, cinnamon, salt, and ginger. Add the eggs, pumpkin, and milk. Pour mixture into unbaked pie shell and bake for 10 minutes. Lower temperature to 300°F and bake for 40-45 minutes more. Watch pie carefully and remove while centre is still a *bit* quivery (don't wait till it is completely firm) as it will thicken as it cools. Serve with whipped cream sweetened with sugar and nutmeg.

Whisks do one of two things: they whip air into whites of eggs or into cream, and they blend and lighten all kinds of mixtures, from vinaigrettes to batters. The balloon whisk is light and flexible and incorporates the maximum amount of air into egg whites or cream; a rigid whisk, of heavy-gauge wire, blends thick sauces, like mayonnaise, and light batters; an all-purpose whisk is of medium wire, and is strong enough to handle light batters and flexible enough to foam eggs and cream. It's a good idea to have one of each in your kitchen.

Rum Pie

Preparation time: 15 minutes
Standing time: about 30 minutes
Cooking time: 20 minutes
Chilling time: 2 hours
Degree of difficulty: moderate
Servings: 6
Calories per serving: 530

Hold on to this recipe for chocolate pie shell: it can be filled with ice cream, chocolate custard or fruit and whipped cream. Barbara Gordon of Beaujolais in Toronto, fills it with rum-flavored custard.

SHELL

1 tablespoon shortening

6 ounces semisweet chocolate chips

FILLING

6 egg yolks

1 scant cup sugar

1 tablespoon unflavored gelatine

½ cup cold water

1 cup whipping cream, whipped

⅓ cup dark rum

2 tablespoons chopped pistachio nuts

Preheat oven to 325°F. To make the shell, line a glass pie plate with foil, smoothing the foil wrap so there are no creases. Add the shortening and chocolate chips and melt in oven for 10 minutes. With a spatula, smear the melted chocolate and shortening over the bottom and sides of the foil until it forms a pie shell. If the chocolate is too runny, let it cool slightly. Chill the chocolate shell in the refrigerator for about 30 minutes. When firmly chilled, carefully peel away the foil and rest the chocolate shell back in the pie plate or on a serving platter. To make the filling, beat the egg yolks until light. Add the sugar and mix. Soften the gelatine in ½ cup cold water and dissolve over low heat. In the top of a double boiler, bring gelatine mixture just to a boil and add the egg yolks, stirring briskly. Let cool, then fold in the whipped cream, then the rum. Pour into the chocolate shell and sprinkle with the pistachio nuts. Chill for at least 2 hours.

Strawberry Tart with Marsala Crust

Preparation time: 30 minutes
Cooking time: 30 minutes (total)
Degree of difficulty: challenging
Servings: 6-8
Calories per serving: 615 (1/6)
460 (1/8)

As part of a sweet table, or as an ending to a special dinner party, this dessert is a hit. Garnish with fresh mint if desired.

CRUST

1½ cups all-purpose flour

1 tablespoon sugar

¾ cup butter at room temperature

4 tablespoons dry Marsala wine

Preheat oven to 375°F. To prepare crust, combine flour and sugar in the bowl of a food processor. Cut butter into 6 pieces and add. Process for 10 seconds. With machine running, add wine through feed tube and let machine run until dough forms a ball, about 10-15 seconds. Press into an 11-inch flan pan with a removable bottom. Chill well. Bake for about 20 minutes or until pastry is golden. Cool.

CUSTARD

5 extra-large egg yolks

5 tablespoons sugar

¼ cup light rum

¼ cup dry Marsala

2 pints fresh strawberries, washed and hulled

1 cup whipping cream

2 tablespoons sugar

1 teaspoon icing sugar

To prepare custard, bring a small amount of water to a boil in the bottom of a double boiler. Put the egg yolks and 3 tablespoons of the sugar in a bowl and beat with a fork or whisk until lemon-colored; stir in rum and Marsala. Put mixture in top half of double boiler and place over boiling water; stir constantly until smooth and thick enough to coat the bottom of a spoon. Remove from heat; stir to cool and to prevent eggs from scrambling; taste, and stir in 2 tablespoons more sugar if desired. When custard has cooled, pour into prepared tart shell. Arrange strawberries around the edge of the tart and chill. At serving time, whip the cream with the sugar; mound cream in centre of pie and sprinkle berries with icing sugar.

Lime Tart with Strawberries

Preparation time: 1¾ hours
Stranding time: 1 hour
Cooking time: 30-35 minutes
Degree of difficulty: moderate
Servings: 6-8
Calories per serving: 350 (1/6)
                    265 (1/8)

A simple supper often demands a spectacular dessert, and this fresh-tasting, pretty tart fills the bill.

PÂTE SUCRÉE

1½ cups all-purpose flour

4 tablespoons sugar

9 tablespoons cold butter, cut into small pieces

1 small egg, lightly beaten

FILLING

⅓ cup plus 2 tablespoons sugar

¼ cup plus 1 tablespoon lime juice

3 egg yolks

3 tablespoons grated lime peel

2 tablespoons softened butter

Fresh strawberries for garnish

Whipping cream (optional)

Sift flour and sugar into a bowl, add butter and egg, and blend until well combined. Form into a ball, knead lightly with the heel of the hand against a smooth surface for a few seconds to distribute the butter evenly, and re-form into a ball. Dust with flour and chill, wrapped in wax paper, for at least 1 hour. Lightly roll out dough ⅛-inch thick, fit into an 8-inch flan ring set on a baking sheet, and chill again for 30 minutes.

Preheat oven to 400°F. Combine filling ingredients except strawberries and whipped cream and beat the mixture for 3 minutes, or until fluffy. Spread mixture in the pastry shell, cover loosely with foil, and bake in the lower third of the oven for 30-35 minutes, or until filling is set. Cool on a rack. Garnish with sliced strawberries and serve with sweetened whipped cream.

PHOTO BY PAT LACROIX/THE BRANT GROUP

Lime Tart with Strawberries

The 18th century a-dored complications in their cuisine. One cook contrived a pas-try ship with guns filled with real pow-der and a castle full of live frogs and birds. After the guns were fired, the ladies threw eggshells full of per-fume at each other, then the lids of the castles were lifted and out jumped the frogs, making the ladies shriek. The birds flew forth, put-ting out the can-dles, and "nobody knows what kisses and struggles and pretty adventures might happen with-out lights." It certainly makes Trivial Pursuit look tame.

Rhubarb and Strawberry Pie

Preparation time: 30 minutes
Standing time: 30 minutes
Cooking time: 45 minutes
Degree of difficulty: moderately challenging
Servings: 8-10
Calories per serving: 400 (1/8)
320 (1/10)

When Barbara Gordon, owner of Toronto's Beaujolais, owned La Cachette in Vancouver — one of Canada's best restaurants — she devised this truly lovely pie.

PASTRY

2 cups all-purpose flour
1 teaspoon grated orange peel
½ teaspoon salt
1¼ cups unsalted butter, chilled
¼-⅓ cup ice water

In a large bowl, combine flour, orange peel, and salt. With a pastry blender or 2 knives, cut in the but-ter until mixture looks like rolled oats. Sprinkle with water while pressing the ingredients to form a dough. Shape into 2 balls and flat-ten; wrap and chill for 30 minutes.

FILLING

1 cup granulated sugar
2 tablespoons instant tapioca
2 teaspoons cornstarch
¼ teaspoon salt
¼ teaspoon nutmeg
3½ cups pink rhubarb,
in 1-inch pieces
¼ cup fresh orange juice
1½ cups coarsely sliced
ripe strawberries
1 tablespoon unsalted butter

Preheat oven to 450°F. To pre-pare filling, blend together the sugar, tapioca, cornstarch, salt, and nutmeg; set aside. Roll out half the dough and place in a deep 10-inch pie plate. Trim the pastry ½ inch from the rim; fold under neatly and flute. Roll out the remaining dough and cut out 24 2½-inch hearts; set aside. Toss the rhubarb in the sugar mixture; stir in the orange juice and spoon mixture evenly into the pie plate. Scatter strawberries over top and dot with butter. Place hearts randomly over the top. Bake for 10 minutes. Lower temperature to 350°F and continue baking 30-35 minutes longer, or until the pastry is golden and the filling is bubbly. Because rhubarb and strawberries are so juicy, place a sheet of alumi-num foil in the bottom of the oven to catch any drips. Let pie cool on a rack.

A Peach of a Pie

Preparation time: 20 minutes
Cooking time: 10 minutes
Chilling time: 1 hour
Degree of difficulty: simple
Servings: 6-8
Calories per serving: 470 (1/6)
350 (1/8)

A glorious dessert both in appear-ance and taste.

1 baked 9-inch pie shell
1 cup whipping cream
1 cup sugar
4 tablespoons cornstarch
2 tablespoons corn syrup
1 cup water
3 tablespoons peach jelly powder
3-4 fresh peaches

Combine sugar, cornstarch, and syrup in a heavy saucepan. Grad-ually add water. Cook until mixture thickens and clears. Stir in jelly powder. Cool to lukewarm. Mean-while, dip peaches in boiling water for 30 seconds, then in cold water for easy peeling. Peel and slice. Combine peaches with glaze, and pour into pie shell. Garnish with whipped cream and refrigerate at least 1 hour before serving.

Raspberry Cranberry Crumble Pie

Preparation time: 15 minutes
Cooking time: 1 hour
Degree of difficulty: moderate
Servings: 8
Calories per serving: 630

This dessert is from Carole Kreid-stein of Willowdale, Ontario.

PASTRY

1 cup all-purpose flour
¼ teaspoon salt
2 teaspoons sugar
¾ cup shortening
1 egg yolk
1 teaspoon almond extract
3 to 4 tablespoons water

FILLING

2 cups cranberries
1 10-ounce package frozen unsweetened red raspberries, thawed and drained
1¼ cups sugar
2 tablespoons quick-cooking tapioca
¼ teaspoon almond extract

TOPPING

1 cup all-purpose flour
½ cup butter
¾ cup granulated sugar

To make the pastry, combine the flour, salt, and sugar in a bowl. Cut in the shortening until the mixture resembles coarse meal. In another bowl, beat together the egg yolk, almond extract, and water. Add to the flour mixture and combine until it forms a soft dough. Roll out dough and line a 9-inch pie plate.

Preheat oven to 350°F. For the filling, chop the cranberries in a food processor or blender. Trans-fer to a bowl and combine with raspberries, sugar, tapioca, and almond extract. Mix well and pour into pie plate. To make the topping, combine the flour with the butter and sugar until the mixture is crumbly. Sprinkle over the top of the pie and bake for 50-60 minutes, or until the topping is golden and the filling is bubbly.

Gingered Pear Mousse Pie

Preparation time: 30 minutes
Chilling time: about 4 hours
Degree of difficulty: simple
Calories per serving: 590

Cuisine '85 Semifinalist
An elegant conclusion to a dinner party.

GRAHAM CRUST

1 cup graham wafer crumbs
3 tablespoons demerara sugar
½ teaspoon ground cinnamon
⅛ teaspoon ground nutmeg
¼ teaspoon ground ginger
¼ cup melted butter

Preheat oven to 350°F. For the crust, combine all ingredients; mix well. Pat into a 10-inch pie plate, making sides thicker than the bottom. Bake for 8 minutes, or microwave 1½ to 2 minutes. When cool, refrigerate until ready to fill.

FILLING

4 large, ripe pears
1 envelope unflavored gelatine
¼ cup cold water
2 tablespoons sugar
1 teaspoon ground ginger
3 large egg yolks, lightly beaten
1 teaspoon vanilla
2 large egg whites
4 tablespoons sugar
1 cup whipping cream, beaten into soft peaks
½ cup toasted walnuts, finely chopped
3 tablespoons dark rum
¼ cup finely chopped crystallized ginger
1 pear, cored and sliced (for garnish)
1 teaspoon lemon juice
Chopped crystallized ginger (for garnish, optional)
Fresh mint sprigs

For the filling, peel and core 2 of the pears, place in a blender and purée to make 1¼ cups. Place purée in the top of a double boiler and add gelatine dissolved in ¼ cup cold water, 2 tablespoons of sugar, and the ground ginger. Stir in egg yolks and cook over simmering water until slightly thickened. Remove from heat and add vanilla. Stir until cool and thickened. Beat egg whites until foamy. Add 4 tablespoons of sugar and beat until stiff. Fold egg whites and whipped cream into purée mixture. Peel, core and dice remaining pears and add along with walnuts, rum, and crystallized ginger. Gently spoon into prepared pie crust. Chill until set — about 4 hours. Garnish with sliced pear painted with lemon juice (to prevent discoloring), crystallized ginger, and mint sprigs.

Mince Tarts

Preparation time: 20-30 minutes
Standing time: 1 hour
Cooling time: 25 minutes
Degree of difficulty: simple
Amount: makes 1 dozen
Calories per serving: 350

FOOD PROCESSOR PASTRY

Using this machine is one of the most reliable ways of making good, flaky pastry.

2 cups all-purpose flour
6 ounces cold butter, in small pieces
2 tablespoons shortening
Large pinch of salt
1 tablespoon lemon juice
¼ cup water
1 24-ounce jar mincemeat

Put the plastic blade in the food processor; add flour, chopped butter, shortening, and salt. Mix briefly. Add lemon juice and again mix briefly. Add water a little at a time and mix until dough forms a ball (not all the water may be needed). Wrap in wax paper and refrigerate for at least 1 hour. Meanwhile, preheat oven to 400°F. Roll out dough ⅛-inch thick. Butter a muffin tin; cut out circles of pastry large enough to line the individual compartments; line, then fill ½ to ¾ with mincemeat (use 1 24-ounce jar). Cut circles of remaining pastry to make lids, and press on firmly, using a little water. Pierce lids with a fork, then bake for about 25 minutes. Serve warm.

NOTES

POULTRY AND GAME

hicken is in most Canadian kitchens on almost a daily basis today, and we should be grateful, because it's one of the most accommodating of birds. It forms the basis for cool summer salads, robust fall soups, even heartier winter stews, and it appears roasted in the spring, along with new potatoes and asparagus, like a newly invented dish. Let's hear it for the chicken.

Ducks, turkey, and geese play lesser roles in Canadian cooking, and are more likely to appear on holidays and special occasion dinners, but they're none the less a welcome change to meat, particularly since the modern breeding of birds has produced smaller turkeys and relatively greaseless ducks and geese. Turkey meat is the least expensive of the three, and provides the most protein per pound.

For the more sophisticated (or experimental) cook, it's possible to find game birds raised in Canadian captivity, one of the most recent being guinea fowl. Pintade Farms, in Cambridge, Ontario, is North America's only year-round supplier of these interesting birds, which are somewhere between chicken and wild game birds. With half the fat of chicken but all of its tenderness, it's a good alternative for barbecuing and oven roasting. Pheasant, Rock Cornish hens, quail, and squab (young pigeons) can be a welcome change, and are all available in Canada, often by mail order.

Chickens worth buying will resemble Elizabeth Taylor, with big breasts and short legs, and smooth, creamy skin. Breastbones should be flexible in chickens and turkeys, indicating youth, while duck and goose bills will be pliable. Whole chickens will spoil faster than will chicken pieces, and most poultry should be eaten within two days of purchase. Marks and Spencer stores sell "chicken with a difference" that is date-stamped, and of high quality. About ¾-1 pound of ready-to-cook birds should be sufficient per person.

Glazed Kebabs (see recipe page 134)

If using a gas barbecue, purchase an extra bag of lava rock to double the volume. Turn the barbecue on high and heat the lava rock for 10-15 minutes. Once rocks are really hot, turn off the gas and begin cooking the meat. The residual heat in the lava rock is sufficient to properly cook the meat. This method avoids open flame, which can make drippings flare up and scorch the meat. A more even cooking takes a little longer but is well worth the extra time. *(Chef Ernst Walder, Ramada Hotel, Don Valley, Toronto).*

Glazed Kebabs

Preparation time: 30 minutes
Cooking time: 20 minutes (oven)
10 minutes (barbecue)
Degree of difficulty: simple
Servings: 4
Calories per serving: 385

Good for barbecue or broiler.

8 chicken thighs

5 tablespoons sesame seeds

½ cup honey

¼ cup lemon juice

1 teaspoon salt

A few drops of Tobasco sauce

8 small white onions

8-16 cubes of squash

1 large green pepper

1 large red sweet pepper

8-16 fresh mushrooms

½ cup oil-and-vinegar dressing

Preheat oven to 350°F. (Or heat coals on barbecue.) Bake chicken for 20 minutes. Sprinkle sesame seeds in an even layer on the bottom of a small saucepan. Toast over low heat, stirring constantly until golden. Stir in honey, lemon juice, salt, and Tabasco. Cut a cross at the end of each onion, and steam onions and squash cubes together for 10 minutes. Seed peppers and cut into 2-inch pieces. Thread chicken thighs onto long skewers with chunks of the squash, onions, and peppers, and whole mushrooms. Brush with oil-vinegar dressing, and barbecue or broil 6 inches from heat for 10 minutes. Brush with sesame glaze, turning and basting until vegetables are done.

Chicken Breasts with Green Peppercorn Sauce

Preparation time: 30 minutes
Cooking time: 30 minutes
Degree of difficulty: simple
Servings: 6
Calories per serving: 310

Green peppercorns warm the flavor of the sauce as nothing else can.

6 large chicken breasts, skinned, boned, and pounded flat

4 tablespoons flour

2 tablespoons olive oil

5 tablespoons butter

3 tablespoons brandy

¼ cup chopped shallots

3 tablespoons green peppercorns, drained

1 cup beef stock

¼ cup whipping cream

Preheat oven to 275°F. Dredge the chicken breasts in flour. Heat olive oil in a large frying pan and add 4 tablespoons of the butter; when bubbly, sauté the chicken breasts on both sides until cooked through and golden, about 10 minutes. Transfer chicken breasts to a large flat casserole dish and place in oven. Wipe pan and add 1 tablespoon butter; when sizzling, add brandy, and flame, shaking the pan until the flame dies. Stir in the shallots and cook over low heat for 3 minutes; add peppercorns. Stir in beef stock and cook over medium-low heat until reduced by ⅓. Stir in the cream and pour over chicken.

Chicken Satay with Peanut Butter Sauce

Preparation time: 30 minutes
Marinating time: overnight
Cooking time: 15 minutes
Degree of difficulty: simple
Servings: 6
Calories per serving: 280
(with sauce)

Adapted from an original, and none the worse for that.

6 chicken breasts, skinned and boned

3 tablespoons lime juice

2 tablespoons soya sauce

1 tablespoon oil

1 tablespoon brown sugar

1 small onion, finely chopped

½ teaspoon grated fresh ginger root

2 cloves garlic, crushed

PEANUT BUTTER SAUCE

½ cup creamy peanut butter

½ cup water

2 tablespoons soya sauce

3 tablespoons lime juice

1 medium onion, finely chopped

½ teaspoon dried chili peppers, crushed

Slice chicken into 1-inch square cubes. Combine remaining ingredients in a medium-size bowl and mix well. Add chicken and marinate several hours or overnight.

To make sauce, cook peanut butter and water over low heat until smooth, about 5 minutes. Add soya sauce, lime juice, onion, and peppers; mix well. Cool to room temperature. Makes about 1 cup.

Prepare barbecue coals. Thread chicken on 12 skewers (wooden ones from the butcher or hardware store are best). Grill 10-15 minutes, turning to brown all sides. Serve with peanut butter sauce.

Chicken with the King

Preparation time: 40 minutes
Standing time: 30 minutes
Cooking time: 30 minutes
Degree of difficulty: challenging
Servings: 4
Calories per serving: 540

Gucheese, an admirable restaurant in Vancouver, used cheese in everything, and an after-theatre specialty was 3 cheeses with appropriate wines.

4 large chicken breast halves, skinned, boned, and flattened
3 tablespoons butter
½ onion, finely diced
½ stalk celery, finely diced
1 small carrot, finely diced
1 small leek, white part only, finely diced
1 tablespoon green peppercorns
2 cups clear chicken stock
1 cup couscous grains (available at health food and specialty shops)
1 cup grated Stilton cheese
Salt to taste
2 tablespoons sunflower or safflower oil
3 shallots, finely chopped
2 tablespoons brandy
¼ cup dry white wine
2 cups brown veal or chicken stock

Heat butter in a saucepan and gently fry the onion, celery, carrot, and leek until soft but not brown. Add peppercorns and clear stock, bring to a boil and simmer for 5 minutes. Add the couscous, mix, cover, remove the pan from direct heat and let the mixture stand for 30 minutes. Preheat oven to 375°F. Add grated Stilton cheese to couscous mixture and after it has melted, taste and add salt if needed. Divide this stuffing on the chicken breast halves, roll up, and secure with toothpicks. In an oven-proof pan, sauté the chicken in oil on all sides until golden, then bake for 10-12 minutes. Remove from oven, add shallots to the pan, and pour in the brandy. Heat gently and flame with a match. Remove chicken and keep warm. Add the wine and reduce sauce by ½. Add the brown stock and reduce again to desired thickness. Slice chicken breasts and arrange on warmed plates. Pour the sauce over chicken, leaving half of each slice unsauced for the color contrast.

Chicken Breasts Stuffed with Prosciutto and Mushrooms

Preparation time: 30 minutes
Cooking time: 20 minutes
Degree of difficulty: simple
Servings: 6
Calories per serving: 290

Somewhat decadent, but not to wretched excess.

6 large chicken breasts
6 tablespoons butter
¼ pound mushrooms, finely chopped
6 thin slices prosciutto ham, chopped
2 teaspoons finely chopped shallots
2 teaspoons finely chopped parsley
¼ teaspoon nutmeg
2 tablespoons lemon juice
½ teaspoon paprika

Bone chicken breasts, keeping skin on. Flatten to an even thickness. Preheat oven to 375°F. Melt 4 of the 6 tablespoons of butter in a frying pan. Add the mushrooms, prosciutto, shallots, and parsley; sauté over medium heat 3-5 minutes. Add nutmeg. Spoon equal portions of the stuffing in the centre of each of the 6 chicken breasts. Roll up. Place chicken breasts seam sides down, in a shallow, lightly oiled baking pan. Melt remaining butter; add lemon juice and paprika, and brush on chicken breasts. Bake 20-25 minutes until tops are golden and juices run clear. (For added color, run under broiler for about 1 minute just before serving.)

Fernand Point's Chicken Fricassee

Preparation time: 10 minutes
Cooking time: 30 minutes
Degree of difficulty: simple
Servings: 6
Calories per serving: 325

Point, turn-of-the-century innovative chef and teacher, developed this and many other dishes suitable for suppers.

1 3- to 3½ pound frying or roasting chicken, cut in serving pieces
4-6 tablespoons unsalted butter
Sea salt and freshly ground pepper to taste
¼ cup tawny port
1 sprig fresh tarragon (or a pinch of dried)
⅔ cup whipping cream
2-3 drops lemon juice
2-3 tablespoons unsalted butter (optional)

In a large frying pan, sauté chicken pieces in butter very gently, without allowing them to color, 15-20 minutes for breasts (cook thighs and legs another 10 minutes or until done). Remove from pan, sprinkle with salt and pepper, and keep warm. Deglaze the pan with port, stirring with a wooden spoon, and add tarragon and cream. Reduce until the mixture lightly coats the spoon. Add lemon juice and taste; if you like a richer flavor, whip in extra butter. Serve sauce over chicken.

Using the incorrect plastic wrap when cooking in the microwave oven can result in melted or dissolved wrapping. Saran Wrap is one of the better-known plastic wraps safe for microwave cooking and can be used to steam, poach, and reheat food correctly. Remember to turn up a small corner of the plastic wrap to allow excess steam to escape during cooking: don't vent the wrap by piercing it, since it might cause it to split during cooking; avoid steam burns by peeling cover away from you as you remove it.

Lemon Ginger
Chicken (right);
Duck with
Blueberries La
Belle Auberge
(below)

Lemon Ginger Chicken

Preparation time: 20 minutes
Cooking time: 30-40 minutes
Degree of difficulty: simple
Servings: 4
Calories per serving: 385

Serve this Chinese-inspired dish with steamed rice, a green salad and chilled white wine.

1 3-pound chicken, quartered
¼ cup butter
2 teaspoons grated lemon peel
2 tablespoons lemon juice
½ teaspoon salt
¼ teaspoon paprika
½ teaspoon powdered or
1 tablespoon grated fresh ginger
Dash of Tabasco sauce

Melt butter in a small saucepan over low heat. Stir in lemon peel, lemon juice, salt, paprika, ginger, and Tabasco. Place chicken, skin side down, on a rack in a shallow pan. Broil 8 inches from heat for 15-20 minutes, brushing occasionally with sauce. Drain fat from pan and turn chicken skin side up. Broil 15-20 minutes longer or until tender, brushing from time to time with the sauce.

Duck with Blueberries La Belle Auberge

Preparation time: 20 minutes
Cooking time: 1½-1¾ hours
Degree of difficulty: simple
Servings: 4
Calories per serving: 480
(with sauce)

Ducks are roasted whole, carved, and served with a wonderful tangy-sweet sauce of blueberries, oranges, and cognac in this recipe from La Belle Auberge in Ladner, B.C.

2 whole ducks
Salt and freshly ground pepper to taste

PHOTOS BY TIM SAUNDERS

SAUCE

1 tablespoon butter
5 tablespoons sugar
⅔ cup wine vinegar
Juice of 4 oranges
⅓ cup chicken stock
¼ cup blueberries, fresh or frozen
1 tablespoon Cognac

Preheat oven to 500°F. Season ducks with salt and pepper. Roast for 30 minutes. Lower temperature to 350°F and roast for 60-75 minutes more, or until ducks are tender. Baste with pan drippings twice during roasting. Cool ducks for 20 min-utes, then carve and arrange on a warm platter.

Meanwhile, heat and stir butter and sugar until caramelized. Add vinegar, orange juice, and stock. Stir until caramel has dissolved, then boil sauce until reduced to a syrup. Add blueberries and Cognac and spoon sauce over duck. Serve with green beans, white rice, and peeled, cubed tomatoes or vegetables of your choice.

Grilled Chicken with Garlic Mayonnaise

Preparation time: 15 minutes
Cooking time: 30 minutes
Degree of difficulty: challenging
Servings: 6-8
Calories per serving: 833 (1/6)
625 (1/8)

4 chicken breasts
1 firm-fleshed fish, prepared for grilling (optional)
½ pound fresh green beans, trimmed
4 carrots, peeled and thinly sliced
1 cauliflower, trimmed and broken into flowerets
Lemon wedges and parsley sprigs
Cherry tomatoes

AIOLI
8-10 cloves garlic, peeled
2 egg yolks at room temperature
Juice of 1 lemon
½ teaspoon Dijon mustard
1½ cups vegetable oil (olive or peanut or a combination)
Freshly ground black pepper to taste

Heat coals on barbecue. Steam the vegetables until tender but crisp; set aside. Place the fish in a barbecue basket and grill until done. Set the chicken breasts over the hot coals and grill until the juices run clear. (If your barbecue is large enough, the fish and chicken may be grilled at the same time.) Meanwhile, prepare the aioli. Place the garlic in a food processor or blender and purée. Add egg yolks, lemon juice, and mustard and process until light and smooth. With the machine still running, slowly pour the oil in a steady stream into the mixture until the sauce is thick and shiny. Add pepper to taste. Transfer to a bowl, cover with plastic wrap, and refrigerate until serving time. Slice the chicken into small serving pieces and arrange on a platter with the fish; surround with vegetables. Garnish with lemon wedges, parsley sprigs, and cherry tomatoes and invite guests to serve themselves. Pass the aioli separately.

Supreme of Duckling with Calvados and Apples

Preparation time: 15 minutes
Cooking time: 45 minutes
Degree of difficulty: simple
Servings: 2
Calories per serving: 760
2 duck breasts, boned and halved
3 tablespoons unsalted butter
2 onions, diced
Salt and freshly ground pepper to taste
¼ cup calvados
¼ teaspoon allspice
1 apple, peeled, cored, and sliced in thick rings
1 cup apple juice
2 tablespoons all-purpose flour

In a heavy frying pan with a cover melt 1 tablespoon butter and fry onion until just transparent. Remove from pan and reserve. Season duck breasts with salt and pepper and sauté in pan until lightly browned on both sides. Add calvados and ignite with a long match. Let burn for 20 seconds before blowing out. Add allspice, sprinkle with onion, top with apple rings, and pour in apple juice. Cover and cook over medium heat for 25 minutes. In another pan, melt remaining butter and mix in flour, stirring until smooth. Slowly stir in gravy from duck and cook for 3 minutes until thick. Pour over duck and serve with wild rice.

Quail Tarragon

Preparation time: 10 minutes
Cooking time: 50 minutes (total)
Degree of difficulty: simple
Servings: 2-3
Calories per serving: 533 (1/2)
349 (1/3)

Domestic quail can be found at many supermarkets, or Cornish hens may be substituted. If possible, use fresh tarragon to complement the other quality ingredients in this festive dish.

6 quail, cleaned

¼ cup all-purpose flour seasoned with salt and pepper

½ cup unsalted butter

½ cup Sauterne

2 tablespoons melted butter

2 tablespoons lemon juice

4 tablespoons fresh or
2 tablespoons dried tarragon

Salt and freshly ground pepper to taste

Brown or wild rice

Dredge quail with seasoned flour. In a frying pan, heat ½ cup butter until it foams and sauté quail until golden brown on all sides. Preheat oven to 400°F. Transfer quail to a rack in a roasting pan, putting a small amount of butter inside each bird. Deglaze frying pan with ½ cup Sauterne. Pour sauce over the birds and roast for 40 minutes, basting with a mixture of remaining Sauterne, melted butter, lemon juice, tarragon, salt, and pepper. Serve with brown or wild rice.

Pheasant and Partridge Pie

Preparation time: 30 minutes
Marinating time: 24 hours
Cooking time: 1½ hours
Baking time: 30 minutes
Degree of difficulty: challenging
Servings: 10-12
Calories per serving: 590 (1/10)
492 (1/12)

This version of pheasant was prepared by Toronto's Delta Chelsea Inn at a heritage luncheon to commemorate Ontario's 200th anniversary. Keep this recipe for a special occasion.

2 pheasants

3 partridge (if partridge is unavailable, substitute squab)

¼ cup vegetable oil

1 tablespoon tomato paste

8 cups beef bouillon

½ cup lardons (these strips of salt pork can be purchased at most butcher shops; if unavailable, substitute bacon)

2 tablespoons brandy

2 tablespoons butter

2 tablespoons all-purpose flour

1 package frozen puff pastry, thawed

1 egg, beaten

MARINADE

1 bay leaf

½ teaspoon whole black peppercorns

1 carrot, sliced

2 cups dry red wine

2 tablespoons wine vinegar

1 celery stalk, sliced

½ teaspoon juniper berries
(or substitute 2 tablespoons gin)

2 cloves garlic, crushed

Bone game birds or have a butcher do this for you. Cut meat into 1-inch cubes and reserve bones. Combine marinade ingredients. Place meat in marinade and refrigerate 24 hours. Strain meat and vegetables from marinade; reserve liquid. Heat oil in a frying pan and brown bones; add vegetables and brown. Add tomato paste, beef bouillon, and marinade liquid. Bring to a boil; reduce heat and simmer for about 1 hour or until liquid is reduced by ½. While sauce is simmering, fry lardons in a saucepan until brown; set aside. In same pan, brown meat. Drain off fat and flame meat with brandy. Strain sauce from bones and add it to meat along with the lardons; simmer until meat is tender (about 20 minutes). Heat butter in a small skillet; add flour, and mix to make a roux. Gradually add roux to sauce, bring to a boil, and thicken to desired consistency. Preheat oven to 425°F. Pour filling into a deep potpie dish (a 10-cup soufflé dish will do nicely). Roll out pastry and place on top of filling; brush with egg. Bake for 15 minutes, then reduce heat to 375°F for another 15 minutes, or until the pastry is golden and the filling is bubbling hot.

Ginger Duck

Preparation time: 10 minutes
Cooking time: 1½ hours
Degree of difficulty: simple
Servings: 4
Calories per serving: 360

The zing of fresh ginger and the sweet saltiness of soya sauce are a good foil for rich domestic duck.

1 4½-pound duck, frozen

¾ cup soya sauce

3 tablespoons ground ginger

Partly thaw the duck, enough to pry open the cavity; pull or cut away as much fat as possible before it is completely thawed. Rub duck with ¼ cup of the soya sauce and ginger, then let stand until fully thawed. Place in a deep casserole, and add remaining soya sauce and ginger, add water to cover, and bring to boil. Reduce heat and simmer for 1 hour. Meanwhile, preheat oven to 450°F. Drain. (Liquid may be cooled, defatted, and used to make duck soup.) Place the duck on a rack in a roasting pan and roast for ½ hour or until crisp and done.

Chicken Livers with Shallots and Madeira

Preparation time: 15 minutes
Cooking time: 35-40 minutes
Degree of difficulty: simple
Servings: 4-6
Calories per serving: 413 (1/4)
275 (1/6)

This brunch dish is standard fare at luxury hotels across Canada. It's even better at home. Serve on buttered toast, noodles, or steamed rice.

| 1½ pounds chicken livers, fresh if possible |
| 15 shallot cloves, or 1 small onion, peeled and finely chopped |
| 2 cloves garlic, peeled and finely chopped |
| 6 tablespoons butter |
| 1 tablespoon all-purpose flour |
| 1¼ cups chicken broth |
| 1½ tablespoons finely chopped parsley |
| Salt and freshly ground pepper to taste |
| ⅓ cup dry Madeira |
| Few drops fresh lemon juice |

In a heavy frying pan, sauté shallots and garlic in 3 tablespoons of the butter. Cook, stirring occasionally, for about 5 minutes until the shallots are soft but not browned. Stir in the flour, simmer for 1 minute, then add the chicken broth. Bring the sauce to a boil, stirring constantly. When thickened, add the parsley, lower heat and simmer for 10 minutes. Stir, remove from heat, and set aside.

Heat the remaining butter in another frying pan. Add the chicken livers, sprinkle with salt and pepper, and sauté briskly for about 5 minutes. Do not overcook; the livers should remain slightly pink in the centre. When they are ready, remove from the pan with a slotted spoon and place on a warm plate. Set aside. Pour the Madeira into the frying pan stirring the pan drippings and scraping in any bits that cling to the pan. Bring to a boil and continue to boil until the wine is reduced to about ½. Stir in the shallot sauce and bring to a boil again. Add the livers and any accumulated juice. Simmer for 1 minute to heat the livers through; do not overcook or they will become tough. Taste for seasoning, add lemon juice, and serve immediately.

Chili Chicken

Preparation time: 15 minutes
Cooking time: 1½ hours
Degree of difficulty: simple
Servings: 4-6
Calories per serving: 580 (1/4)
390 (1/6)

As a variation on traditional beef chili, Winnipeg's Marlene Proctor makes her chili with chicken, serves it in individual bowls, and tops each with a crunchy phyllo pastry crust.

| 4 chicken breasts, skinned, boned, and chopped |
| 2 tablespoons butter |
| 6 cloves garlic, minced |
| 2 medium onions, chopped |
| ¼ cup beef stock |
| 1 19-ounce can plum tomatoes, drained, seeded, and chopped |
| 1 4-ounce can green chilis, drained, and chopped |
| ½ cup beer |
| ½ teaspoon cumin |
| 2 teaspoons oregano |
| 1 teaspoon chili powder |
| 2 cups grated Cheddar cheese |
| Phyllo pastry sheets |
| Melted butter |

Melt the 2 tablespoons of butter in a large saucepan. Add the garlic and onions and sauté for 5 minutes. Stir in the chicken, beef stock, tomatoes, chilis, beer, cumin, oregano, and chili powder. Bring to a boil, reduce heat, and simmer, uncovered, for 1 hour. Preheat oven to 350°F. Ladle the chili chicken into ovenproof soup bowls and top each with Cheddar cheese. Cut 3 or 4 sheets of phyllo pastry to fit over tops of soup bowls and brush lightly with melted butter. Bake until pastry is golden, about 15 minutes.

Chicken Ston Easton Park

Preparation time: 20-25 minutes
Cooking time: 15-20 minutes
Degree of difficulty: moderate
Servings: 4
Calories per serving: 335

The herbs in this dish can be tricky — the amount of each depends entirely on how much you like the herb. Go slow, but don't be a coward about it.

| 4 chicken breasts |
| ½ cup dry white wine |
| ½ cup dry sherry |
| Pernod to taste |
| 1 leek, julienned |
| 2 medium carrots, julienned |
| 2 stalks celery, julienned |
| Fennel |
| Basil |
| Mint |
| Lemon thyme |
| Tarragon |
| 1 cup light cream |
| Salt and freshly ground pepper to taste |

Place chicken breasts in a shallow pan and cover with white wine, sherry, and Pernod. Place the vegetables on top of the chicken breasts, cover with foil, and cook over moderate heat for 15-20 minutes until breasts are cooked. Remove pan from heat, take out chicken breasts, and keep warm.

For the sauce, add herbs to the liquid and reduce by ½ over high heat. Add the cream and reduce until sauce coats the back of a spoon. Salt and pepper to taste. Arrange chicken breasts on a serving plate and coat with sauce.

If you cook more than one vegetable, start cooking those that take the longest, such as parsnips or carrots, before adding the quick-cooking ones, like broccoli or cauliflower.

Whiskey Chicken, Shaken Peas (see recipe page 187), and Rice Pilaf Mold (see recipe page 112)

Whiskey Chicken

Preparation time: 20 minutes
Marinating time: 1 hour
Cooking time: 45 minutes
Degree of difficulty: simple
Servings: 6
Calories per serving: 275

An interesting taste, and certainly a conversation piece.

6 chicken breasts
⅓ cup Scotch whiskey
3 tablespoons butter
¼ cup light olive oil
4 ounces button mushrooms
2 shallots (or 1 onion), chopped
Juice of 1 lemon
Salt and freshly ground pepper to taste
1 cup light cream
Toasted flaked almonds (optional)

Marinate chicken in whiskey for at least 1 hour; discard marinade. Heat butter and oil in a large, heavy casserole or frying pan with a lid. Fry the chicken until golden brown on both sides. Add the mushrooms, chopped shallots, and lemon juice. Cook for a further 5 minutes. Season, cover, and cook on low to medium heat for 30 minutes, or until tender. Remove the chicken pieces and keep warm. Skim excess fat from the pan juices and stir in cream. Pour sauce over chicken and garnish with a scattering of toasted almonds.

Roast Duck with Fruit Stuffing

Preparation time: 25 minutes
Cooking time: 2½-3 hours
Degree of difficulty: simple
Servings: 4
Calories per serving: 570

The fruitiness of the stuffing helps cut the richness of the bird.

1 5-6-pound duck, prepared for stuffing
1 orange
½ cup water
2 tablespoons red currant jelly
1 tablespoon lemon juice

FRUIT STUFFING

1 medium onion, chopped
1 tablespoon butter
4 cups soft, fresh breadcrumbs
½ cup chopped dates or raisins
¾ cup fresh cranberries
Salt and freshly ground pepper to taste
1 tablespoon lemon juice
1 egg, beaten

Preheat oven to 350°F. Remove excess fat from duck. Prepare the stuffing: in a small saucepan, sauté onion in butter until soft, about 5 minutes. Combine with remaining ingredients. Fill the duck with stuffing. Place duck breast side down on a rack in a shallow roasting pan. Prick skin well and roast for 45 minutes. Turn breast side up, prick skin, pour off fat, and continue roasting 90 minutes more, pouring off fat as it accumulates. Meanwhile, shred orange peel and cook in water 10 minutes. Add the juice from the orange, jelly, and lemon juice to the peel and liquid in the saucepan. Simmer until slightly thickened and remove from heat. Baste duck with glaze. Continue roasting and basting several times until duck is tender — about 20 minutes more.

Stuffed Chicken Legs with Apricot Orange Sauce

Preparation time: 1 hour
Chilling time: overnight
Cooking time: 30 minutes
Degree of difficulty: simple
Servings: 4
Calories per serving: 675

Cuisine '85 Semifinalist

4 boned chicken legs (drumstick plus thigh)

¼ cup orange liqueur

2 tablespoons butter

¼ cup pine nuts

3 ounces chopped Italian pancetta (or bacon or prosciutto)

¼ cup finely chopped shallots

½ cup dried, diced apricots

½ pound spinach, washed, drained, squeezed of excess water and chopped

⅔ cup breadcrumbs

1 egg, slightly beaten

Salt and freshly ground pepper to taste

¼ cup clarified butter

Juice and peel of 2 oranges

2 cups chicken stock

3 tablespoons butter

3 tablespoons all-purpose flour

Rub the skin and flesh of the chicken with the orange liqueur, cover with foil, and refrigerate overnight. In a frying pan, melt 2 tablespoons of butter and gently sauté the pine nuts until golden. Remove with a slotted spoon and set pine nuts aside. Fry the pancetta in the same pan until crisp but not dried out. Remove with a slotted spoon and set aside. In the same pan, sauté the shallots until softened. Stir in ¼ cup of the dried apricots and cook over low heat for 5 minutes. Transfer the sautéed apricots and shallots to a bowl and combine with the pancetta, pine nuts, spinach, and breadcrumbs; bind with the beaten egg and add salt and pepper to taste.

Preheat oven to 350°F. Meanwhile stuff each chicken leg with ¼ of the stuffing and sew up each leg with thread or metal skewers. Brown the legs in the clarified butter; transfer the legs to an oven-proof dish and bake for 20 minutes or until the chicken juices run clear. While the chicken is baking, make the sauce. To the remaining butter in the pan, stir in the remaining diced apricots, the orange juice and peel, and the chicken stock. Bring the mixture to a boil, and cook until the sauce is reduced to about 1¾ cups. Strain, pressing the apricots and peel to extract all the liquid. In another saucepan, melt the 3 tablespoons of butter and, when bubbly, stir in the 3 tablespoons of flour, mixing well to make a roux. Continue cooking until the roux is smooth and golden. Slowly add the strained liquid; cook over medium-low heat, stirring until the sauce is smooth and thick. Serve the sauce over the chicken legs.

Sesame Chicken Wings

Preparation time: 15 minutes
Cooking time: 1 hour
Degree of difficulty: simple
Servings: 12
Calories per serving: 150

Good finger food for a buffet.

3 pounds chicken wings (about 25)

1 egg

½ cup milk

¼ cup sesame seeds

½ cup all-purpose flour

1 teaspoon salt

¼ teaspoon freshly ground pepper

¼ teaspoon ground ginger

4 tablespoons butter

Preheat oven to 350°F. Wash wings and pat dry. Beat egg and milk together in a bowl. In another bowl combine sesame seeds, flour, salt, pepper, and ginger. Melt butter in a large baking pan. Dip wings in egg mixture and then in seed mixture to coat. Place in baking pan, rolling in butter to coat all sides. Bake until brown and tender, about 1 hour.

Rabbit Flemish Style

Preparation time: 10 minutes
Cooking time: 1-1½ hours
Degree of difficulty: simple
Servings: 4-6
Calories per serving: 735 (1/6)
490 (1/4)

Although Flemish style doesn't *always* mean cooking with beer, it's most often the case. Use an ale with character to make this dish, and drink it as an accompaniment.

1 3-4-pound rabbit, cut into serving pieces

7-8 tablespoons butter

4 large onions, coarsely chopped

⅓ cup white vinegar

1 tablespoon sugar

2 teaspoons Dijon mustard

4 slices crustless bread

2 sprigs fresh parsley

1 sprig fresh or ¼ teaspoon dried thyme

1 small bay leaf

4 cups ale

Salt and freshly ground pepper to taste

Melt 3-4 tablespoons of the butter in a frying pan; add rabbit pieces and brown well. In a large casserole, brown the onions in 4 tablespoons of the butter. Add white vinegar, sugar, and rabbit pieces. Spread ½ teaspoon of mustard on each slice of bread; distribute bread around the rabbit pieces. Add herbs, pour in the ale, and season lightly. Cook, covered, over low heat for 1-1½ hours, or until rabbit is tender. Serve rabbit pieces with sauce.

The guinea fowl is a native of West Africa and has been domesticated in England since the 15th century, when it was known as turkey, probably because it was introduced from that country before the real thing was seen in Europe. There are several different varieties of guinea fowl, but all have two things in common — they never run to fat, and the flesh is naturally dry. Guinea fowl are obtainable across Canada.

Pierre Dubrulle's Chicken in Cointreau

Preparation time: 10 minutes
Cooking time: 20-25 minutes
Degree of difficulty: simple
Servings: 8
Calories per serving: 324

4 whole chicken breasts, halved, boned, and skinned

2 small oranges

1 lemon

1½ cups demiglace or 1 10-ounce can beef bouillon

1 tablespoon red wine vinegar

¼ cup Cointreau

Salt and freshly ground pepper to taste

½ cup all-purpose flour

3 tablespoons butter

1 tablespoon vegetable oil

Parsley sprigs for garnish

Peel the oranges and lemon, slice peel into thin strips, and blanch for 2 minutes in 2 cups boiling water. Strain and reserve the peel. Segment the peeled oranges. Bring the demiglace to a boil (if using bouillon, reduce to desired consistency). Stir in the vinegar, Cointreau, blanched peel, and orange segments. Salt and pepper to taste. Set sauce aside and keep warm. Dip each chicken breast in flour. Heat butter and oil in a frying pan. Cook the chicken breasts over medium heat for 5 minutes on each side. Line a warm serving plate with some Cointreau sauce. Slice chicken breasts thinly and arrange on top of the sauce: garnish with parsley. Pass remaining sauce.

Savory Baked Chicken

Preparation time: 10 minutes
Cooking time: 1¼ hours
Degree of difficulty: simple
Servings: 6
Calories per serving: 375

Yogurt isn't only for dessert.

¾ cup plain yogurt

1 tablespoon lemon juice

1 teaspoon salt

1 teaspoon paprika

½ teaspoon Worcestershire sauce

⅛ teaspoon garlic powder

1 2½-3-pound broiler-fryer, cut up

1¼ cups fine, dry breadcrumbs

¼ cup butter

Preheat oven to 350°F. Combine yogurt, lemon juice, salt, paprika, Worcestershire sauce, and garlic powder. Dip chicken pieces in mixture and roll in crumbs. Place in a broad, shallow baking dish and dot with butter. Cover and bake for 45 minutes. Remove cover and cook another 30-35 minutes.

Quail with Black Peppercorns and Strawberries

Preparation time: 30 minutes
Marinating time: 2-3 hours
Cooking time: 1¼ hours
Degree of difficulty: moderate
Servings: 2
Calories per serving: 615
(with sauce)

Bizarre though it may seem, black peppercorns and fresh strawberries have an established link in French cookery. The following recipe was designed by Le Manoir Mauvide-Genest, a charming inn on the Île d'Orléans, Quebec.

4 quail

2 carrots, sliced

1 stalk of celery, sliced

1 onion, diced

½ cup plus 2 tablespoons strawberry liqueur

3 cups chicken broth

8-12 black peppercorns

3 cups strawberries

4 teaspoons butter

½ cup whipping cream

Salt to taste

Place the quail in a bowl and add the carrots, celery, onion, ½ cup strawberry liqueur, and chicken broth. Marinate 2-3 hours. Preheat oven to 300°F. Remove the quail from the marinade and put 2-3 peppercorns and 1-2 strawberries inside each one. Place the vegetables and marinade in a heavy-bottomed stewpot. Arrange the quail on top, dot with butter and bake, uncovered, for 15 minutes. Lower temperature to 275°F, add the rest of the strawberries, cover, and continue baking for 1 hour. When the quail are tender, remove from oven, cover, and keep warm. Purée the vegetable and strawberry mixture, then return to stewpot. Add the cream slowly, stirring constantly. Add the 2 tablespoons of strawberry liqueur and salt to taste. Serve with baked potatoes and a steamed green vegetable.

PHOTO BY TIM SAUNDERS

Walper Goose

Preparation time: 20 minutes
Cooking time: 4-5 hours
Degree of difficulty: simple
Servings: 8
Calories per serving: 490
(with dressing)

This version of a Kitchener, Ontario, recipe calls for dry white wine in the stuffing.

1 10-12-pound goose

1 medium onion, finely chopped

¼ cup butter, melted

5 cups soft breadcrumbs

1 teaspoon savory (or to taste)

2 teaspoons dried sage (or to taste)

Salt and freshly ground pepper to taste

½ cup crisply cooked bacon bits

½ cup finely chopped cooked lean ham

1 cup halved gooseberries (fresh if you can find them, otherwise canned and drained)

Dry white wine

Preheat oven to 450°F. Sauté onion in butter until soft and transparent. Sprinkle seasonings over breadcrumbs and toss. Add onion and butter and toss again. Add bacon bits, ham, and gooseberries and distribute evenly through dressing. Add enough dry white wine to moisten dressing so it holds together. Fill goose cavity without packing too tightly. Place on rack in roasting pan and cover loosely with brown paper tent. Place in oven and reduce heat to 350°F. Roast for 25 minutes per pound. Since goose tends to be fat, you may wish to pour off drippings from time to time.

Be careful when substituting fresh herbs for dried, or vice versa. The formula usually given is to use two to three times as much fresh as dried, but a lot depends on how fresh the herbs are to begin with, and your own personal taste.

Chicken in Sour Cream

Preparation time: 5 minutes
Cooking time: 1¼-1½ hours
Degree of difficulty: simple
Servings: 8
Calories per serving: 245
(with sauce)

A special favorite, from former hockey great Carl Brewer's kitchen.

7 to 11 chicken breast halves
Butter
Salt, pepper, paprika
1 large (or 2 small) cans cream of mushroom soup
2 packages dry onion soup mix
1 cup sour cream
1 tablespoon lemon juice
1 teaspoon dill seed

Preheat oven to 350°F. Place chicken breasts in buttered baking dish, skin side up. Dot each with butter; sprinkle with salt, pepper and paprika. Combine remaining ingredients and pour over chicken. Bake until chicken is tender and sauce is brown. Serve with rice, a green vegetable and a tossed salad.

Chichester Chicken

Preparation time: 15 minutes
Cooking time: 1¼ hours
Degree of difficulty: simple
Servings: 6
Calories per serving: 315
(with sauce)

An English classic: chicken oven-steamed in cream, with nutmeg to give it fragrance, curry for flavor, green onion or watercress for texture, rice and carrots for color.

3 to 4 pounds chicken, cut in pieces
1 teaspoon salt
¼ teaspoon pepper
¼ teaspoon nutmeg or mace
1 teaspoon curry powder
3 tablespoons butter or margarine
2 cups cream
1 teaspoon Worcestershire sauce
6 to 10 green onions or scallions
1 bunch of watercress (optional)

Preheat oven to 350°F. In a plate, blend together the salt, pepper, nutmeg or mace, and curry powder. Roll the chicken in this mixture, until each piece is well coated. Heat the butter or margarine in a frying pan, brown each piece of chicken until golden and place in an elegant baking dish. Stir together the cream and Worcestershire sauce. Add to fat remaining in frying pan. Stir to clean up pan juices, and pour over the chicken. Cover and bake for about 1 hour or until the chicken is tender and the cream is reduced to a lovely thick yellowish clotted cream.

While the chicken is cooking, clean the green onions, leaving as much green as possible. Then shred each one thinly, starting in the middle of the white part up to the end of the green part. Place side by side in a flat plate and cover with ice cubes. Set in refrigerator. They will become crisp and the stems take very interesting shapes.

When ready to serve, set the cold shallots on top of the hot chicken and surround with a crown of watercress.

Roast Cornish Hens with Raspberry Tarragon Sauce

Preparation time: 20 minutes
Cooking time: 1½ hours
Degree of difficulty: simple
Servings: 6
Calories per serving: 475
(with sauce)

Raspberries and tarragon sharpen the sauce for this tasty litte bird.

3 Cornish hens, washed and dried
1 lime, sliced
Sprigs of fresh herbs (parsley, summer savory, dill, or rosemary)
1 onion, cut in 3
Salt and freshly ground pepper to taste
Pinch of nutmeg
½ cup Dijon mustard
3 tablespoons bacon fat or butter

RASPBERRY-TARRAGON SAUCE
6 tablespoons butter
6 tablespoons flour
3 cups hot chicken stock
4 tablespoons raspberry vinegar
2 bay leaves
4 tablespoons fresh or
3 tablespoons dried tarragon
Salt and freshly ground pepper to taste

Preheat oven to 375°F. Squeeze lime juice into the cavities of the birds. Stuff each with fresh herbs, onion, salt, and pepper and a pinch of nutmeg. Tie the legs together and brush the outside of each bird with Dijon mustard. Melt the bacon fat or butter in a large frying pan and brown the birds all over. Transfer to a large casserole and bake, uncovered, for about 45 minutes. To make the sauce, melt the butter and mix in the flour to make a roux. Gradually stir in the chicken stock, mixing until smooth. Add the raspberry vinegar, bay leaves, and tarragon and cook over low heat for 15 minutes. Salt and pepper to taste. Pour the sauce over the birds and return to the oven for 15 minutes more. Halve birds and transfer to a warm serving platter. Strain the sauce into a gravy boat and pass separately.

Chicken Stew with Dumplings

Preparation time: 20 minutes
Cooking time: 50-60 minutes
Degree of difficulty: simple
Servings: 4 or more
Calories per serving: 574
(with dumplings)

This traditional stew will warm you to your toes. Serve with a green salad and a simple dessert.

1 3-pound fryer, cut in 8 pieces

2 tablespoons oil or chicken fat

2 medium onions, coarsely chopped

2 stalks celery, coarsely chopped

3 cups chicken stock

1 small winter squash, peeled and cubed

2 potatoes, peeled and cubed

½ turnip, peeled and cubed

1 cup peas (fresh or frozen)

Salt and freshly ground pepper to taste

DUMPLINGS

¾ cup all-purpose flour

1 teaspoon baking powder

½ teaspoon salt

1½ tablespoons butter

½ cup milk

1 teaspoon chopped parsley or chives

In a heavy-bottomed Dutch oven, heat the oil and sauté the chicken pieces, onion, and celery. Stir over high heat until the chicken is browned on all sides. Add the chicken stock and simmer for 15 minutes. Add the squash, potatoes, and turnip and simmer 10 minutes.

Meanwhile, prepare the dumplings: Sift together flour, baking powder, and salt. Cut in the butter with 2 knives, a pastry cutter or your fingers. Stir in the milk and parsley or chives. Set aside.

When the stew has simmered, add salt and pepper to taste, and the peas. Then drop the dumpling dough by teaspoonfuls into the simmering stew, cover and simmer for 15 to 20 minutes. *Do not peek*! (Uncovering dumplings is a sure way to ruin them.) After 15 minutes, cut 1 dumpling open to make sure it is cooked through. Serve immediately when the dumplings are done.

Waterzooi au Poulet

Preparation time: 10-15 minutes
Cooking time: 45 minutes-1 hour
Degree of difficulty: simple
Servings: 4
Calories per serving: 315

Neither soup nor stew, but a delicious compromise of a main dish, this would be well served by a side dish of garden peas or tiny new carrots.

1 2½-pound chicken, cut into serving pieces

2 leeks, white part only, finely chopped

2 stalks celery, finely chopped

1 small onion, finely chopped

1 carrot, finely chopped

2 tablespoons butter

4 cups chicken broth

1 egg yolk

⅓ cup heavy cream

2 teaspoons chopped parsley

In a casserole just large enough to hold the chicken, sauté the leeks, celery, onion and carrot in butter for 5 minutes. Arrange the chicken pieces over the vegetables, add broth and simmer, covered, for 30 minutes, or until chicken is very tender.

Put pieces of chicken in 4 large heated soup bowls. In a bowl beat the egg yolk with the cream, and stir in ½ cup of the broth. Return mixture to the casserole, stirring, and heat the soup but don't let it boil. Season with salt and pepper to taste, and pour it over the chicken. Sprinkle each portion with ½ teaspoon of chopped parsley, and serve French bread to mop up the juices.

NOTES

PRESERVES

In the days of Canada's past, preserving was done partly because very sweet foods didn't spoil during the long winters and partly because those same long winters added a new dimension to the word "tedium" when it came to tastebuds taxed by yet another boring bowl of porridge or dry toast for breakfast. Today, too, a slather of tangy grape jam or dollop of bright red currant or elderberry jam makes all the difference between a yawn and a smile at the breakfast table. A house that smells of the sweetness of cooking fruit is a wonderful thing to come home to, but, if you both work, why not cook up a few batches of summer sunshine together on the weekends?

Jams and jellies are rather more taxing to make than one might think. A marmalade recipe that has worked for years might suddenly be too thick or thin because the fruit is being imported from another country, or there was more rain before the fruit crop was harvested. Fruit can be grown in the shade, the sun, or a mixture of both — any method can affect the flavor of the fruit and the quantity of preserve that results, particularly if you're making jelly.

Still, nothing major will go wrong with those pounds of freshly picked fruit that the cook will combine with sugar and perhaps pectin to turn into glowing dishes of brightness for the breakfast table or as filling for small tarts.

PHOTO BY SKIP DEAN, FOOD STYLING BY KATE BUSH

Always read your recipe completely through before you start cooking, to avoid arriving at the step that says "Marinate overnight" about an hour before dinner is to be served. (It has happened to the best of us!) As well, it will avoid last-minute trips to the local delicatessen for that spice, herb, or vinegar you've never used before and therefore don't have on your shelf.

Sweet Pickled Prunes

Preparation time: 5 minutes
Marinating time: overnight
Cooking time: 12-13 minutes
Degree of difficulty: simple
Amount: makes about 3 cups
Calories per cup: 840

The lowly prune takes on a new lustre with this delicious garnish for cold turkey, beef, or lamb.

12 ounces dried pitted prunes

1 cup malt vinegar

1/2 cup water

2 cups brown sugar

2-3-inch stick cinnamon

Put the prunes in a pottery mixing bowl and add vinegar, water, sugar, and cinnamon. Cover with a cloth and leave overnight to allow the prunes to soften and the sugar to dissolve. Next day, turn contents of bowl into a nonaluminum saucepan, bring to a simmer, and cook gently, covered, until the prunes are tender, about 10 minutes. Allow to cool slightly, drain prunes, reserving syrup, and pack into an 8-ounce jar. Return syrup to heat, bring to a boil and simmer for 1 to 2 minutes only. Pour the syrup over the prunes to cover. Let cool before storing.

The Very Best Marmalade

Preparation time: 20 minutes
Cooking time: 1 1/2 hours
Standing time: 20 minutes
Degree of difficulty: simple
Amount: makes about 6-8 pounds
Calories: 9,310 (total)

Tart without being bitter, this old English recipe can be made in late January and February when the Seville oranges are in the markets.

3 pounds Seville oranges

6 cups water

2 lemons

5 pounds sugar

Scrub oranges, place in a large saucepan, and cover with 4 cups of water. Cover with a lid and simmer about 1 hour, until oranges are quite soft. Lift out oranges, reserving cooking water. Cut each orange in half, scoop out the pith and pips from the centres into a saucepan. Add remaining 2 cups water to pith and pips, bring to a boil, and simmer for 10 minutes. Finely chop or mince soft peel and return to the pan containing water. Add sugar, finely grated peel, and strained juice of lemons and strained water from pith and pips. Stir over low heat until all sugar has dissolved, then bring up to the boil and cook rapidly until a set is obtained, about 20 minutes. Remove pan from heat, spoon away scum that may have risen to the surface, and allow marmalade to stand for 20 minutes to cool, and to ensure even distribution of peel. Pour into sterilized jars and seal.

Lemon Curd

Preparation time: 5 minutes
Cooking time: 20 minutes
Degree of difficulty: simple
Amount: makes about 1 1/2 cups
Calories per tablespoon: 79

Wonderful in little tarts with crisp pastry crust, even better on hot toast for breakfast.

2 large lemons

8 tablespoons chopped butter

1 cup less 1 tablespoon sugar

4 large eggs, beaten

Remove peel with a peeler, being careful not to take any bitter white pith with it, and chop finely. Put in top of a double boiler with butter and sugar, with simmering water beneath, and stir until dissolved. Pour eggs through a strainer into lemon mixture, stirring until the mixture is thick. Don't boil, or it will curdle. Pour into small jars and cover. It will keep best in the refrigerator, and not longer than 3 months.

Date and Lemon Chutney

Preparation time: 20 minutes
Degree of difficulty: simple
Amount: makes about 2 1/2 cups
Calories per tablespoon: 42

The sweetness of the dates and the tartness of the lemon are a good foil for curried dishes or the richness of roast goose or duck.

1 pound pitted dates, coarsely chopped

1 cup unsweetened shredded coconut

1/2 cup fresh lemon juice, strained

4 tablespoons chopped fresh ginger

4 tablespoons finely chopped parsley

1 teaspoon anise seeds

1 teaspoon salt

Freshly ground black pepper to taste

Combine dates, coconut, lemon juice, ginger, and parsley and mix thoroughly. Bruise the anise seeds with a mortar or rolling pin and add to the mixture. Season to taste. Stir thoroughly.

Three-Fruit Marmalade

Preparation time: 10 minutes
Standing time: overnight
Cooking time: about 4 hours
Degree of difficulty: moderate
Amount: makes about 10 cups
Calories per tablespoon: 50

The Marshlands Inn at Sackville, N.B., has shelves that are always filled, and this homemade marmalade is served at every breakfast.

| *1 large grapefruit* |
| *1 large orange* |
| *1 large lemon* |
| *10 cups cold water* |
| *10 cups sugar* |

Quarter fruit and then slice paper-thin. Put into a large preserving kettle with 10 cups of cold water, and let stand overnight. In the morning, boil until the fruit is tender and the liquid has thickened (at least 4 hours). Then add 10 cups of sugar. Stir well until sugar is dissolved. Continue to boil until mixture is 222°F on a candy thermometer. Pour immediately into sterilized jars and seal. (The last 2 degrees of temperature are crucial in getting this to set, so don't stop at 220°F.)

Celery Cranberry Relish

Preparation time: 10 minutes
Degree of difficulty: simple
Amount: makes about 4 cups
Calories per tablespoon: 23

This isn't a preserve — three weeks is about maximum keeping time but it's very good while it lasts.

| *1 pound cranberries* |
| *2 cups chopped celery* |
| *1 unpared, cored apple* |
| *1½ cups sugar* |
| *2 tablespoons lemon juice* |

Coarsely chop the cranberries, celery, and apple. Stir in sugar and lemon juice. Cover and refrigerate.

Red Pepper Jelly

Preparation time: 30 minutes
Draining time: 3 hours
Cooking time: 15 minutes
Degree of difficulty: simple
Amount: makes about 4 cups
Calories per tablespoon: 60

This is sensational with good cream cheese, spread on light rye or crusty French bread.

| *3 red peppers, coarsely chopped* |
| *1 medium onion, coarsely chopped* |
| *4 2½-inch fresh hot red chili peppers or 1 teaspoon red pepper flakes* |
| *1 tablespoon salt* |
| *4½ cups sugar* |
| *1¼ cups white vinegar* |
| *½ cup fresh lemon juice* |
| *6 whole cloves* |
| *1 6-ounce bottle liquid pectin* |

In a food processor fitted with a steel blade, grind the red peppers, then transfer mixture to a colander. Ingredients may also be chopped by hand — use rubber gloves when chopping chili peppers. Toss vegetables with 1½ teaspoons of the salt, let drain for 3 hours, then gently press dry. In a heavy stainless steel or enamelled saucepan, combine vegetables with sugar, vinegar, lemon juice, cloves, and remaining 1½ teaspoons salt. Bring liquid to a boil, stirring, and boil for 10 minutes. Add pectin and boil, stirring, for 1 minute. Pour jelly into sterilized jelly glasses immediately and seal with paraffin. Store in a cool, dark place.

Peach Chutney

Preparation time: 20 minutes
Standing time: overnight
Cooking time: 1-1½ hours
Degree of difficulty: moderate
Amount: makes about 10 cups
Calories per tablespoon: 34

Chutney is traditionally served with hot curry dishes, but it's also great with cold meat and in sandwiches. A dollop on plain yogurt makes a zesty snack.

| *4 pounds peaches, peeled* |
| *1 cup seedless raisins* |
| *2 cloves garlic, minced* |
| *½ cup chopped onion* |
| *⅔ cup chopped preserved ginger* |
| *1-2 tablespoons chili powder* |
| *1 tablespoon mustard seed* |
| *1 teaspoon curry powder* |
| *1½ teaspoons salt* |
| *4 tablespoons mixed pickling spices* |
| *4 cups cider vinegar* |
| *2 pounds brown sugar* |

Slice peaches and combine with remaining ingredients (tie mixed pickling spices in a cheesecloth bag). Stir together in a large mixing bowl and let stand overnight. Turn into a heavy pot and simmer uncovered until chutney is of desired consistency. Stir frequently to prevent scorching. Remove spice bag and ladle chutney into sterilized jars. Seal immediately.

If a recipe calls for both juice and grated citrus peel, grate the peel first. It's easier to do this if the fruit is placed in the freezer for 10-15 minutes, and pushed diagonally across the grater instead of straight up and down. Peel can be frozen for future use — once it's grated and frozen, put it in a jar with a tight lid and store in the freezer.

Mexican Barbecue Sauce

Preparation time: a few minutes
Cooking time: less than 10 minutes
Degree of difficulty: simple
Amount: about 1½ cups
Calories per tablespoon: 24

With so many Canadians occasionally braving the cold to barbecue outdoors in winter or using indoor stovetop barbecue grills, this sauce (developed by the test kitchens at Best Foods) is appropriate. Refrigerated, it keeps well for up to 1 week, and may also be used to oven-baste pork chops or chicken.

⅓ cup corn syrup
⅓ cup strong coffee
¼ cup ketchup
¼ cup cider vinegar
¼ cup Worcestershire sauce
2 teaspoons chili powder
1 tablespoon corn oil
2 teaspoons dry mustard
½ teaspoon salt
Dash of hot pepper sauce

In a large saucepan, mix all the ingredients. Stirring frequently, bring to a boil over medium-high heat and boil 5 minutes. Cool and pour into sterilized jars.

PHOTOS BY TIM SAUNDERS

Barney's Rock 'n' Rye

Preparation time: 5 minutes
Marinating time: 3 days
Degree of difficulty: simple
Amount: 4 cups
Calories per ounce: 80

1 large orange, cut in 8
½ lemon, cut in 8
5 to 8 ounces rock candy or crystallized sugar
24 ounces rye whiskey

Place the fruit and rock candy or sugar in a wide-mouthed 1-quart screwtop jar. Or, for gift giving, use one or more hinged glass-lidded canning jars. Pour in the whiskey, cover and let stand at least 3 days before drinking.

Marinated Goat Cheese

Preparation time: 5 minutes
Marinating time: a few days
Degree of difficulty: simple
Servings: 6-8
Calories per serving: 214 (1/6)
160 (1/8)

Friends who embrace new food ideas should welcome this as a food gift. It's lovely when eaten with crusty French bread or over salad greens.

8 ounces goat cheese

1 clove garlic, peeled

1 shallot, peeled

10 whole black peppercorns

¼ teaspoon hot red pepper flakes

1 teaspoon dried rosemary

1 teaspoon dried thyme

1 bay leaf

⅓ cup pitted black olives

1½ cups olive oil

Fit work bowl of food processor with metal blade. With machine running, drop garlic and shallot through feed tube and chop coarsely. Add peppercorns, pepper flakes, rosemary, thyme, bay leaf, and olives. Process with 3 or 4 on/off pulses, or until olives are barely chopped. Add oil and process just to blend. (To make by hand: Mince garlic and shallots; mix with peppercorns, pepper flakes, rosemary, thyme, and bay leaf. Chop olives finely; mix with olive oil. Combine olive oil mixture with herb and spice mixture.) Cut cheese into 4 pieces and place in a jar or bowl. Add marinade. Coat cheese well. Marinate a few days in the refrigerator (oil will become cloudy but will clear at room temperature), or overnight at room temperature. Note: After a few days in the marinade, the peppercorns soften and become edible.

PHOTO BY TIM SAUNDERS

Sardine Butter

Preparation time: 1 minute
Degree of difficulty: simple
Calories per tablespoon: 90

One of life's simple pleasures is this wonderful flavored butter spread on toast.

Canned sardines

Unsalted butter

Lemon juice to taste

Cayenne pepper to taste

Clarified butter

Drain sardines well and mix with soft unsalted butter in the proportion of 1 ounce sardines to ½ ounce butter (or about 2 to 1). Add lemon juice and cayenne pepper to taste and mash thoroughly. Pack into containers and cover with clarified butter. (Melt unsalted butter and allow to settle. Pour off the clear liquid, which is the clarified butter.) Cover and refrigerate before giving. Keeps well for 2 weeks refrigerated.

Cardamom Orange Olives

Preparation time: 5 minutes
Marinating time: 2 weeks
Degree of difficulty: simple
Calories per olive: 20

Flavored olives are lovely gifts when packed into glass jars whose lids have been covered with gingham. The following recipe can be doubled or tripled as desired.

1 14-ounce can black olives, drained and rinsed

Peel of 1 orange, cut in long strips

1 tablespoon cardamom seeds, bruised but not pulverized

Olive oil to cover

Place all ingredients in a glass jar; cover tightly and shake gently to disperse the seeds. Store in a cool place. The flavor will develop nicely in about 2 weeks.

Sardine Butter, Cardamom Orange Olives, and Marinated Goat Cheese

Pickling salt should be used only when it's called for in preserving recipes, since it is pure and contains no preservatives, iodine, or additives. Plain table salt has iodine, which darkens pickles and interferes with the fermentation process, resulting in soft pickles. As well, table salt and kosher salt contain anti-caking agents that make the brine unpleasantly cloudy.

Ginger Marmalade

Preparation time: 20 minutes
Cooking time: 2⅔ hours (total)
Degree of difficulty: simple
Amount: makes 7-8 cups
Calories per tablespoon: 80

You either like ginger or don't. For those of you who do, this is pleasing.

2 large grapefruit
5 oranges
4 lemons
6 cups water
5 pounds sugar
3 tablespoons finely chopped candied ginger

Squeeze the juice from the grapefruit, oranges, and lemons and blend with 3 cups of water. Finely chop pulp and peel. Mix juice, water, and pulp and boil for 20 minutes. Mix sugar with 3 cups water and cook for 20 minutes. Blend the two mixtures together and add the candied ginger. Mix well and simmer for 2 hours. While hot, pour into sterilized jars and seal.

Tomato Apple Chutney

Preparation time: 20 minutes
Standing time: 10 minutes
Cooking time: 1-1½ hours
Degree of difficulty: simple
Amount: makes about 7 pints
Calories per tablespoon: 22

This excellent chutney makes good use of abundant seasonal produce. Serve it with roast meats

4 pounds ripe tomatoes
3 teaspoons salt
5 pounds tart cooking apples
2 cups white vinegar
6 cups sugar
18 whole cloves, tied in a cheesecloth bag

Scald tomatoes in boiling water, a few at a time; plunge into cold water and slip off skins. Chop into small pieces. Sprinkle lightly with salt, let stand 10 minutes, then drain in a colander to remove excess water and seeds. Peel, core, and finely chop apples. Place vinegar, sugar, and cloves in a preserving kettle and bring to a boil, stirring to dissolve the sugar. Add tomatoes and apples and cook over medium-low heat until apples are soft and chutney is as thick as desired. Stir frequently to prevent scorching. Remove cloves. Bottle in sterilized jars while boiling hot and seal.

Onion Jam

Preparation time: 10 minutes
Cooking time: 1¾ hours
Degree of difficulty: simple
Servings: 6
Calories per serving: 110

Sliced onions are simmered slowly with red wine to produce this delicious condiment. The recipe is from Au Tournant de la Rivière, in Quebec, where it's served with pâté.

6 medium onions, thinly sliced
2 tablespoons butter
½ cup dry red wine
2 tablespoons grenadine syrup
2 tablespoons red wine vinegar
1 tablespoon sugar

Sauté the onions in the butter slowly until they begin to brown. Press the onions to remove excess butter and drain the pan of all surplus butter. Add remaining ingredients. Cook slowly, uncovered, over low heat for 1½ hours, stirring occasionally to prevent the onions from sticking to the bottom of the pan. Serve slightly warm or at room temperature.

Freezer Apricot Jam

Preparation time: 20 minutes
Standing time: 20 minutes
Cooking time: 2-3 minutes
Degree of difficulty: simple
Amount: 9 cups
Calories: 31 per tablespoon

3 cups pitted and chopped apricots
5 cups sugar
1 tablespoon ascorbic acid
1 teaspoon lemon juice
1 package powdered pectin
¾ cup water

Combine sugar and ascorbic acid; add to fruit with lemon juice. Let stand 20 minutes. Combine pectin and water in a small saucepan and bring to a boil, stirring constantly. Boil hard 1 minute. Add to fruit and stir for 2 minutes. Ladle into sterilized jars, cover and let stand at room temperature for 24 hours. Freeze. After thawing to use, store in refrigerator.

Jalapeño Jelly

Preparation time: 10 minutes
Draining time: 15 minutes
Cooking time: 30 minutes
Degree of difficulty: simple
Amount: makes 4 6-ounce jars
Calories: 66 per tablespoon
*   or 22 per teaspoon*

If you like hot and spicy food tastes, this will be a welcome addition to your kitchen pantry.

14-ounce can jalapeño peppers, in natural brine, roasted and peeled
1 green pepper, seeded and chopped
1 cup white or cider vinegar
4 cups sugar
1 bottle pectin
Green food coloring (optional)

Drain, seed, and chop the jalapeño peppers. (Handle them with care: do not touch eyes when working with them and wash hands after handling.) Purée jalapeños and green pepper in a blender or food processor. Combine purée and vinegar in a saucepan and bring to a boil. Reduce heat and simmer for 10 minutes. Pour purée into a fine-mesh strainer over a large saucepan and let drain for 15 minutes. Press gently with the back of a wooden spoon to extract all the liquid. Discard pulp. Add sugar to liquid in saucepan and bring to a boil. Add pectin and boil for 1 minute. Remove from heat and add green food coloring, if desired. Skim off foam and pour into sterilized bottles. Seal immediately.

Sweet and Sour Prunes

Preparation time: 5 minutes
Cooking time: 30 minutes (total)
Standing time: 24 hours
Marinating time: 6 weeks
Degree of difficulty: simple
Amount: 2 cups
Calories per prune: 84

1 package large prunes
2 cups tea, preferably linden
1⅓ cups sugar
2 cups white wine tarragon vinegar
1 cinnamon stick
2 whole cloves
1 tablespoon vodka

Simmer the prunes in the tea for 10 minutes; let stand 2 to 3 hours. Heat the sugar and vinegar in an enamelled saucepan, stirring until the sugar dissolves. Add the cinnamon stick and cloves and simmer for 10 minutes. Remove from the heat and let stand until cool. Drain the prunes, reserving their liquid, and roll them in paper towels to dry. Place the prunes in a bowl and strain the cool vinegar mixture over them. Let stand 24 hours. Strain the vinegar mixture back into a saucepan and slowly boil for 6 to 8 minutes. Cool completely. Place the prunes in a very clean glass preserving jar. Cover them with the cold vinegar mixture. Add the vodka, close jar tightly and store in a dry, dark place for 6 weeks. Keep refrigerated after opening.

NOTES

SALADS

Far from the pale iceberg lettuce salads of the '50s, with bottled dressing and a limp slice or two of tomato, today's gorgeous greens gracing our tables are a medley of curly endive, dandelion leaves, red radicchio, tender Boston lettuce, lightly bitter arugula, romaine, and such previously scorned "weeds" as lamb's quarters and mâche. Sometimes salads are topped with sprouts, watercress, or spinach leaves, and it isn't that unusual to find bok choy (a Chinese cabbage), young turnip greens, Belgian endive, or nasturtium leaves dwelling happily among the lettuces. This is not to ignore the colorful mélanges of mango, kiwi fruit, apples, and often nuts or raisins, or the mixtures of bulgur wheat, barley, or lentils that appear on winter buffet tables. Lucky us.

Salads make the health-conscious happy, because although greens are low in calories, they're quite high in vitamins C and A: just remember that the darker the color, the higher the vitamin content. There's also some iron and calcium in salad greens.

This always presupposes that all your greens are free of brown spots, tears, or yellow leaves, and not wrapped in plastic. Wash your greens well in cold running water, blot with paper towels, and wrap in additional paper towels until needed. A spin dryer, which removes water from greens with centrifugal force, is a handy addition to your kitchen utensils, but make sure it's plastic, which is easier on fragile leaves.

Do clean your wooden salad bowl with a quick sudsy wash, rinse, and drying between each use. If you prefer a gentle touch of garlic, rub a stale piece of bread with a cut clove of garlic and rub the bowl with it. Experiment with various combinations of oil and vinegar — there are many different kinds of oil to be pondered over, from olive oils with varying degrees of virginity, to walnut and hazelnut oils, and they can be happily mixed with vinegars that range from simple red or white wine and tarragon vinegar to sherry or balsamic and fruit vinegars.

PHOTO BY SKIP DEAN, FOOD STYLING BY KATE BUSH

The word "salad" comes from the Latin *herba salata*, salad greens. The Romans garnished raw and cooked vegetables with fresh and dried herbs, and tossed the vegetables with ingredients that included vinegar and oil. Mary Queen of Scots liked a salad made of diced boiled celery root and lettuce topped with mustard-flavored cream and garnished with cooked egg slices, truffles, and chervil, a recipe that would be right at home with today's new cuisine.

Autumn Harvest Salad

Preparation time: 15 minutes
Degree of difficulty: simple
Servings: 6
Calories per serving: 225

Vancouver's Sidney Shadbolt contributed this wonderful salad to *Homemaker's* Cuisine '85 contest — a twist on the traditional spinach and mushroom. It's delicious with roast beef, omelets, lamb, and chicken, he says.

1 clove garlic, crushed (or more, to taste)
4 cups spinach leaves, washed, dried, and torn into pieces (or 2 cups lettuce and 2 cups spinach)
12 firm fresh mushrooms, washed, dried, and thinly sliced
1 large sweet red pepper, washed, seeded, and sliced into rings
½ cup roasted shelled pumpkin seeds
⅓ cup crumbled feta cheese

APPLE CIDER HONEY DRESSING
2 teaspoons liquid honey
6 tablespoons apple cider vinegar
9 tablespoons sunflower oil
Salt and freshly ground pepper to taste

Rub a salad bowl with crushed garlic. Combine spinach, mushrooms, red pepper, pumpkin seeds, and feta cheese in the salad bowl. Combine dressing ingredients in a blender or food processor and process until well blended. Pour dressing over and toss.

Fresh Spinach, Orange, and Mango Salad

Preparation time: 15 minutes
Standing time: 10 minutes
Degree of difficulty: simple
Servings: 4-6
Calories per serving: 345 (1/4)
230 (1/6)

The tart dressing is a perfect foil for the sweet, juicy fruit in this unusual recipe. Soft, ripe honeydew or cantaloupe may be substituted for the mango.

1 pound fresh spinach
2 navel oranges
2 mangoes

DRESSING
3 teaspoons grated onion
½ teaspoon salt
Freshly ground pepper
1 tablespoon Dijon mustard
2 tablespoons white wine vinegar
1 teaspoon lemon juice
⅔ cup olive oil

Wash and thoroughly dry the spinach. Strip the leaves from the stems. Peel and section the oranges. Peel the mangoes and remove pit. Cut mango into ½-x-1½-inch strips. To prepare the dressing, combine the onion, salt, pepper, mustard, vinegar, and lemon juice in a small bowl. Mix well, then beat the olive oil in very slowly. Continue beating until dressing thickens. Arrange the spinach, orange, and mango in a chilled salad bowl, pour dressing over, and toss thoroughly. Let stand for 10 minutes, then serve on chilled plates.

Cabbage Salad

Preparation time: 15 minutes
Cooking time: 10 minutes
Standing time: 30 minutes
Degree of difficulty: simple
Amount: makes 5 cups
Calories per serving: 75

The Marshlands Inn, Sackville, N.B., serves this often, with their own homemade dressing.

2 cups shredded cabbage
¼ cup chopped green onion
¼ cup chopped green pepper
¼ cup grated raw carrot
¼ cup diced radish

Mix together with enough Marshlands Dressing to bond the ingredients.

MARSHLANDS DRESSING
1 cup hot water
¾ cup white vinegar
¼ cup butter
¾ cup sugar
¾ cup all-purpose flour
1 tablespoon dry mustard
¼ teaspoon celery salt
¼ teaspoon cayenne pepper
2 teaspoons salt
2 eggs
2 cups milk
½ cup evaporated milk

In the top of a double boiler (over hot water), mix together the hot water, vinegar, and butter until the butter melts.

Mix together the sugar, flour, dry mustard, celery salt, cayenne pepper, and salt.

Beat the eggs, add milk and evaporated milk. Sift the dry ingredients into the milk and egg mixture, beating with a whisk. Pour all slowly into the hot mixture, whisking all the time to prevent lumps. Cook over hot water until thick. Turn off the heat, and let sit over the hot water for another ½ hour. Cool and refrigerate. This will be a thick dressing, and can be thinned down with milk or cream for various purposes.

Red Lettuce Salad with Pecans

Preparation time: 10 minutes
Cooking time: 30-40 minutes
Degree of difficulty: simple
Servings: 8-10
Calories per serving: 245 (1/8)
196 (1/10)

This delicious salad is tossed with a warm bacon and vinegar dressing. The ingredients can be prepared ahead of time, but it should be assembled just before serving.

2 small heads or 1 large ruby leaf lettuce

1 small head curly endive or 6 Belgian endives or 2 bunches watercress or a combination

1 cup pecan halves

8 ounces thickly sliced bacon, cut into 1-inch pieces

1 tablespoon dark brown sugar

⅓ cup cider vinegar

Salt and freshly ground pepper to taste

Preheat oven to 325°F. Wash greens and tear into bite-size pieces (leave Belgian endive leaves whole if small and use some for garnish). Place pecan halves in a shallow roasting pan and toast in oven for 20-30 minutes. Cook bacon pieces in a large frying pan until crisp; drain on paper towels. Pour off all but ⅓ cup bacon fat from the pan and add brown sugar. Stir with a wire whisk to dissolve. Add vinegar and stir till bubbling. Put the greens in a large salad bowl, add toasted pecans and toss; add bacon pieces and toss again. Add hot dressing at the last minute; salt and pepper to taste, toss quickly and serve at once.

Fresh Vegetable Salad with Italian Sausage

Preparation time: 20 minutes
Degree of difficulty: simple
Servings: 6-8
Calories per serving: 325 (1/6)
245 (1/8)

Served with cheese and crusty Italian bread, this salad makes a picnic.

½ pound fresh mushrooms

½ pound fresh green beans, trimmed

1 pint cherry tomatoes

1 head cauliflower

1 English cucumber

1 head romaine lettuce

1 bunch green onions

½ cup mixed green and black olives

1 cup sliced cooked Italian sausage

1 cup olive oil

½ cup white wine vinegar

Salt and freshly ground pepper to taste

4 hard-cooked eggs, halved

Wash and prepare the vegetables. If the mushrooms are large, slice them in half; parboil the green beans for 1 minute; remove stems from the cherry tomatoes; separate the cauliflower into flowerets; cube the cucumber; break the lettuce into bite-size pieces; chop the green onions.

Combine vegetables, olives, and sausage in a large salad bowl. Toss together with the oil and vinegar. Add salt and pepper to taste and decorate with hard-cooked eggs. Chill.

Spinach Salad with Strawberries

Preparation time: less than 15 minutes
Degree of difficulty: simple
Servings: 6
Calories per serving: 234

Cuisine '85 Semifinalist
This lovely, refreshing summer salad, submitted by Paula Dillon of Markham, Ontario, is a winner any time — but especially during summer when produce is fresh and when it can accompany barbecued lamb or beef.

1 pound fresh spinach, washed, dried, and torn into pieces

1 pint fresh strawberries, washed and hulled

½ cup slivered toasted almonds

SESAME-POPPYSEED DRESSING

¼-½ cup sugar

2 tablespoons sesame seeds

1 tablespoon poppyseeds

1½ teaspoons chopped onion

¼ teaspoon Worcestershire sauce

¼ teaspoon paprika

½ cup vegetable oil

¼ cup cider vinegar

Place spinach in a serving bowl. Halve berries and arrange over the spinach. To prepare the dressing, combine ingredients in a food processor or blender and process until smooth. Just before serving, pour the dressing over the salad and toss. Garnish with slivered almonds.

Vary your vinegars, perhaps using a sprinkle of wine vinegar, sugar, and freshly ground pepper on fresh strawberries (odd, but delightful); deglaze your frying pan with herb vinegars to complement the dish you're cooking; and by all means make your own.

Jim's Cold Beef Summer Salad with Honey Garlic Dressing and Red Pepper Soup (see recipe page 178)

Jim's Cold Beef Summer Salad with Honey Garlic Dressing

Preparation time: less than 30 minutes
Cooking time: less than 30 minutes
Chilling time: at least 2 hours
Degree of difficulty: simple
Servings: 6
Calories per serving: 685

Cuisine '85 Semifinalist

2 pounds leftover roast beef

2 cups beef stock

½ teaspoon salt

6 red potatoes, washed and cut into wedges

½ pound fresh green beans, trimmed and julienned

2 green onions, finely chopped

1 teaspoon finely chopped fresh basil

1 teaspoon finely chopped fresh tarragon

1 tablespoon finely chopped fresh parsley

Salt and freshly ground pepper to taste

Romaine lettuce

Trim all fat from the roast beef and cut beef into small cubes. Add salt to beef stock and boil the potatoes in the stock for 10-15 minutes or until tender; drain, reserving leftover broth for another use, and set aside. Steam the beans until tender-crisp and set aside. When the potatoes and beans have cooled, combine with the beef, green onions, fresh herbs, and salt and pepper.

PHOTO BY PETER CHOU

HONEY GARLIC DRESSING

1 egg yolk

¼ cup olive oil

¼ cup vegetable oil

2 tablespoons liquid honey

2 large cloves garlic, finely minced

1 teaspoon Dijon mustard

½ teaspoon salt

Freshly ground pepper

1 teaspoon finely chopped fresh basil

3 tablespoons raspberry vinegar

To prepare dressing, combine ingredients in order listed in a blender or food processor. Pour over salad, toss, and chill in the refrigerator for at least 2 hours. Serve on a bed of romaine lettuce leaves.

Spinach Salad

Preparation time: 15 minutes
Degree of difficulty: simple
Servings: 6-8
Calories per serving: 190 (1/6)
140 (1/8)

The spinach must be young and fresh — either bought regionally in the spring or from a specialty store during other months.

2 pounds fresh spinach

1 cup sour cream

Juice of ½ lemon

1 teaspoon hot mustard

½ pound crisply fried, crumbled bacon

¼ cup chopped parsley

Salt and freshly ground pepper to taste

Wash spinach thoroughly. Drain, dry and chop medium-fine. Toss spinach with a mixture of sour cream, lemon juice, and mustard. Sprinkle with crumbled bacon and parsley. Season to taste.

Quilter's Potato Salad

PHOTO BY SKIP DEAN

Preparation time: 15 minutes
Cooking time: 10-12 minutes
Chilling time: several hours
Degree of difficulty: simple
Servings: 8
Calories per serving: 410

So called because it was often eaten during a quilting bee on a bee-booming, hot summer day.

OLD-FASHIONED BOILED DRESSING

¼ cup sugar

2 teaspoons salt

1½ teaspoons dry mustard

4 large eggs, lightly beaten

⅓ cup melted butter

1 cup cider vinegar

¾ teaspoon Tabasco sauce

1 cup whipping cream, whipped

SALAD

3 pounds new red potatoes, boiled, peeled, and cut in ½-inch cubes

4 hard-cooked eggs, peeled and coarsely chopped

6 green onions, trimmed and coarsely chopped (include some tops)

⅓ cup coarsely chopped sweet red pepper

To prepare the dressing, combine sugar, salt, and mustard in the top of a double boiler, pressing out all lumps. Mix in eggs, butter, vinegar, and Tabasco. Set over simmering water and cook, stirring constantly, 10-12 minutes, until mixture has the consistency of mayonnaise. Quick-chill dressing by setting in an ice bath. When cool, fold in whipped cream; taste and correct seasonings and set aside.

Place potatoes, eggs, onions, and red pepper in a large bowl. Pour as much dressing as desired over salad, toss well, cover, and chill several hours before serving.

**Quilter's
Potato Salad**

Winter salads can happily take the place of summer salads when supplies of fresh local tomatoes and greens are expensive and limited. Avocado salads are delicious spiced with anise seeds, ground ginger, or allspice; pasta and rice salads can be found in many cookbooks; and it's simple to steam broccoli, cauliflower, carrots, and potatoes and dress them in a spicy vinaigrette while still warm.

Lentil Salad

Preparation time: 10 minutes
Cooking time: 40 minutes
Chilling time: a few hours
Degree of difficulty: simple
Servings: 6
Calories per serving: 215

This easy summer salad of marinated lentils is not only very French but also very refreshing. The recipe, compliments of Michel Guérard, one of the granddaddies of nouvelle cuisine, is from his book, *Cuisine for Home Cooks.*

1 cup dry brown lentils

Salt and freshly ground pepper to taste

1 bouquet garni

½ onion, chopped

1 carrot, chopped

½ clove garlic, chopped

4 tablespoons peanut oil

4 tablespoons wine vinegar

1 small shallot, finely chopped

1 tablespoon chopped capers

Wash the lentils thoroughly and place them in a saucepan with water to cover. Bring to a boil, skim off foam, then add salt and pepper as desired, the bouquet garni, onion, carrot, and garlic. Lower heat, cover, and simmer until lentils are tender but not mushy, about 30 minutes. Drain, remove bouquet garni, and chill. To make the dressing, whisk together the oil, vinegar, and shallot in a large bowl. Salt and pepper to taste. Toss with lentil-and-caper mixture.

Tortellini and Fontina Salad

Preparation time: 10 minutes
Cooking time: 5-6 minutes
Degree of difficulty: simple
Servings: 4-6
Calories per serving: 555 (1/4)
370 (1/6)

Cold pasta, Fontina cheese, and tomatoes make an innovative salad that's as good on a buffet table as it is stolen out of the refrigerator at midnight. From Toronto's Bersani & Carlevale.

1 pound fresh or frozen green tortellini

4 ripe tomatoes, chopped and seeded

½ cup Fontina cheese, diced or grated

½ package frozen spinach, thawed, drained and chopped

½ teaspoon salt

Freshly ground pepper to taste

DRESSING

1 cup vegetable oil

½ cup white vinegar

2 tablespoons Dijon mustard

2 tablespoons chopped parsley

½ tablespoon chopped garlic

Cook the pasta in several quarts of rapidly boiling water until tender. Fresh pasta will take 2-5 minutes to cook; frozen, a minute or two longer. *Do not overcook.* Drain, and rinse in cold water.

To prepare the salad dressing, combine ingredients in a blender and mix at high speed for 1 minute or until the dressing is the consistency of thin mayonnaise.

Combine the pasta, tomatoes, cheese, and spinach in a large bowl. Toss with the dressing. Add salt and freshly ground pepper to taste. Chill.

Hot and Cold Salad

Preparation time: 15 minutes
Cooking time: 20 minutes (total)
Degree of difficulty: simple
Servings: 4
Calories per serving: 360

This is a wonderful dish that encourages children to eat vegetables. Serve and watch it disappear.

COOKED VEGETABLES

½ cup chopped marrow

½ cup chopped zucchini

½ cup green beans

½ cup peas, fresh or frozen

½ cup coined carrots

(These vegetables may be changed to suit your child's taste.)

SALAD

½ cup chopped or finely sliced spinach

1 tomato

½ cup sunflower seeds or toasted soya nuts

½ cup chopped dates

½ cup chopped nuts (filberts, almonds, walnuts)

½ cup grated apple

½ cup chopped celery

Juice of lime or lemon, and grated peel

CHEESE SAUCE

1 tablespoon butter

1 tablespoon whole wheat flour

¾ cup grated mild cheese

1 cup milk or tomato juice

Melt butter in a heavy saucepan and slowly stir in the flour. Blend until smooth and cook gently to eliminate raw taste of flour. Gradually add the liquid, blend and stir in the cheese. Keep hot over low heat or a double boiler. Just before serving, toss salad ingredients and vegetables in a large salad bowl and pour on the sauce.

Squid and Mussel Salad

Preparation time: about 1 hour
Cooking time: about 1 hour
Degree of difficulty: simple
Servings: 4 for lunch or 8
as an appetizer
Calories per serving: 460 (1/4)
230 (1/8)

Helen Kates, a wonderful cook, is co-owner of Arowhon Pines in Algonquin Park, in Ontario. Her recipe is quite sublime and easy, although a bit time-consuming. Try it on weekends, or for buffets.

1 1-pound squid, including tentacles, cleaned
Coarse (kosher) salt
6 shallots, finely chopped
1 clove garlic, finely chopped
1 cup dry white wine
5 sprigs Italian parsley, chopped
1/2 bay leaf
Salt and freshly ground pepper to taste
3 pounds mussels, well scrubbed and bearded
3 large tomatoes, skinned and coarsely chopped, plus tomato juice to make 3 cups
6 tablespoons olive oil
2 tablespoons Marukan Japanese spice vinegar (available at Chinese or Japanese food stores)
2-3 sprigs each fresh Italian parsley, dill, and fennel, leaves coarsely chopped
1 tablespoon fresh lemon juice
1/2 English cucumber, unpeeled, cut lengthwise, and sliced
1 small white onion, halved and finely sliced
1/2 yellow or red pepper, julienned
1/2 lemon, peeled, halved lengthwise, and thinly sliced
Dill sprigs for garnish

Rinse squid well with cold water and cut into 1/2-inch rings, leaving tentacles whole for interest. Soak in cold salted water for 30 minutes. Put the shallots, garlic, wine, parsley, bay leaf, salt, and pepper in a large, heavy saucepan and simmer, covered, for about 5 minutes. Add mussels, cover and cook over high heat, shaking pan occasionally. Remove from heat as soon as shells open. Remove mussels and cool. Strain the liquid back into the saucepan and add tomatoes and juice. Simmer gently for 10 minutes. Drain squid and rinse well; add to saucepan and simmer gently, covered, for 45 minutes, or until squid is easily pierced with a fork. Cool.

Shell 2/3 of the mussels, discard any that don't open. Add shelled and unshelled mussels to the squid. Taste and correct seasonings and refrigerate. Whisk together the oil, vinegar, herbs, and lemon juice in a bowl and refrigerate (recipe may be prepared in advance to this point). Just before serving, add the remaining ingredients except dill to the seafood. Pour dressing over salad and toss well. Garnish with dill sprigs and serve on chilled plates with garlic bread.

Sunomono

Preparation time: 6 minutes
Degree of difficulty: simple
Servings: 4
Calories per serving: 130

A light, Japanese style vinegared salad, used as an accompaniment.

1 cucumber
1/2 cup white vinegar
1/2 cup sugar
1/2 cup small cooked clams, shrimp or crabmeat
Slice of lemon for garnish

Peel the cucumber only if it has been waxed. Slice in half lengthwise and scoop out seeds. Slice the cucumber halves into thin slices. Combine the sugar and vinegar. Add the cucumber slices and the clams, shrimp or crabmeat. Chill. Serve in small bowls, garnished with lemon wedges.

Terrific Tomato Aspic

Preparation and cooking time: 15 minutes
Chilling time: 4 hours
Degree of difficulty: simple
Servings: 6-8
Calories per serving: 45 (1/6)
35 (1/8)

This aspic gives color to a tossed salad, or it can be molded as an accompaniment to lunch.

1 28-ounce can tomatoes
1/2 cup water (preferably vegetable water from carrots or a green vegetable)
1 medium onion, chopped very fine
2 packages unflavored gelatine
2 teaspoons lemon juice or vinegar
Chopped parsley for garnish

Lift the whole tomatoes out of their liquid and set aside. Bring the tomato liquid and other liquid and the onion to the boil, so the onions aren't quite raw. Sprinkle gelatine over cold water and allow to soften; then heat over low heat until dissolved, 3-5 minutes. Pour the tomato-and-onion mixture, the lemon juice, or vinegar, and the gelatine quickly over the whole tomatoes (or tomato pieces if your can doesn't contain whole ones), and stir thoroughly. Sprinkle a little chopped parsley, chopped celery or finely shredded green pepper over. It will take about 4 hours to set in the refrigerator. In summer you can add 1/4 cup fresh chopped mint for a refreshingly cool flavor. Or try adding some chopped radishes and cucumber.

Balsamic vinegar is made from the unfermented must of white Trebbiano grapes that has been boiled to concentrated sweetness. By law it is aged for at least 10 years, but sometimes for 30-50 years, in a series of ever-smaller wooden barrels containing some older vinegar. Both the older vinegar and the barrels add flavor; the resulting vinegar is about 6 percent acidity and highly aromatic with an intense flavor. Just a few drops will season a salad or fish, and is delightful on ripe strawberries.

Tomatoes and Mozzarella in Basil Vinaigrette

Preparation time: 15 minutes
Degree of difficulty: simple
Servings: 6
Calories per serving: 215

A simple, traditional salad that perks up the taste buds.

3 large tomatoes, washed and cut into ¹/₂-inch slices

¹/₂ pound fresh Mozzarella cheese, thinly sliced

¹/₄ cup olive oil

2 tablespoons wine vinegar

1 teaspoon Dijon mustard

¹/₄ cup chopped, fresh basil

Freshly ground pepper to taste

Alternate slices of tomatoes and cheese on a serving dish. In a clean jar with a lid, mix together olive oil, vinegar, mustard, and basil; shake until well blended. Pour dressing over tomatoes and cheese; sprinkle liberally with pepper.

Pasta Salad Niçoise

Preparation time: 20 minutes
Cooking time: 5-10 minutes
Chilling time: several hours
Degree of difficulty: simple
Servings: 6
Calories per serving: 380

¹/₃ cup oil

3 tablespoons lemon juice

3 tablespoons tarragon or white wine vinegar

¹/₂ teaspoon salt

¹/₂ teaspoon Dijon mustard

¹/₂ teaspoon paprika

¹/₂ teaspoon basil

8 ounces linguine

¹/₄ pound green beans, cooked, drained, and chilled

1 cup halved cherry tomatoes

¹/₄ cup sliced and pitted black olives

1 7-ounce can tuna, chilled and drained

3 hard-cooked eggs, quartered

To prepare dressing, combine oil, lemon juice, vinegar, salt, mustard,

Tomatoes and Mozzarella in Basil Vinaigrette and Baked Trout with Lemon (see recipe page 82)

PHOTOS BY PAT LACROIX/THE BRANT GROUP

**Pasta Salad
Niçoise (left);
Marinated Four-
Pepper Salad**

paprika, and basil in a screw-top jar. Cover and shake well to mix; set aside. Cook linguine *al dente*, drain and rinse under cold water. Pour dressing over linguine and toss gently to coat. Cover and chill for several hours. Combine chilled linguine, green beans, cherry tomatoes, and olives in a salad bowl, tossing to mix. Break tuna into bite-size chunks and mound on top of salad. Garnish with eggs.

Marinated Four-Pepper Salad

Preparation and cooking time: about 40 minutes
Marinating time: 1 hour or more
Degree of difficulty: challenging
Servings: 10-12
Calories per serving: 200 (1/10)
165 (1/12)

Supermarkets offer a variety of imported or hothouse peppers, so you can make this wonderful dish any time of year.

4 large sweet red bell or shepherd peppers

2 large green peppers, preferably Cubanelle

2 large yellow peppers

6 large banana peppers, preferably hot

Assorted salad greens

DRESSING

½ cup olive oil

3 tablespoons red wine vinegar

1 teaspoon salt

¼ teaspoon freshly ground pepper

¼ teaspoon paprika

¼ teaspoon coriander

1 large clove garlic, minced

2 tablespoons finely chopped onion

Roast peppers by broiling them 4 inches from the heat or by setting them on a rack over an electric element; turn peppers until they blister and char. Set aside in a covered container for 10 minutes, then steam for 10 minutes in a closed saucepan; cool. Cut out stem ends; peel, slit, and discard membranes and seeds. Rinse off any sticky seeds and patches of charred skin. Pat dry and slice into strips. Prepare dressing by combining all ingredients in a jar; shake well and pour over peppers; marinate 1 or 2 hours at room temperature, stirring occasionally. Line a bowl with salad greens and place marinated peppers in centre.

The olive was brought to Marseilles by the Phoenicians; the Greeks introduced the fruit to the Romans, who developed new varieties. Cato wrote about 7 varieties in the 2nd century B.C.: a writer in the 5th century described 16 — and still, demand outstripped supply. By the 9th century, olive oil was so scarce that a religious council authorized priests to make anointing oil from bacon. Today, oil tastings in Canada are as prestigious (at least, among aficionados) as wine tastings.

German Hot Potato Salad with Bacon

Preparation time: 5 minutes
Cooking time: 15-20 minutes
Degree of difficulty: simple
Servings: 8-10
Calories per serving: 165 (1/8)
135 (1/10)

Derived from a traditional Mennonite recipe, this salad is not served often enough in Canada.

8 boiling potatoes

Salt

¼ pound bacon, diced

2 small onions, chopped

¼ cup vinegar

¼ cup water or beef stock

2 tablespoons sour cream

Minced parsley

Boil potatoes in their jackets in lightly salted water to cover. Do not overcook or potatoes will crumble in the salad. Peel and slice while hot and place in serving dish. Fry bacon and just before it's crisp, add onion. Sauté slowly until onion is transparent. Remove from heat and pour in combined vinegar and water mixture. Do this carefully so the liquid doesn't cause the hot fat to sputter. Bring to a boil and pour over sliced potatoes. (Lift the potatoes with a wooden spoon so the dressing runs evenly over them.) Fold in sour cream carefully. Sprinkle with parsley.

Supreme of Chicken and Avocado Salad

Preparation time: 15 minutes
Cooking time: 45 minutes
Marinating time: overnight
Degree of difficulty: simple
Servings: 4-6
Calories per serving: 275 (1/4)
210 (1/6)

4 boneless chicken breasts

2 cups oil-and-vinegar dressing

2 ripe avocados

Lettuce

1 lemon, cut in wedges

Preheat oven to 325°F. Bake chicken breasts until cooked but not dry, about 45 minutes. Or microwave breasts for 7-8 minutes per pound covered with wax paper or plastic wrap. Skin breasts and cut into strips about 2 inches long and ¼-inch thick. Marinate overnight in oil-and-vinegar dressing. Just before serving, peel and slice avocados. Place slices of avocado and chicken alternately on bed of lettuce. Ladle a little dressing over and serve with lemon wedges.

Endive and Orange Salad

Preparation time: 10 minutes
Degree of difficulty: simple
Servings: 6
Calories per serving: 105

Light, colorful, and pretty, this salad is perfect for a spring day.

6 Belgian endives, washed and dried

6 large oranges, peeled and thinly sliced

French dressing

Chopped watercress

With a sharp knife, cut out a small cone at the base of each endive and halve them. Arrange the endives like a fan on a serving dish, surround with orange slices, and drizzle with a few tablespoons of a good French dressing mixed with a generous amount of finely chopped watercress. Serve with additional dressing on the side.

Onion and Ripe Olive Salad

Preparation time: 10 minutes
Chilling time: at least 1 hour
Degree of difficulty: simple
Servings: 8
Calories per serving: 180

A spicy side dish to be served in small quantities.

1 bunch green onions, coarsely chopped

1 medium Spanish onion, peeled and sliced paper thin

½ cup wine vinegar

1 teaspoon salt

1 cup green olives with pimento, sliced

1½ cups black pitted olives, sliced

1 clove garlic, peeled and crushed or minced

1 cup olive oil

¼ teaspoon freshly ground pepper

Put onions in a bowl, pour vinegar over, sprinkle with salt, and place in the refrigerator for at least 1 hour. Add olives and garlic, then pour the olive oil over. Add pepper and mix well before serving.

Crabmeat and Watercress Salad with Kiwi Vinaigrette

Preparation time: 5 minutes
Degree of difficulty: simple
Servings: 1
Calories per serving: 230

For dieters, a salad is often appreciated more if it has extra oomph — as in this low-calorie treat .

3 ounces crabmeat, drained and picked over

1 bunch watercress, washed, stems trimmed, and dried

1 tablespoon vegetable oil

2 tablespoons white wine vinegar

1 teaspoon Dijon mustard

2 teaspoons puréed kiwi fruit

Salt and freshly ground pepper to taste

Place crabmeat on a bed of watercress. Combine remaining ingredients well and pour over crab and watercress.

Lobster and Spinach Salad

Preparation time: 20 minutes
Degree of difficulty: simple
Servings: 4
Calories per serving: 475

The secret of this delightful salad is in the dressing, a Caesar salad taste-alike invention of the restaurant Eight One Nine in Vancouver.

½ pound chopped lobster meat, fresh or canned

1 egg yolk

1½ tablespoons mayonnaise, preferably homemade

½ teaspoon Dijon mustard

1 cup vegetable oil

¼ cup dry white wine

1 anchovy fillet, diced

1 teaspoon puréed garlic

Dash of lemon juice

Dash of Worcestershire sauce

Pinch of oregano

Salt and freshly ground pepper to taste

2 bunches fresh spinach, washed, stems removed

Lemon wedges

Mix the egg yolk, mayonnaise, and mustard together in a bowl. Add oil in a slow stream while whisking steadily. As it thickens, dilute gradually with white wine. Add the anchovy and garlic and continue whisking, but don't overmix or dressing will form lumps. Whisk in lemon juice, Worcestershire sauce, oregano, salt, and pepper. Taste and correct seasonings if necessary. Overlap spinach leaves on plates and place lobster meat in the centre. Pour dressing over. Garnish with lemon wedges and pass remaining dressing separately.

Pierre Franey's Carrot and Orange Salad

Preparation time: 30 minutes
Chilling time: 30 minutes
Degree of difficulty: simple
Servings: 6
Calories per serving: 215

3 cups grated new carrots

4 seedless oranges, peeled, sectioned, membranes removed

1 medium red onion, cut in 2-inch lengths

½ cup currants, soaked in water for 10 minutes and drained

¼ teaspoon hot red pepper flakes

3 tablespoons olive oil

Juice of 1 lemon

¼ cup chopped walnuts

½ teaspoon salt

Freshly ground black pepper to taste

Put all ingredients in a bowl and toss. Chill for 30 minutes or more before serving.

Dinah Koo's Wild Rice Salad

Preparation time: 10 minutes
Cooking time: about 1 hour (total)
Degree of difficulty: simple
Servings: 6-8
Calories per serving: 300 (1/6)
320 (1/8)

This special recipe using Manitoba wild rice was developed by Toronto caterer Dinah Koo. (Long-grain rice may be substituted for ½ the wild rice quantity.)

2 cups wild rice

3 cups cold water

Salt and freshly ground pepper to taste

½ cup butter

1 onion, chopped

1 cup slivered almonds

2 tablespoons chopped parsley

Wash the rice well and place in a pot with water. Cover and bring to a boil. Simmer for 20 minutes; uncover and continue to cook for another 20-30 minutes, or until all the water is absorbed and the kernels just open. Season well. In a frying pan, melt butter and sauté onion until soft; add almonds and sauté. Fold into rice. Garnish with parsley. Cool.

NOTES

SOUPS

There's hardly anything as satisfying as a pot full of homemade soup simmering slowly on the stove, redolent of onions, leeks, and the various bones and carcasses of meat or chicken making their last triumphant bow on the kitchen stage. Of course, that seductive smell could be a *bouillabaisse* or *cioppino*, with contributions of fish stock, herbs, orange peel, and lobster, fish, mussels, and clams. In the summer, there might be an aggressive, garlicky gazpacho made with red, ripe tomatoes and cold cucumber, or satin-smooth spoonfuls of vichysoisse (please pronounce the "s" at the end), a mixture of common ingredients — onions and potatoes — that results in elegance.

Many good cooks insist that vegetables should be cooked and slightly browned before adding them to the stock, and all agree that vegetables should be simmered with their skins on for better flavor (unless the soup is destined to be light in color). Any strong-flavored soup, such as minestrone or oxtail, picks up flavor when dry red table wine is added, but not more than ½ cup to 4 cups of soup. Vegetable soups can often be raised to the level of a luncheon dish with the addition of rice, barley, breadcrumbs, or pasta.

Most soups taste better if they're made one or two days ahead of time, and it's easier to degrease them if they're chilled, by simply lifting off the layer of cold fat. You should always taste a soup that is to be served cold before serving it, since cold food usually needs more seasoning than hot food. If you have oversalted the soup (it won't happen if you add slowly and taste as you do), try adding a peeled, halved raw potato and simmering about 15 minutes. It should absorb some of the salt: remember to take it out before serving. Generally, 4 cups of soup will serve 6 people as a first course. And, if you have a microwave oven, consider using it to make soup stock — refer to your specific oven's cookbook for directions.

Seven-Vegetable Broth with Walnut Garnish (see recipe page 170)

The garden carrot was at first so highly esteemed that ladies wore leaves of it in their headdresses in 16th-century Elizabethan England.

Seven-Vegetable Broth with Sour Cream and Walnut Garnish

Preparation time: 20 minutes
Cooking time: 20 minutes
Degree of difficulty: simple
Servings: 6
Calories per serving: 125

Spring is a good time to search out the ingredients for this interesting soup.

4 cups chicken stock
2 large carrots, scraped and minced
2 leeks, white part only, thinly sliced
1/2 stalk celery, minced
1 cup fresh spinach, chopped
1/4 pound mushrooms, sliced
1 small red pepper, seeded and julienned
1/4 pound asparagus, cut in 1-inch pieces
1/2 cup sour cream
1/4 cup chopped walnuts

Bring chicken stock to a boil. Add carrots, leeks, celery, spinach, mushrooms, red pepper, and asparagus. Lower heat and simmer 20-25 minutes. Ladle into soup bowls and top each serving with a dollop of sour cream and a sprinkling of chopped walnuts.

Canadian Pea Soup

Preparation time: 15 minutes
(total — including cutting up bone and puréeing)
Cooking time: 3-3 1/2 hours
Degree of difficulty: simple
Servings: 6-8
Calories per serving: 794 (1/6)
595 (1/8)

What's a Canadian cookbook without one of the soups that has made our cuisine famous?

1 pound green or yellow split peas, washed and picked over
1/4 cup bacon dripping or other fat
2 medium onions, chopped
3 carrots, sliced
8 cups water
1 bay leaf
1/2 teaspoon dried thyme
2 teaspoons salt
1 ham bone or smoked pork hock
2 tablespoons butter
2 teaspoons sugar
1 1 1/2-2 pound piece of ham or 1/2 pound sliced bacon

Soak peas overnight. Sauté onions and carrots in fat in a large pot until soft but not brown. Add peas, water, seasonings, and ham bone or hock, cover, and bring to the boil. Turn heat low and simmer for about 2 1/2-3 hours. Remove bone and cut off meat into bite-size pieces to be served in each soup plate. Purée soup and vegetables in a blender, return to the pot, and add sugar, butter, and meat pieces. Season to taste and cook gently again until ham is heated thoroughly.

Curried Lentil Soup

Preparation time: 15 minutes
Cooking time: 1 hour
Degree of difficulty: simple
Servings: 6
Calories per serving: 220 (with garnish)

Spicy, but not painfully so.

1 tablespoon oil
1 tablespoon butter
1 small bunch green onions, sliced
1 teaspoon ground cumin
1 teaspoon turmeric
1/2 teaspoon ground coriander
1/4 teaspoon cayenne pepper
4 cups cold water
1/2 cup red lentils, rinsed and drained
2 cups peeled, diced eggplant
1 cup peeled, diced potato
1 tomato, peeled, seeded, and chopped
1/2 cup finely chopped parsley
1 tablespoon lemon juice
1 cup light cream
Salt and freshly ground pepper to taste
1 tablespoon butter (optional)
1/4 cup slivered almonds (optional)

Heat the oil and butter in a large saucepan over medium heat. Sauté onions until transparent. Stir in cumin, turmeric, coriander, and cayenne and cook 1 minute more. Add water, lentils, eggplant, potato, tomato, and half the parsley. Bring to a boil, reduce heat, and simmer, partially covered, for 40 minutes. Purée in a food processor or blender, in batches if necessary. Heat through; stir in lemon juice and cream. Salt and pepper to taste. In a small saucepan, melt butter and sauté almonds until golden. Garnish soup with almonds and parsley.

Cream of Fiddlehead Soup

Preparation time: 10 minutes
Cooking time: about 45 minutes (total)
Degree of difficulty: simple
Servings: 6-8
Calories per serving: 230 (1/6)
175 (1/8)

Fiddleheads, so named because the shape of this green vegetable is like the head of a violin, make an excellent cream soup. This recipe may be served hot or cold.

2 10-ounce packages of fiddleheads, thawed and drained
3 cups water
Salt
3 tablespoons butter
4 tablespoons all-purpose flour
6 cups fresh or canned chicken broth
1/2 cup whipping cream
4 egg yolks
1/8 teaspoon freshly grated nutmeg, or to taste
Cayenne pepper to taste
2 tablespoons fresh lime or lemon juice

Boil fiddleheads for about 6 minutes and drain in a colander. Run under cold water, drain, then squeeze between the hands to extract excess moisture. Chop fiddleheads fine. Do not add liquid.

Melt the butter, then add the flour, blending with a wire whisk. When blended, rapidly stir in the broth. Simmer for about 30 minutes, stirring frequently.

Blend the cream and egg yolks. Remove the soup from the heat and stir in the yolk-and-cream mixture. Add the fiddleheads and bring the soup almost but not quite to the boil, stirring vigorously. Add the remaining ingredients.

Cream of Fennel Soup

Preparation time: 10 minutes
Cooking time: 30-35 minutes
Degree of difficulty: simple
Servings: 6-8
Calories per serving: 235 (1/6)
175 (1/8)

This smooth, light soup can be sprinkled with croutons and served hot with sandwiches or casual lunches, or chilled for a more elegant dinner.

6 tablespoons butter
1 medium onion, thinly sliced
3 fennel bulbs, thinly sliced
4 tablespoons all-purpose flour
4 cups chicken stock
1 cup milk
1 bay leaf
Salt and freshly ground pepper to taste
2 egg yolks
1/2 cup light cream

Melt the butter in a heavy saucepan, add the onion and fennel, stir until well coated with butter. Cook over low heat until softened, but on no account let them brown. Remove from heat and stir in the flour. Cook 3 minutes, then gradually blend in the stock and milk. Add bay leaf, cover, and simmer 20 minutes. Remove bay leaf and pass soup through a fine sieve or whir in a blender; return to a clean saucepan. Add salt and pepper to taste. Mix egg yolks and cream and slowly whisk in about 1/2 cup hot soup; gradually whisk mixture into soup. Reheat gently, never letting it boil, and serve.

Cream of Parsnip Soup

Preparation time: 15 minutes
Cooking time: 20 minutes
Degree of difficulty: simple
Servings: 6
Calories per serving: 140

Not everyone likes parsnips — but for those who do (or those who have the courage to risk), this will be gratifying.

2 tablespoons butter
1 medium onion, chopped
1 stalk celery, chopped
1 pound parsnips, peeled and sliced
4 cups chicken broth
1/2 cup light cream
1/4 teaspoon curry powder
1 orange
Salt and white pepper to taste
2 tablespoons minced parsley

In a medium saucepan, sauté onion and celery in butter until soft. Add parsnips and chicken broth. Cover and bring to a boil. Lower heat and simmer 10-15 minutes, or until parsnips are soft. Cool slightly and purée, in batches if necessary, in a food processor or blender. (Soup can be made ahead of time to this point. Cover and refrigerate until just before serving.) Return to pot and add cream and curry. Add the grated peel of the whole orange and the juice of half the orange. Simmer until heated through. Taste and season with salt and pepper. Sprinkle each serving with parsley.

Herbs with long stems, such as mint or parsley, can be stood in a glass of water, covered with a plastic bag, and refrigerated for up to a week; short-stemmed herbs like chives or thyme should be rinsed, dried, and wrapped in paper towels, put in a plastic bag, and refrigerated. Leave no moisture on the leaves or they will rot quickly.

Dried Fruit Soup

Preparation time: 15 minutes
Cooking time: 2½ hours
Soaking time: overnight
Degree of difficulty: moderate
Servings: 6-8
Calories per serving: 453 (1/6)
*   340 (1/8)*

Dried fruit, lentils, and lamb combine with turmeric, cardamom, and cumin for a delicious and colorful soup. An excellent winter dish.

½ cup dried kidney beans

3 tablespoons olive oil

1¼ pounds boneless lamb, cubed

⅔ cup minced onion

¼ teaspoon turmeric

⅛ teaspoon each cardamom and cumin

6 cups chicken stock

½ cup dried, rinsed lentils (soaked in water overnight)

1 large beet, peeled and cut in thin strips

1 cup chopped mixed dried fruit (apricots, prunes, pears, peaches)

Salt and freshly ground pepper to taste

2 tablespoons lemon juice

1 tablespoon minced parsley

Soak kidney beans overnight. Drain beans, place them in a large saucepan, and cover with cold water. Bring to a boil, reduce heat, and simmer, uncovered, for 1 hour or until tender. Heat olive oil in a large pot; when hot, add lamb and cook, turning frequently, until nicely browned. Add the onion, turmeric, cardamom, and cumin; stir and cook for 2 minutes. Add the chicken stock, beans with their liquid, drained lentils, and beet strips. Bring to a boil, lower heat, cover and simmer for 1 hour. Add the dried fruit and simmer, covered, for an additional 30 minutes. Season to taste. Just before serving, stir in lemon juice and add more stock (or water) if the soup is too thick. Garnish with minced parsley.

Icy Borscht

Tomato Bisque

Preparation time: 10 minutes
Cooking time: 35 minutes
Degree of difficulty: simple
Servings: 4-6
Calories per serving: 240 (1/4)
160 (1/6)

Served hot with a green salad and brown bread, or cold as partner to a main dish, this is a lovely soup.

1/4 cup butter
1/4 cup all-purpose flour
1 1/2 cups milk, scalded
1 cup hot chicken stock
1 28-ounce can tomatoes
1/2 cup minced onion
1 tablespoon honey
2 tablespoons minced parsley
1 teaspoon dill seed
1/4 teaspoon each basil and marjoram
1 bay leaf, crushed
Salt and freshly ground pepper to taste

Melt butter in a large saucepan and stir in flour; cook gently over low heat for 3 minutes. Remove pan from heat and add milk and stock, whisking vigorously. Return to heat and bring to a boil, stirring constantly until thick and smooth. Purée the tomatoes in a blender and add to the milk with onion, honey, and seasonings. Simmer for 20 minutes, stirring frequently.

Icy Borscht

Preparation time: 15 minutes
Chilling time: 1 hour
Degree of difficulty: simple
Servings: 6
Calories per serving: 202

This iced soup contributed by Diana Bennett is stunning in both appearance and flavor. It's versatile too: without the buttermilk and stock, it's a super dip.

2 cups buttermilk
1 cup sour cream
1/2 cup plain yogurt
1/2 cup chicken stock
1/2 cup or more pickled beet juice
1 cucumber, chopped
15 red radishes, chopped
1 bunch green onions, chopped
3 hard-cooked eggs, chopped
1-1 1/2 cups small cooked shrimp
Fresh dill to taste
Salt and freshly ground pepper to taste

Mix together buttermilk, sour cream, yogurt, and chicken stock. Add enough pickled beet juice to color soup bright pink. Pour over cucumber, radishes, green onions, eggs, and shrimp. Season to taste with salt, pepper, and dill. Chill for about 4 hours. Serve very cold. You may want to add some crushed ice immediately before serving.

Tinned crabmeat will be close to fresh crab in flavor if you run cold water over it, squeeze it dry, and pat lightly with paper towels.

Green Bean Chowder

Preparation time: 20 minutes
Cooking time: 35-40 minutes
Degree of difficulty: simple
Servings: 8
Calories per serving: 185

A satisfying, warming vegetable chowder that's as pretty to serve as it is good to eat. Offer with chunks of warm buttered bread and a dilled tomato salad.

4 slices bacon

1 onion, minced

1 pound green beans, cut into 1-inch pieces

1 cup beef bouillon

2 cups raw potato cubes

1 bay leaf

2 tablespoons chopped parsley

4 cups milk

Freshly ground pepper

Paprika

Few drops of Tabasco sauce

Chop the bacon very fine and sauté until the fat has been rendered. Add onion and cook, stirring, until soft. Add beans, cook over low heat for 5 minutes. Add bouillon, potato cubes, bay leaf, and parsley. Cook 15-20 minutes until vegetables are tender. Add milk, and pepper to taste. Cover and simmer 10 minutes. Discard bay leaf. Dust with paprika; add Tabasco to taste.

Zwicker Inn Seafood Chowder

Preparation time: 15 minutes
Cooking time: 30 minutes (total)
Standing time: overnight
Degree of difficulty: simple
Servings: 6-8
Calories per serving: 510 (1/6)
380 (1/8)

Jack Sorenson, owner-chef of the outstanding Zwicker Inn in Mahone Bay, N.S., claims a fisherman's grandmother as the source of his famous, though heretical, chowder.

½ pound haddock or halibut fillets, or a combination of both

⅓ pound scallops, chopped

⅔ cup chopped cooked lobster meat

½ cup minced onion

1 tablespoon butter

1⅓ teaspoons dried thyme

1¼ teaspoons celery salt

2 cups whipping cream

¾ cup sour cream

3½ cups diced cooked potato

1¼ cups milk

Salt and freshly ground pepper to taste

Paprika

Fry the minced onion in the butter until transparent. Add the thyme and celery salt, then remove from heat. Poach the fish in the 2 cups cream. When cooked, remove with a slotted spoon, cool, then break up and remove bones. Add the onion mixture and the scallops to the poaching liquid. Poach until scallops are opaque, about 1 minute. If chowder is not to be used immediately, refrigerate everything at this stage. If eating right away, add the sour cream, diced potato, fish, lobster meat, and milk. Heat through, but do not allow to boil. When reheating refrigerated chowder, if may be necessary to add a little more milk, water or cream because the fish will have absorbed some of the liquid. Season to taste and ladle into soup bowls. Sprinkle with paprika.

Hot-Sour Soup

Preparation time: 20 minutes
Soaking time: 30 minutes
Cooking time: 20-30 minutes
Degree of difficulty: moderate
Servings: 4
Calories per serving: 165

The wonderful contrasts in tastes have made this soup popular in Chinese restaurants.

4 dried black Chinese mushrooms (available in Oriental markets)

2 ounces lean pork

6 raw shrimp

1 green onion

2 eggs

2 tablespoons cornstarch

4 tablespoons water

3 tablespoons white vinegar

1 tablespoon soya sauce

¼ teaspoon salt

¼ teaspoon white pepper

6 cups chicken stock

¼ cup bamboo shoots, cut into ¼-x-⅛-inch strips

6 snow peas, cut into ⅛-inch-wide strips

½ teaspoon Tabasco sauce

Soften the mushrooms in enough hot water to cover for 30 minutes. Cut the pork across the grain in ¼-inch-thick slices, then cut the slices into ⅛-inch strips. Shell and devein the shrimp. Squeeze the excess liquid from the mushrooms. Remove the stems and cut the caps into strips. Mince the green onion. Beat the eggs lightly in a cup. In a second cup, combine the cornstarch and water, blending well. Combine the vinegar, soya sauce, salt, and pepper in a third cup. In a soup pot, bring the stock to a boil. Add the pork, bamboo shoots, and mushroom strips; bring to a boil again, then reduce heat. Skim the soup if necessary and add the shrimp. Stir the vinegar-soya sauce mixture again and stir it into the soup until well blended. Stir the cornstarch mixture again and add it to the soup, stirring constantly, until the soup thickens, about 2 minutes. Add the green onion, snow pea strips and Tabasco. Beat the egg again and add it, stirring constantly, in a thin stream to form yellow threads as its sets. Serve at once.

Joanne Ferrari's Brandied Pumpkin Soup

Preparation time: 30 minutes
Cooking time: about 40 minutes
Degree of difficulty: simple
Servings: 4-6
Calories per serving: 540 (1/4)
360 (1/6)

Cuisine '85 Winner

Joanne Ferrari of Burnaby, British Columbia, developed this soup after many post-Hallowe'en experiments with leftover jack-o'-lanterns and pie pumpkins.

Meat of 1 1½-2-pound pie pumpkin (or 1 14 -ounce can pure pumpkin purée)
2 tablespoons olive oil
1 large onion, finely chopped
1 stalk celery, finely chopped
1 small carrot, finely chopped
2 ounces mild Italian pancetta (or prosciutto or bacon)
4 tablespoons brandy
6 cups chicken stock
6 tablespoons light cream
1 egg yolk
Salt and freshly ground pepper to taste
2 ounces Parmesan cheese, grated
2 ounces Asiago cheese, grated (available at Italian grocery stores)
2 ounces old white Cheddar cheese, grated

To prepare pumpkin, discard pulp and seeds; peel, then cut flesh into chunks, place in a saucepan with water just to cover, bring to a boil, reduce heat, and simmer until tender. Purée in a blender, adding a little more water if necessary. Heat oil in a large saucepan; add onion, celery, carrot, and pancetta and sauté until onion and celery are translucent and pancetta is crisp. Stir in brandy and cook 2 minutes. Add chicken stock and puréed pumpkin; bring to a boil, reduce heat and simmer for 35 minutes. Remove from heat. Mix together the cream and egg yolk; stir a ladleful of hot soup into the cream mixture, then slowly add to the soup, stirring constantly. Add salt and pepper. Combine cheeses. Serve the soup sprinkled with the cheese mixture.

Tomato Soup Elana

Preparation time: 30 minutes
Cooking time: 30 minutes if using beef marrow bones; 1 hour or more if using oxtail
Degree of difficulty: simple
Servings: 4-6
Calories per serving: 495 (1/4)
330 (1/6)

Cuisine '85 Semifinalist

1 pound oxtail, in pieces, or beef marrow bones
1 thick slice smoked ham, chopped
2 pounds ripe tomatoes, peeled, seeded, and chopped, or
1 28-ounce can tomatoes
2 medium leeks, washed and white parts chopped
1 stalk celery, chopped
1 small bunch fresh dill
2-3 cups fresh beef stock
Salt and freshly ground pepper to taste
½ teaspoon sugar (optional)
¼ cup freshly squeezed or canned pink grapefruit juice
¼ cup soft ripe goat cheese
Paper-thin grapefruit slices and dill sprigs for garnish

Place the oxtail or beef marrow bones, the smoked ham, tomatoes, leeks, celery, dill, and beef stock in a large saucepan, cover, and bring to a boil. Uncover and simmer 30 minutes (longer if oxtail pieces are used). Remove bones or oxtail pieces and place mixture in a food processor or blender; purée, in batches if necessary. Before transferring mixture back to saucepan, press through a fine sieve, using the back of a spoon. Reheat soup. Taste and season with salt, pepper, and sugar if desired. Whisk in grapefruit juice and goat cheese and continue whisking until smooth. Serve in heated soup bowls garnished with grapefruit slices and dill sprigs.

Netley Marsh Wild Rice Soup

Preparation time: less than 1 hour
Cooking time: less than 1 hour
Degree of difficulty: simple
Servings: 6-8
Calories per serving: 165 (1/6)
124 (1/8)

Cuisine '85 Semifinalist

This hearty but sophisticated soup was named for Manitoba's famous wild rice region.

8 cups beef stock
2 ounces dried shiitake mushrooms (or equivalent)
2 tablespoons butter
1 large carrot, diced
1 large onion, diced
1 cup wild rice, well washed
½ teaspoon thyme
1 large bay leaf
Freshly ground pepper
Chopped parsley or watercress sprigs

Soak the mushrooms in 2 cups of the stock until softened (about 20 minutes); drain, reserving liquid. Discard stems and chop. In a large saucepan, melt the butter and sauté the carrot and onion until soft (about 5 minutes). Add the remaining 6 cups of stock, the mushrooms and their broth, the wild rice, thyme, and bay leaf. Bring to a boil, reduce heat, cover and simmer 45 minutes or until the wild rice is tender. Add pepper to taste. Garnish with chopped parsley or watercress sprigs.

If the soup had been
as warm as the claret
If the claret had been
as old as the chicken
If the chicken had
been as fat as our
host
It would have been
a splendid meal.

Christmas Soup

PHOTO BY PETER CHOU

Christmas Soup

*Preparation time: less than
30 minutes*
Cooking time: about 3 hours
Chilling time: 2-3 days
Degree of difficulty: simple
Servings: 8-10
Calories per serving: 622 (1/8)
                    498 (1/10)

Cuisine '85 Semifinalist
This soup is a hearty, stick-to-your-ribs main-course potage devised by Calgary's Aileen Lamont.

4 pounds smoked pork hocks

3 pounds fresh or canned sauerkraut

sausages, sliced

6 prunes

6 peppercorns

2-3 whole chili peppers

10 juniper berries

2 medium onions, chopped

1 tablespoon vegetable oil

2 tablespoons all-purpose flour

2 teaspoons paprika

1 5½-ounce can tomato paste

Salt and freshly ground pepper to taste

Sour cream for garnish

Place the smoked pork hocks, the sauerkraut, smoked sausages, prunes, peppercorns, chili peppers, and juniper berries in a large soup pot. Add enough water to cover all the ingredients; bring to a boil, reduce heat, and simmer for 2½ hours. Remove pork hocks, debone, trim fat, slice meat and return to soup. Sauté the chopped onions in the oil, add the flour, and brown lightly. Stir in the paprika and transfer mixture to soup. Stir in the tomato paste, bring to a boil, and simmer 30 minutes more. Skim fat from the soup and add salt and pepper to taste. Serve with a dollop of sour cream and rye bread. (For best results, refrigerate soup 1-2 days to allow flavors to blend.)

Corn Soup with Tomato Relish Chez Panisse

Preparation time: 30 minutes
Cooking time: 20 minutes
Degree of difficulty: simple
Servings: 6
Calories per serving: 280

4 tablespoons unsalted butter

6 to 7 ears fresh corn, kernels scraped with dull side of a knife (reserve liquid)

Salt and freshly ground pepper to taste

3 cups water

4 to 6 tablespoons whipping cream (optional)

Melt butter in a heavy pot, add corn, corn liquid, salt and pepper. Toss over medium heat about 3 minutes; add water and cook over low heat, stirring occasionally, for 15 minutes. Cool slightly.

TOMATO RELISH

2 ears fresh corn, kernels cut, not scraped

2 ripe tomatoes, peeled, seeded and diced

6 to 8 basil leaves, chopped

Salt and freshly ground pepper to taste

To prepare tomato relish, combine corn, tomatoes, basil, salt and pepper in a bowl; let stand a few minutes before adding to the soup. In a food processor or blender, blend soup until smooth. Add whipping cream and heat until just hot. Stir in tomato relish just before serving.

Carrot and Orange Soup

Preparation time: 10 minutes
Cooking time: 25 minutes
Degree of difficulty: simple
Servings: 8
Calories per serving:
> *160 (with cream)*
> *140 (with yogurt)*

This is a beautiful soup to look at and is even more beautiful to eat. Serve it hot in the winter and chilled in the summer, or as you please. Frozen concentrated orange juice gives a better result than fresh.

1 onion, chopped
4-5 tablespoons butter
1 pound carrots, diced
3½ cups light chicken stock
1 6¼-ounce can frozen concentrated orange juice, thawed
Salt and freshly ground pepper to taste

Either ½ cup light cream and grated peel of 1 orange

Or ½ cup plain yogurt and chopped mint

Sauté the onion in the butter until soft but not brown. Add carrots and stock and simmer, covered, until the carrots are tender, about 20 minutes. Purée in a blender. Return soup to pot and gradually add orange juice concentrate, tasting to make sure orange flavor doesn't get too strong. Season to taste.

To serve soup hot, reheat with cream and extra stock or water if you like a thinner soup. Add orange peel just before serving. Crisp croutons of bread fried in clarified butter go well with the soup.

For chilled soup, mix in the yogurt, add water if you wish to thin it, or more yogurt to your taste. Correct the seasonings and chill several hours. Serve with two ice cubes in each bowl and a scatter of chopped mint.

PHOTO BY SKIP DEAN

Tomato Basil Soup with Salted Cognac Cream

Preparation time: 30 minutes
Cooking time: 1 hour (total)
Degree of difficulty: simple
Servings: 6
Calories per serving: 350

Classic tomato soup is updated with panache in this recipe from Faye Schmidt of Victoria, B.C. It's good hot or cold.

2 tablespoons butter
1 tablespoon olive oil
1½ cups chopped onion
2 cloves garlic, minced
7 medium tomatoes, peeled, seeded, and chopped
4 cups vegetable or chicken stock
1 bay leaf
1½ teaspoons herb pepper (or substitute 1 teaspoon finely chopped mixed herbs and ½ teaspoon freshly ground pepper)
1 7½-ounce can tomato sauce
2 tablespoons dried sweet basil
4 tablespoons Cognac
1 cup whipping cream
½ teaspoon salt
Fresh basil leaves for garnish (optional)

Heat butter and oil in a heavy saucepan. Add onions and garlic and sauté over medium-low heat until onion is transparent. Add tomatoes, stock, bay leaf, herb pepper, tomato sauce, and basil. Bring to a boil, reduce heat and simmer for about 45 minutes. Remove from heat and purée soup, in batches if necessary, in a food processor or blender. Stir in 2 tablespoons of the Cognac. If served cold, place in refrigerator for at least 2 hours. Before serving, make the Cognac cream: whip the cream and stir in the salt and remaining Cognac. Serve soup with a dollop of whipped Cognac cream and garnished with basil leaves.

Only five short paragraphs in the papers paid tribute to the death in May 1953 of the woman who shaped Canadian cooking for three decades. Nellie Lyle Pattinson, of Bowmanville, Ontario, was a key figure in the introduction of domestic science into schools, and published her *Canadian Cook Book* in 1923. It's a classic reflection of what Canadians of that era thought fine food should taste and look like.

Watercress Soup

Preparation time: 10 minutes
Cooking time: 20-30 minutes
Degree of difficulty: simple
Servings: 4-6
Calories per serving: 245 (1/4)
163 (1/6)

This light soup is ideal at lunch, or to begin a hearty dinner. Taste the watercress when buying it to make sure it isn't bitter.

1 medium bunch watercress
3 medium onions, coarsely chopped
2-3 stalks celery, coarsely chopped
3-4 medium potatoes, coarsely chopped
6 cups water
4 tablespoons unsalted butter
4 tablespoons whipping cream
Salt and freshly ground pepper to taste

Rinse the watercress, shake dry, and reserve about ⅓ of the leaves. Put the rest, including stalks, in a saucepan with the onions, celery, and potatoes. Add water and simmer about 20 minutes, until tender. Put butter and cream in a blender, add the vegetables and reserved watercress, and blend until smooth. Add seasonings and reheat but do not boil.

Red Pepper Soup

Preparation time: 30 minutes
Cooking time: 30 minutes
Chilling time (optional): at least 2 hours
Degree of difficulty: simple
Servings: 6
Calories per serving: 180

Cuisine '85 Semifinalist
This is a beautiful color, and has an interesting, unusual flavor. Serve it to an adventurous family or for a dinner party.

3 tablespoons butter
6 red bell peppers, cored and finely chopped
1 small bunch green onions, trimmed and finely chopped
2 small red onions, finely chopped
2 medium potatoes, peeled and finely chopped
4 carrots, peeled and finely chopped
4 stalks celery, finely chopped
4 cups fresh or canned chicken stock
1 teaspoon dried basil
1 teaspoon dried tarragon
Salt and freshly ground pepper to taste
2 cups plain yogurt

In a medium soup pot, melt the butter, add the vegetables, and sauté until tender. Add the stock and seasonings and simmer 30 minutes, or until the vegetables are cooked. Purée in a food processor in batches or put through a food mill. Let cool slightly, then gradually whisk in yogurt. To serve cold, chill for 2 or more hours. To serve hot, reheat soup gently; do not allow to boil or the yogurt will separate.

Smoked Ham and Black Bean Soup

Preparation time: 30 minutes (total)
Cooking time: 3½ hours
Degree of difficulty: moderate
Servings: 8
Calories per serving: 295

The salt-smokiness of the ham and the heartiness of the dried beans combine wonderfully in this soup. Build a meal around it with dark bread, green salad, and a jug of ale.

2 cups dried black beans
10 cups cold water
1 large onion, peeled and finely chopped
2 celery stalks with leaves, finely chopped
1 bay leaf
2 smoked ham hocks
2 tablespoons red wine vinegar
4 hard-cooked eggs, coarsely chopped
Salt and freshly ground black pepper to taste
1 lemon, cut into paper-thin slices, seeds removed
8 sprigs parsley

Wash the beans under cold running water until water runs clear. Bring the water to a boil in a 4-5-quart heavy casserole. Add the beans, onion, celery, bay leaf, and ham hocks. Return water to the boil, stirring constantly. Partially cover the pot, lower the heat, and simmer for about 3 hours, or until beans are tender.

Remove the ham hocks and reserve; discard the bay leaf. Purée the soup in a processor or blender or, with the back of a large spoon, force through a fine sieve set over a bowl. If the soup is too thick for your taste, thin with more water, adding it by the tablespoon until it reaches the desired consistency. Dice the lean meat from the ham hocks. Immediately before serving, stir in 1-2 tablespoons of vinegar and gently stir in the eggs and ham. Season with salt and pepper. Serve in individual soup bowls, garnished with a slice of lemon and a sprig of parsley.

Harira

Preparation time: 15 minutes
Cooking time: 70 minutes (total)
Standing time: overnight
Degree of difficulty: simple
Servings: 6-8
Calories per serving: 270 (1/6)
200 (1/8)

A peppery, lemony, hearty soup, traditionally served after the Ramadan fast.

½ cup dried chickpeas

¾ pound boneless lean lamb, cubed

2 tablespoons olive oil

3 large stalks celery (including leaves), minced

2 onions, minced

2 tomatoes, chopped

¾ cup minced parsley

1 teaspoon each cinnamon, coriander, and cumin

½ teaspoon turmeric

6 cups water

⅔ cup lentils

Salt and freshly ground pepper to taste

2 eggs

½ cup lemon juice

1 lemon, thinly sliced

Soak the chickpeas in cold water to cover overnight. Drain and reserve.

In a large, deep saucepan, brown the lamb in olive oil over moderately high heat, stirring constantly, for 1-2 minutes. Add celery, onion, tomato, ½ cup parsley, cinnamon, coriander, cumin, and turmeric, and cook over moderate heat, stirring, for 3 minutes. Add water, chickpeas, and lentils. Bring the liquid to a boil over moderate heat and simmer, partially covered, for 1 hour, or until the chickpeas and lentils are tender. Season with salt and pepper.

In a small bowl, beat the eggs and lemon juice. Add to the simmering soup in a steady stream, whisking constantly, then remove the pan from the heat (the eggs will separate and form strands). Ladle the soup into heated bowls and garnish with thin slices of lemon and remaining parsley.

More Than Just Potato Soup

Preparation time: 15 minutes
Cooking time: 25 minutes
Degree of difficulty: simple
Servings: 6-8
Calories per serving: 180 (1/6)
135 (1/8)

Serve this comforting soup with hot garlic sausage and sliced tomatoes sprinkled with freshly ground pepper and dill.

2 tablespoons butter

1 medium onion, diced

2 large potatoes, peeled and diced

1 stalk celery, finely chopped

1 cup cabbage, diced

4 cups chicken stock

½ cup milk

1 tablespoon all-purpose flour

1 cup sour cream

Salt and freshly ground pepper to taste

Fresh or dried dill for garnish

In a soup pot, melt the butter and sauté the onion until wilted. Add the potatoes, celery, cabbage, and chicken stock and simmer for 15 minutes or until vegetables are tender. Remove 2 cups of the cooked vegetables, combine with milk, flour and sour cream and purée in a blender or food processor, or mash with a fork until well blended. Stir mixture into the soup and reheat. Add salt and pepper to taste. Garnish with dill and serve.

NOTES

VEGETABLES

*L*ong regarded as being good for us (eat your spinach), vegetables have only recently become a joy to eat on their own account.

Nothing on our menus has more variety than vegetables. Imagine the number of dishes that can be made from the potato alone, starting with the sheer delight of a baked potato with creamy insides and crisp brown skin, going on to home fries with bits of onion and perhaps snips of bacon, and segueing into a puffy potato soufflé. We can learn from the Chinese and Japanese, who use almost no water, but stir-fry vegetables in a few drops of oil, thus preserving most of the vitamins and resulting in vegetables with a wonderful crunch: we can also regard the French, who blanch many vegetables in boiling salted water, then rinse in ice water before cooking again, briefly, in butter. This procedure sets color and flavor, and means that the cook can have things ready for several hours ahead of dinner without vegetables losing vitamins or looks.

It's better not to wash vegetables before you refrigerate them, except of course salad ingredients. Instead, wash just before cooking. Keep any liquids left over from cooking vegetables and add them to your soup stock. Boil vegetables whole whenever possible (even better, steam them) since this prevents nutrient loss, and reheat them in a double boiler, steamer, or microwave oven. For that matter, cook them from the start in a microwave, since vegetables respond very well to that method, retaining color, taste, texture, and nutritive value.

In these days of rapid transport, it's easy to fall into the expensive habit of buying strawberries or asparagus in December, rather than waiting for their annual appearance. But fresh means relatively fresh-picked, seasonal fruits and vegetables, at the peak of their flavor, color, and vitamin content. Try to buy in one of the many produce markets that have sprung up over the past few years, from Saint John in New Brunswick to Vancouver in British Columbia. Many markets, in smaller versions, exist outside our big cities. Failing a true market source, find out when your local supermarket receives its supplies, and buy on that day.

If a vegetable is old, add flavor with herbs and spices; if it's new, just scrub it and cook a minimum amount of time, tossing it in butter when it's finished. Steam vegetables whenever possible, using a collapsible metal steamer or one made of bamboo — make sure the water is boiling before you put the steamer and contents over it. And do eat a good selection from the family of vegetables called brassicas — cabbage, broccoli, sprouts, etc., — since there is some evidence that they help in the prevention of cancer of the colon.

Stir-Fried Vegetables

Julienned vegetables, usually used for garnish or added to soups at the last minute, need a flat surface to be cut easily. Put the cut side down, slice lengthwise into ⅛-inch strips, then put some of the pieces on their side and cut the same size strips in the same direction.

Boston Baked Beans

Preparation time: 10 minutes
Soaking time: overnight
Cooking time: 2 hours (total)
Degree of difficulty: simple
Servings: 6
Calories per serving: 560

Beans are full of fibre, and they taste so good, you'll soon be full of beans.

1 pound white beans
¾ cup brown sugar
½ cup molasses
⅓ cup catsup
2 teaspoons salt
1 cup tomato juice
1 teaspoon mustard
3 strips bacon

Soak beans overnight. Drain, add water to cover beans by about 2 inches, cook 1½ hours until soft but not mushy. Preheat oven to 350°F. Mix ½ cup brown sugar and all other ingredients except bacon with 2½ cups water from beans. Put beans in shallow pan or ovenproof casserole and pour mixture over them so they are covered. Spread strips of bacon on top and sprinkle with remaining ¼ cup brown sugar. Bake for 20-25 minutes.

Brussels Sprouts

Preparation time: 10 minutes
Cooking time: 20-25 minutes
Degree of difficulty: simple
Servings: 6-8
Calories per serving: 260 (1/6)
195 (1/8)

Brussels sprouts have not been traditionally a Canadian favorite. This method of cooking them has put them right on the hit parade.

2 pounds Brussels sprouts
5 tablespoons butter
1 tablespoon oil
1 large or 2 medium onions, finely chopped
½ pound fresh mushrooms, finely chopped
Salt and freshly ground pepper to taste
Pinch of nutmeg
Juice of 1 lemon
½ cup broken walnuts

Trim stems, remove wilted outer leaves, and wash Brussels Sprouts. Cut an X in the stem ends, simmer until tender-crisp, about 10 minutes. In a frying pan, melt 2 tablespoons of butter with the oil. Add finely chopped onion. Cover with a sheet of buttered wax paper and a lid. Fry for 3 minutes at a high heat, shaking frequently. Add chopped mushrooms, salt and pepper to taste, and a pinch of nutmeg. Lower the heat, replace the buttered wax paper and lid, and cook for 5 more minutes, shaking pan frequently. Add lemon juice and 3 tablespoons butter, stirring until butter melts. Mix very well, scrape pan, and pour mixture over the drained Brussels sprouts in a preheated oven dish. Keep warm in the oven. Just before serving, add walnuts.

Eggplant and Tomato Casserole

Preparation time: 15 minutes
Standing time: 10 minutes
Cooking time: 20-25 minutes
Degree of difficulty: simple
Servings: 6
Calories per serving: 245

The Mozzarella cheese makes this dish a complete meal. Serve it with crusty bread and dry red wine.

1 medium eggplant, peeled and cut into ½-inch slices
4 tablespoons olive oil
1 onion, finely chopped
1 clove garlic, finely chopped
1 zucchini, sliced
5 fresh tomatoes, peeled and chopped
Salt and freshly ground black pepper to taste
1 stalk celery, diced
½ teaspoon dried basil
⅓ cup Parmesan cheese, freshly grated
⅓ cup chopped parsley
¾ cup soft breadcrumbs
4 ounces roughly grated Mozzarella

Sprinkle the eggplant slices with salt and let stand about 10 minutes. Rinse and dry well. Heat 2 tablespoons of the olive oil in a frying pan and brown the eggplant quickly. Add the onion, garlic, and zucchini and cook 3 minutes, adding more olive oil if needed. Add the tomatoes, salt and pepper to taste, celery, and basil. Bring to a boil and simmer, covered, for 15 minutes or until zucchini is barely tender.

Stir in the Parmesan and parsley. Turn the mixture into a serving dish and sprinkle with grated Mozzarella. Heat the remaining 2 tablespoons of oil in a frying pan and brown the breadcrumbs. Sprinkle over the casserole and serve immediately or keep warm in the oven until ready to serve.

Homestyle Beans

Preparation time: 15 minutes
Standing time: 1 hour
Cooking time: 7-8 hours (total)
Degree of difficulty: simple
Servings: 10-12
Calories per serving: 725 (1/10)
605 (1/12)

Winnie Allen of Pleasant River, Nova Scotia, is known for her baked beans because they are unusually rich and delicious. Serve them with brown bread, sausages, and a glass of ale.

2 pounds yellow-eyed
or navy beans

1 teaspoon dry mustard

2 teaspoons salt

1/4 teaspoon freshly ground pepper

1 onion, sliced

1/4 cup brown sugar

1/2 cup molasses

1/2 cup catsup

1/2 pound bacon ends

1/2 pound salt pork

In a large pot, cover beans with cold water, bring to a boil, and simmer for 2 minutes. Remove from heat and let stand, tightly covered, for 1 hour. Bring again to a slow boil, reduce heat, and simmer for about 1 hour — until the skins burst when you take a few on a spoon and blow on them. Drain beans, reserving cooking water. Place beans in a large crock or covered casserole. Combine the mustard, salt, pepper, onion, sugar, molasses, and catsup with 1 cup of the reserved water. Pour over the beans and add more water if necessary to cover. Stir in the bacon ends.

Preheat oven to 250°F. Cover the salt pork with boiling water and let stand for 2 minutes. Drain and cut 1-inch gashes every 1/2-inch without cutting through the rind. Push the salt pork down into the beans until all but the rind is covered. Cover the crock and bake for 6-8 hours. Add boiling water as needed to keep the beans moist. Uncover for the last hour of baking so the rind will brown.

Eggplant Gratinée

Preparation time: 10 minutes
Standing time: 30 minutes
Cooking time: 1 hour (total)
Degree of difficulty: simple
Servings: 6-8
Calories per serving: 270 (1/6)
205 (1/8)

Serve this as a main course with crusty bread and red wine, or as a side dish with a simple roast.

1 large eggplant

2 tablespoons salt

1 green pepper, seeded and chopped

1 small onion, chopped

2 cloves garlic, chopped

2 large stalks celery, chopped

1/2 cup unsalted butter

6 ripe fresh tomatoes, chopped

1/2 cup water

1 cup grated Cheddar cheese

Slice the eggplant crosswise into 1/2-inch-thick slices; do not remove skin. Salt the slices and let stand for 30 minutes. Meanwhile, make a tomato sauce: sauté the green pepper, onion, garlic, and celery in 2 tablespoons butter until soft. Add the chopped tomatoes and the water and simmer slowly for 15 minutes.

Preheat oven to 350°F. Wipe the eggplant slices with a paper towel to remove the liquid and excess salt. Melt 2 tablespoons butter and a little oil in a heavy-duty frying pan, and fry the eggplant slices on both sides over medium heat until brown (they will absorb a lot of butter and oil, so add more butter to the pan as required). Layer the eggplant in the bottom of a large baking dish and pour the tomato sauce over. Bake for 30-45 minutes. Remove from the oven and sprinkle evenly with the cheese. Return to the oven until the cheese melts and just starts to bubble.

Braised Belgian Endives

Preparation time: 10 minutes
Cooking time: 40-50 minutes
Degree of difficulty: simple
Servings: 6
Calories per serving: 110

Among the dozens of ways to cook endive, this is one of the simplest and best.

2 pounds Belgian endives

1/2 cup water

Juice of 1/2 lemon

2 tablespoons butter

1 tablespoon sugar

1/2 teaspoon salt

Extra butter

Preheat oven to 350°F. With a sharp knife, cut out a small cone at the base of each endive. Wash endives, drain well, and arrange in a single layer in a flame-proof casserole with a lid. Add all other ingredients except extra butter. Cut a piece of wax or parchment paper the size of the casserole and cut a small hole in the centre. Lay the paper on top of the endives, bring liquid to a boil, cover the casserole, and braise the endives in oven or over low heat for 40-50 minutes. Remove endives to a heated dish, reduce the liquid to about 1/2 cup, and swirl in a large chunk of butter. Pour the sauce over endives and serve hot.

J.B. Platina, a Vatican librarian and gifted amateur in gastronomy, produced the first printed cookbook in 1474, but it's modern compared to the *Culinaria* of Celius Apicius, a rich epicure of Rome in the time of Augustus and Tiberius, the first century of the Christian era. The Romans cooked as many things as we do today including asparagus, which was cooked the correct way — bunching the stems down and heads out, so the bottoms boiled and the heads steamed at the same rate.

Baked Onions Stuffed with Veal and Spinach

Preparation time: 20 minutes
Cooking time: 35-45 minutes (total)
Degree of difficulty: simple
Servings: 6
Calories per serving: 255

Whole sweet Spanish onions are stuffed with cooked veal and fresh spinach, sprinkled with Parmesan, and drizzled with butter before they're roasted to let the juices sizzle and blend.

6 Spanish onions
8 tablespoons butter
1 teaspoon finely chopped garlic
½ teaspoon dried thyme
½ cup cooked fresh spinach
1 cup ground or finely chopped cooked veal
¼ cup dry breadcrumbs
4 tablespoons whipping cream
Salt and freshly ground pepper to taste
2 tablespoons dry breadcrumbs
2 tablespoons Parmesan cheese
½ cup chicken stock

Drop the unpeeled onions into a pot containing enough boiling water to cover and cook for 10 minutes. Drain the onions and plunge into cold water. Peel them, starting at the root end. Cut a 1-inch slice off the root end of each onion and with a large fork pull out the centres, leaving a hollow cup composed of the outside 2 or 3 layers of onion. Chop the scooped-out onion pulp very finely. Melt 4 tablespoons of the butter in a large, heavy frying pan, add the onion pulp and cook until all the moisture has evaporated and it has started to brown. Add the garlic and thyme. Squeeze excess fluid from spinach, chop finely, and mix with the onion pulp. Cook over medium heat until all moisture is gone, being careful not to let it burn. Preheat oven to 375°F. Scrape the spinach and onion mixture into a large bowl and add the ground veal and ¼ cup breadcrumbs. Moisten with the whipping cream and season with salt and pepper. Pack the mixture into the onion cups and arrange them compactly in a shallow baking pan. Combine the 2 tablespoons breadcrumbs with the Parmesan and sprinkle the mixture over the tops of the onions. Pour the chicken stock around them. Melt remaining 4 tablespoons of butter and pour over the tops of the onions. Cover the pan with aluminum foil and bake in the centre of the oven for 15 minutes. Remove the foil and bake for another 15 minutes, until the onions are tender and the tops lightly browned.

PHOTOS BY TIM SAUNDERS

Cauliflower with Pecans

Preparation time: 5 minutes
Cooking time: 15 minutes
Degree of difficulty: simple
Servings: 6
Calories per serving: 95

Cauliflower that's crisp and crunchy.

1 head cauliflower, trimmed and cut into flowerets
2 tablespoons butter
¼ cup chopped pecans
Salt and freshly ground pepper to taste

Boil the cauliflower in lightly salted water for 10-12 minutes, or until tender-crisp. Drain. Melt butter in a large saucepan and quickly sauté the cauliflower and pecans for 2-3 minutes. Salt and pepper to taste.

Leeks Vinaigrette

Preparation time: 10 minutes
Cooking time: 10 minutes
Degree of difficulty: simple
Servings: 6
Calories per serving: 190

An interesting beginning to a meal, standard fare in French bistros.

6 large leeks
1 tablespoon Dijon mustard
3 tablespoons tarragon vinegar
¾ cup vegetable or corn oil
½ teaspoon dried tarragon

Wash leeks well to remove dirt between leaves. Trim the green tops so that leeks are about 4-5-inches long; split in half lengthwise. Place in a large saucepan, cover with cold water, bring to a boil, then reduce heat to simmer for 10 minutes, or until tender but not mushy. Drain leeks, pat dry, and set aside. To prepare dressing, combine mustard, vinegar, oil, and tarragon in a jar; cover, shake, then spoon over leeks. Divide leeks with dressing among 6 plates.

Baked Fennel

Preparation time: 10 minutes
Cooking time: 1 hour and
20 minutes
Degree of difficulty: simple
Calories per serving: 112

Prized for its delicate anise flavor, fennel comes from the Mediterranean, and is now grown in Canada.

1½ pounds fennel
⅓ cup butter
Finely grated peel of 1 large, thin-skinned lemon
2 tablespoons fresh lemon juice
Salt and freshly ground pepper to taste

Preheat oven to 350°F. Trim base and top stems of the fennel, reserving some of the feathery green tops for garnish. Quarter each head lengthwise. Blanch in boiling salted water 5 minutes. Melt butter in a shallow ovenproof casserole. Remove from heat and add lemon peel and juice. Season to taste. Arrange fennel in casserole in a single layer and add salt and pepper to taste. Bake 1 to 1¼ hours.

Baked Fennel and Creamed Broccoli

Creamed Broccoli

Preparation time: 10 minutes
Cooking time: 50 minutes
Degree of difficulty: simple
Servings: 6
Calories per serving: 220

Wonderful for a simple, elegant supper, or to accompany a roast of beef.

1½ pounds broccoli
1½ cups milk
Salt and freshly ground pepper to taste
4 tablespoons butter or margarine
4 tablespoons all-purpose flour
½ teaspoon grated nutmeg
2 eggs, separated
½ cup fresh white breadcrumbs

Preheat oven to 325°F. Trim and discard any thick broccoli stems, cut florets into small pieces, then wash and drain well. Place broccoli in a medium saucepan with the milk, salt, and pepper and bring to a boil. Cover pan tightly and simmer gently 10 to 15 minutes. Strain milk and reserve. In a clean saucepan, melt butter and stir in flour. Cook 1 to 2 minutes. Gradually stir in the reserved milk (there should be about 1¼ cups) and bring to a boil; allow to bubble for 2 minutes, stirring.

Remove from heat and beat in broccoli, nutmeg and egg yolks; adjust seasoning to taste. Whisk egg whites until stiff and fold into the sauce. Spoon into a well-greased shallow ovenproof dish. Scatter breadcrumbs over the top and bake about 50 minutes, or until just set. Serve immediately.

The term "gratin" refers to the thin crust formed on the surface of dishes when browned in a hot oven or under the broiler. Grated cheese and bread-crumbs usually form the topping. A gratin dish is a shallow, oval ovenproof dish, sometimes with handles, often found in colorful enamel-led iron attractive enough to serve at the table.

Broccoli Casserole

Preparation time: 10 minutes
Cooking time: 15-20 minutes
Degree of difficulty: simple
Servings: 6
Calories per serving: 300

Olives, capers and feta cheese provide wonderful contrasts in flavor and color with the broccoli. This may be served as a side dish or as a main course for lunch.

3 pounds broccoli

½ cup crumbled feta cheese

½ cup grated Romano cheese

SAUCE

1 large onion, thinly sliced

1 clove garlic

⅓ cup olive oil

1 tablespoon capers

6 black olives, pitted and coarsely chopped

½ cup dry red wine

Trim broccoli into flowerets. Peel and slice remaining stalks. Steam for 10 minutes, or until bright green and crisply tender.

Sauté onion and garlic gently in olive oil. Add capers, olives, and wine and simmer uncovered for 10 minutes. Remove and discard garlic.

Place broccoli in a large oven-proof serving dish and toss with sauce; add feta cheese and toss again. Sprinkle Romano cheese over broccoli and place under broiler for a few minutes until lightly browned.

Parsnip Pie

Preparation time: 20 minutes
Cooking time: 1¼ hours (total)
Degree of difficulty: simple
Amount: makes 1 10-inch pie
Calories per serving: 385

This sweet and lovely pie may be served at room temperature with heavy cream, as it is in England, or less traditionally and just as deliciously, warm, as a side dish with roast meat.

3½ pounds parsnips, scraped and cut into 1-inch lengths

2 tablespoons butter

½ cup honey

3 tablespoons orange peel

2 eggs, lightly beaten

½ teaspoon cinnamon

¼ teaspoon each allspice and powdered cloves

1 teaspoon strained, fresh lemon juice

½ cup prunes, pitted and chopped, or raisins

1 10-inch pastry shell, partially baked

2 tablespoons honey

Bring the parsnips to a boil in 3-4 quarts of water. Reduce heat and simmer until soft and easily mashed with a fork. Drain thoroughly. Purée in a blender, food processor, or food mill. Measure 3 cups and, in a mixing bowl, blend with the butter, honey, orange peel, eggs, spices, and lemon juice, beating with a wooden spoon so the mixture is very smooth. Fold in the prunes.

Preheat oven to 375°F. Bake pastry shell until lightly browned. Spoon the mixture into pastry shell, smooth the top, and spread a thin film of honey on top. Bake in the centre of the oven until the filling is firm and the top is lightly browned, 50-60 minutes. Serve warm.

Charcoal-Grilled Zucchini

Preparation time: 10 minutes
Cooking time: 40 minutes
Degree of difficulty: simple
Servings: quantities vary
Calories per serving: about 110

A simple dish to take advantage of the last days of summer. Quantities vary according to the number of people being served.

1 zucchini, crookneck or other summer squash, sliced

Tomatoes, quartered

Green peppers, quartered

Small onions, peeled

New potatoes, scrubbed

Salt and freshly ground pepper to taste

Salt and pepper each vegetable, then wrap each in buttered, heavy-duty aluminum foil. Place on coals to bake. Start the potatoes first since they take about 40 minutes; other vegetables take 20 minutes. Turn packages once during baking.

Carrots with Lettuce and Cream

Preparation time: 10 minutes
Cooking time: 5 minutes
Degree of difficulty: simple
Servings: 6
Calories per serving: 95

3 tablespoons butter

1 shallot, peeled and minced

4 carrots, scraped and shredded

½ head iceberg lettuce, washed, dried, and shredded

¼ cup chicken stock

1 tablespoon whipping cream

Salt and freshly ground pepper to taste

Melt butter in pan, add shallot, and sauté until transparent. Add carrots and sauté until cooked but crisp, about 2 minutes. Add shredded lettuce and chicken stock; cover and cook 2 minutes more. Stir in cream. Salt and pepper to taste.

Potatoes Romanoff

Preparation time: 15 minutes
Cooking time: 1 hour (total)
Chilling time: overnight
Degree of difficulty: simple
Servings: 8-10
Calories per serving: 265 (1/8)
212 (1/10)

This wonderful dish can be made ahead of time.

6 good-size potatoes

2 cups sour cream

1 1/2 cups shredded sharp Cheddar cheese

1 bunch green onions, chopped

1 1/2 teaspoons salt

1/4 teaspoon freshly ground pepper

Paprika

Preheat oven to 350°F. Cook potatoes in jackets until fork-tender. Peel. Shred potatoes into large bowl. Stir in sour cream, 1 cup grated cheese, onion, salt, and pepper. Turn into buttered 2-quart casserole. Top with remaining cheese; sprinkle with paprika. Cover and refrigerate several hours or overnight. Bake, uncovered, about 30-40 minutes, or until heated through.

Parsnip and Pear Purée

Preparation time: 10 minutes
Cooking time: 30 minutes
Degree of difficulty: simple
Servings: 6-8
Calories per serving: 180 (1/6)
135 (1/8)

Even parsnip haters tend to like this dish.

2 cups chicken stock

6-8 medium parsnips, pared and sliced

1 pear, peeled, cored, and sliced

Salt and freshly ground pepper to taste

Bring stock to boil. Add parsnips, lower heat, and simmer for 30 minutes until tender. Purée parsnips, with their cooking liquid, and pear in a blender or food processor. Add salt and pepper to taste. Serve hot.

Sautéed Parsnips, Carrots, and Zucchini

Preparation time: 10 minutes
Cooking time: 10 minutes
Degree of difficulty: simple
Servings: 6
Calories per serving: 125

3 tablespoons butter

3 medium carrots, peeled and julienned

3 medium parsnips, peeled and julienned

1 medium zucchini, julienned

Salt and pepper to taste

Juice of 1/2 lemon

Melt butter in a large skillet. Add carrots and stir-fry over medium heat for 5 minutes. Add parsnips and zucchini, cover and reduce heat to low. Cook until vegetables are tender-crisp, about 4 to 5 minutes. Season with salt and pepper and sprinkle with lemon juice.

Shaken Peas

Preparation time: 10 minutes
Cooking time: 15 to 20 minutes
Degree of difficulty: simple
Servings: 6
Calories per serving: 105

1 teaspoon butter

1 teaspoon flour

3 tablespoons butter

1 small onion, finely chopped

1/2 pound frozen baby peas

1/2 head lettuce, finely shredded

2 tablespoons cold water

4 mint leaves, finely chopped (or pinch of dried mint)

1/2 teaspoon sugar

Salt and freshly ground pepper to taste

1 tablespoon whipping cream

In a saucer, work the teaspoon of butter and flour into a soft paste. Melt the 3 tablespoons of butter in a heavy pan with a lid, add onion and sauté without browning. Add frozen peas, cover and shake well over low heat until peas begin to give off some juices. Add lettuce and water and continue to shake the pan over low heat. Add mint, sugar, salt and pepper. When the peas are almost tender, gently stir in a little of the flour and butter mixture, letting the sauce thicken and come to a boil after each addition. Add the cream, reheat peas and serve in a heated bowl.

Fennel and Broccoli Purée

Preparation time: 10 minutes
Cooking time: 30 minutes
Degree of difficulty: simple
Servings: 6
Calories per serving: 135

A wonderful combination, both to look at and to taste.

1 pound fennel bulb

1/4 cup unsalted butter

1 medium potato, peeled and sliced

1 pound broccoli, cleaned and chopped

1/2 cup water

1/2 teaspoon dried thyme

1/2 cup chicken stock

Salt and freshly ground pepper to taste

2 tablespoons chopped parsley

To prepare fennel, trim and discard upper stalks, shoots, tough outside stalks, and core of fennel bulb; slice and clean. Melt butter in a large saucepan until bubbling. Add fennel and sauté for a few minutes. Add potato, broccoli, water, and thyme; cover pan and simmer over low heat for 20-25 minutes, or until vegetables are tender. Drain. Transfer vegetables to a food processor, blender, or food mill and purée with the chicken stock. Correct seasoning and garnish with chopped parsley.

A *coulis* is just a fancy name (after all, it has to be called something) for a reduced purée or sauce, usually of vegetables. Tomato coulis is the most used and best known: it should be made only with really fresh and good tomatoes, and seasoned with whatever herbs and spices a recipe calls for. For best visual results, it should be spooned onto a plate, and the food set in the middle of the pool of sauce.

Evan Jones's Gratin of Sliced Tomatoes

Preparation time: 15 minutes
Cooking time: 45 minutes
Degree of difficulty: simple
Servings: 6
Calories per serving: 200

3 pounds firm tomatoes, peeled and sliced

6 teaspoons sherry

Chopped fresh basil to taste

Salt and freshly ground pepper to taste

12 tablespoons whipping cream

6 heaping tablespoons grated Cheddar cheese

Chopped parsley

Preheat oven to 300°F. Divide the tomatoes among 6 buttered gratin dishes, about 6 inches in diameter. Dribble a teaspoon of sherry over each, then sprinkle with basil, salt, and pepper. Bake uncovered for 30 minutes. Remove from the oven, pour 2 tablespoons of cream over each and sprinkle cheese on top. Bake for another 15 minutes on the top rack, then sprinkle with parsley. Serve with plenty of good bread to mop up the juices.

Roasted Garlic

Preparation time: 15-20 minutes
Cooking time: 30 minutes
Degree of difficulty: simple
Servings: 4
Calories per serving: 135

When roasted, fresh garlic loses its sharp bite and assumes a wonderful sweetness. Serve with roasted meat and home-fried potatoes.

4 large heads garlic

2 tablespoons olive oil

Salt and freshly ground pepper to taste

1 tablespoon finely minced parsley

Preheat oven to 350°F. Peel enough garlic cloves for your guests — as many as 200 small cloves for six guests. Toss with the olive oil and season with salt and pepper. Place in a covered earthenware dish and bake for 30 minutes. Serve sprinkled with minced parsley.

Evan Jones's Gratin of Sliced Tomatoes, Pierre Franey's Carrot and Orange Salad (see recipe page 167), and Corn Soup with Tomato Relish Chez Panisse (see recipe page 176)

Onion Custard

Preparation time: 15 minutes
Cooking time: 1¼ hours
Degree of difficulty: simple
Servings: 6
Calories per serving: 150

This goes well with roast beef and Yorkshire pudding.

¼ cup butter

6 medium-size onions, diced

2 eggs, lightly beaten

1 cup milk

1 teaspoon salt

Pinch each of pepper and nutmeg

Preheat oven to 350°F. Melt butter in a saucepan and add the onions. Stir until well coated with butter, then cook over medium heat until pale gold, about 10-15 minutes. Combine remaining ingredients, add to onions, and pour mixture into a buttered 1-quart casserole. Bake uncovered for 45 minutes or until set (a knife pushed gently into the middle comes out clean).

Scalloped Potatoes with Rosemary

Preparation time: 15 minutes
Cooking time: 30 minutes
Degree of difficulty: simple
Servings: 6
Calories per serving: 288

Rosemary, symbolizing remembrance, adds a fitting touch.

2 pounds potatoes, scrubbed, unpeeled, and sliced about ⅛-inch thick

½ clove garlic, crushed

5 tablespoons butter

1 cup grated Parmesan cheese

2 tablespoons fresh or 1 tablespoon dried rosemary

1 cup beef bouillon

Preheat oven to 425°F. Rub a baking dish (about 10 inches in diameter and 2 inches deep) with garlic and smear with 1 tablespoon butter. Spread a layer of potatoes on the bottom of the dish, dot with butter, and sprinkle with some of the cheese. Repeat layers until potatoes are used up. Sprinkle rosemary and remaining cheese over top. Pour on bouillon. Bake for 30 minutes, or until potatoes are tender, bouillon has been absorbed, and the top is golden brown.

Red Potatoes with Chives

Preparation time: 5 minutes
Cooking time: 15 minutes
Degree of difficulty: simple
Servings: 6
Calories per serving: 150

18-24 red potatoes, washed, skins left on, quartered or halved

½ teaspoon salt

2 tablespoons butter

1 tablespoon freshly ground pepper

2 tablespoons snipped fresh chives

1 teaspoon chopped parsley

Half fill a large pot with water and bring to a boil. Add salt and potatoes and cook until tender, about 10-15 minutes. Drain. Toss with butter and pepper. Garnish with snipped chives and chopped parsley.

Bok Choy with Bacon

Preparation time: 15 minutes
Cooking time: 10 minutes (total)
Degree of difficulty: simple
Servings: 6
Calories per serving: 120

The saltiness of the bacon and the spicy chili-based sauce lend this crunchy dish special flavor.

1 2-pound head bok choy

2 tablespoons water

2 tablespoons sugar

2 tablespoons vinegar

2 teaspoons Worcestershire sauce

¼ cup chili sauce

1 tablespoon cooking oil

6 slices bacon, cooked and crumbled

Break bok choy apart, wash, and drain. Cut the white stems in thin diagonal slices and the green tops in thicker slices. To prepare sauce, combine water, sugar, vinegar, Worcestershire sauce, and chili sauce in a small saucepan and heat thoroughly. Heat oil in a wok or frying pan at medium-high heat. Add stems and stir-fry until tender but still crisp, about 4 minutes. Add leaves and stir-fry an additional 2 minutes. Place on a serving dish, spoon hot sauce over, and sprinkle with crumbled bacon. Serve immediately.

PHOTO BY TIM SAUNDERS

Bok Choy with Bacon

Savory Squash Rings

Preparation time: 10 minutes
Cooking time: 30 minutes
Degree of difficulty: simple
Servings: 8
Calories per serving: 180 (with sour cream) 140 (with yogurt)

Squash is always an autumn favorite.

2 medium pepper squash

¼ cup butter

½ cup thinly sliced onion

1½ teaspoons salt

⅛ teaspoon freshly ground pepper

½ teaspoon basil

1 cup sour cream or plain yogurt

¼ cup mayonnaise

Preheat oven to 350°F. Cut squash into ½-inch-thick slices. Peel and remove seeds. Sauté onion in butter. Spread squash rings in large, buttered pan. Sprinkle with salt, pepper, and basil, and cover with foil. Bake for 20-30 minutes, or until tender. Meanwhile, mix together sour cream or yogurt and mayonnaise; add to onion in frying pan and heat through. Spoon over squash to serve.

Zesty Carrots and Onions

Preparation time: 10 minutes
Cooking time: 30 minutes (total)
Degree of difficulty: simple
Servings: 4-6
Calories per serving: 105 (1/4)
70 (1/6)

Since carrots and onions go so well together in stew, why not in a vegetable dish of their own?

½ cup chicken broth or 1 chicken-flavored bouillon cube

½ cup boiling water

1 pound carrots (about 6 medium), peeled and julienned, 2-inches long

2 medium onions, sliced

1 tablespoon butter

1 tablespoon all-purpose flour

½ teaspoon salt

Dash of freshly ground pepper

Pinch of sugar

⅛ teaspoon dried thyme (optional)

¾ cup water

Bring chicken broth to a boil, or add bouillon cube to ½ cup boiling water in a medium-size saucepan; stir until dissolved. Add carrots and cook, covered, for 10 minutes. Do not drain. Meanwhile, cook onions for 5 minutes in melted butter in a covered frying pan, shaking the pan so the onions don't stick. Uncover; stir in flour, salt, pepper, sugar, and thyme. Remove from heat; add ¾ cup water. Return to moderate heat and cook, stirring, until boiling, thickened, and smooth. Add carrots and their cooking liquid. Simmer, uncovered, until carrots are tender, about 5 minutes.

Rutabaga and Apple Purée

Preparation time: 10 minutes
Cooking time: about 45 minutes
Degree of difficulty: simple
Servings: 6
Calories per serving: 90

Even people who don't like rutabagas (yellow turnips, or swedes, as they're sometimes called) respond well when the vegetable is softened by the sweetness of apple.

1 medium rutabaga, peeled and diced

1 apple, peeled and chopped

2 cups water

2 cups chicken stock

2 tablespoons butter

½ teaspoon cumin

¼ teaspoon curry

1 teaspoon chopped parsley

Salt and freshly ground pepper to taste

In a large pot, combine water and stock; bring to a boil. Add rutabaga and apple; cook until tender, about 15 minutes. Remove with a slotted spoon. Boil down stock to 1 cup. Purée rutabaga and apple with stock in blender or food processor. Add butter and seasonings and mix.

Zucchini Dill Soufflé

Preparation time: 5 minutes
Cooking time: 1¼ hours (total)
Degree of difficulty: simple
Servings: 4
Calories per serving: 195

This light and tasty soufflé could be served as a first course.

4 medium zucchini, peeled and cubed

1 tablespoon lemon juice

2 teaspoons salt

2 tablespoons butter

2 tablespoons all-purpose flour

1 cup chicken broth or milk

4 eggs, separated

2 tablespoons chopped fresh dill or dill seed

Simmer zucchini and lemon juice in boiling, salted water to cover for 15 minutes. Drain and set aside.

Preheat oven to 350°F. Melt butter, add flour, and stir in broth. Cook until thickened. Beat egg yolks and add to sauce. Stir in zucchini and dill. Beat egg whites until stiff and fold into mixture. Pour into a 6-cup prepared soufflé dish. Place soufflé dish in a pan of water and bake for 50 minutes or until set.

Super Succotash

Preparation time: 15 minutes
Cooking time: 40-45 minutes
Degree of difficulty: simple
Servings: 8
Calories per serving: 230

This has the very smell of summer to it. Make a baked potato your second vegetable and try teaming these two with chicken, baked with a little lemon and tarragon.

1 medium onion, finely chopped

3 tablespoons finely chopped parsley

1 clove garlic, minced

3 slices bacon, diced

1 tablespoon paprika

6 cobs of corn

1 green pepper, chopped

2 tomatoes, chopped

1 cup chopped zucchini

1 pound fresh or 1 package frozen lima beans

¼ cup water

Salt and freshly ground pepper to taste

In a large heavy saucepan with a tightly fitting lid, sauté onion, half the parsley, and garlic with bacon until lightly browned. Add paprika and cook 2 minutes longer. Cut kernels from cobs. Add corn to the bacon mixture with the tomatoes, pepper, zucchini, and shelled lima beans. Mix. Add the water and seasoning and simmer, tightly covered, for 30 minutes, or until tender. Remove lid and bring to boil to reduce liquid. Sprinkle with remaining parsley.

Imam Bayildi (The Priest Fainted)

Preparation time: 10 minutes
Standing time: 30 minutes
Cooking time: 1 ¾ hours
Degree of difficulty: simple
Servings: 6-8
Calories per serving: 235 (1/6)
175 (1/8)

Imam Bayildi is similar to ratatouille.

3 medium eggplants
4 tablespoons plus 2 teaspoons salt
6 medium onions, sliced and separated into rings
7 large cloves garlic, finely chopped
5 medium fresh ripe tomatoes, finely chopped
8 tablespoons olive oil
1 cup water
4 tablespoons finely chopped parsley

Cut off stems and slice eggplants lengthwise. Sprinkle with 2 tablespoons salt and let stand at least 30 minutes. Repeat with the onion rings. Drain the eggplant and pat dry with paper towels; rinse the onion rings and pat dry.

Combine onion, garlic, and tomatoes in a bowl and sprinkle with 2 teaspoons salt. Pour 2 tablespoons olive oil into a wide-bottomed frying pan with a cover. Layer the eggplant and the tomato-onion-garlic mixture, and add 6 tablespoons olive oil and the water. Bring the mixture to a boil, reduce heat, cover and let simmer slowly for 1 ½ hours. Sprinkle with parsley and serve at room temperature.

Green Beans with Pecans and Yogurt

Preparation time: 5 minutes
Cooking time: 30 minutes (total)
Degree of difficulty: simple
Servings: 6
Calories per serving: 125

The contrast in texture between the crunchy vegetables and nuts and the creamy and pungent yogurt lends this dish special interest.

1 pound green beans, or broccoli, trimmed
½ cup pecans
1 tablespoon butter
Salt
1 bunch green onions, chopped
1 teaspoon dill
1 cup plain yogurt
Freshly ground black pepper

Wash and steam the beans until they are barely tender. Sauté the pecans in the butter until just brown; remove with a slotted spoon, leaving the butter in the pan. Salt the nuts. To the pan add the chopped green onion and the dill. Sauté for 1 minute, then add the yogurt. Stir and cook over low heat for 3 minutes to reduce the volume of yogurt. Just before serving, add the green beans and pepper and heat through. Place in a serving dish and sprinkle with the nuts.

Chilled Asparagus with Yogurt Sauce

Preparation time: 15 minutes
Cooking time: 5 to 7 minutes
Chilling time: 1 hour
Degree of difficulty: simple
Servings: 6
Calories per serving: 60

1 ½ pounds fresh asparagus, ends trimmed
1 cup plain low-fat yogurt
2 teaspoons minced fresh parsley
1 teaspoon snipped fresh chives
½ teaspoon dried tarragon leaves, crumbled
½ teaspoon sugar
¼ teaspoon salt (optional)
¼ teaspoon paprika
Dash cayenne pepper
Leaf lettuce, parsley and cherry tomatoes for garnish (optional)

Steam asparagus 5 to 7 minutes until tender-crisp. Cut into 2-inch pieces, cover and refrigerate. In a small bowl, combine remaining ingredients except garnish. Mix thoroughly and refrigerate for at least 1 hour. Just before serving, toss asparagus with yogurt sauce. Serve on a bed of lettuce, garnished with parsley and cherry tomatoes.

NOTES

THE HOMEMAKER'S ENTERTAINMENT GUIDE

*E*ntertaining friends is rather like being on stage — you must plan, rehearse, mount the best production you can muster — and then be ready to respond to last-minute emergencies with grace (at least on the surface). If the sauce curdles, know how to bring it back; if some ingredient is missing for a recipe (which shouldn't happen if you have planned in advance), know what to substitute; if a disaster occurs, be a survivor. One of the best desserts I ever tasted came about because I dropped a rich nut torte upside down on the counter while taking it out of the oven, about an hour before guests were due to arrive. In desperation I hurriedly thawed some frozen raspberries by pouring a lot of port over them and layered the crumbled nut torte in a bowl with boozy raspberries and a dollop of whipped cream. Although I've never wanted to repeat the experience, the dessert was a success.

If the cheesecake cracks in the baking, put tiny fresh flowers in a pattern all over the cake, or grate nuts on the top; if your child makes a mess on the dining-room wallpaper with crayons or spills something awful on the carpet the afternoon of your scheduled party, clean it as best you can, lower the lamps, light the candles, and try to ignore it. Whatever you do, try to be relaxed. If you're tense and nervous, your guests will sense it and get uptight, too. They're here because they want to see you, not rate your expertise in the catering department (particularly if you've already hired a caterer), so why not join the party?

Eating is, has always been, and probably always will be one of life's greatest pleasures. If you put it together with old friends, and some possible new ones, add lots of flowers, music, and conversation, you can only increase the enjoyment. Don't save up your entertaining debts to have people over three or four times a year: do entertain smaller groups as often as once a month so that it becomes more a casual habit and pleasure than a chore. Mix up your

PHOTO BY SKIP DEAN, FOOD STYLING BY KATE BUSH

guests so that an accountant sits next to an actress (however aspiring she may be), a quirky neighbor who's a fanatic on organic gardening and someone who adores rally driving. The food will fuel conversation, and your party will be a success.

The thing is, some people are born party givers. They seem to have the knack of pulling a group of people together almost at will. Their caterer never lets them down, their flowers never arrive wilted and too late to be exchanged, their soufflés never collapse even before they are taken from the oven. For the rest of us, however — and believe me we are legion — planning is probably the single most important part of a successful party.

The menu is of primary importance, and there are some people so well organized that they keep a file of 3-x-5-inch cards that show at a glance the guests at dinner, brunch, or whatever, on a given date, the food and wines served, the flower arrangements, and the success of the individual dishes. If you plan sufficiently ahead of time, the menu isn't really much of a problem. For a small number of guests — 8 to 20 — try a cold soup or appetizer, a hot entrée, and a cold or frozen dessert (in summer, you might try a cold appetizer or perhaps a small arranged salad, a cold or barbecued entrée, and a room-temperature dessert). The idea is to present the best possible food to your guests with the least possible hassle for you.

The composition of the menu is mostly a matter of balance. You wouldn't, for instance, serve a white cream cheese mousse appetizer, chicken in a pot with cauliflower and boiled potatoes, and floating island dessert — too much of the same color and texture. The mousse would be better served before glazed, stuffed lamb with lightly steamed snow peas and Lyonnaise potatoes, with perhaps a chocolate-raspberry combination for dessert. You should know how long each dish will take to prepare and cook, so there are no blockage points in the kitchen. If you're serving a cold soup or dessert, perhaps they can be made the day before or early in the morning, while sauces can often be made in advance and refrigerated.

Of course, you must consider the taste and tendencies of your guests. If they're business acquaintances, you might go more middle of the road than is your normal inclination … time for the garlicky gazpacho when you know them better. Allergies should be taken into account, as should certain dislikes, such as anise, broccoli, or oysters. Phone people who are new to you and ask them if there's anything they can't or don't want to eat. Dieters are generally considered to be on their own — they don't have to eat the chocolate pecan pie you think is perfect for your menu. On the other hand, it doesn't hurt to have a fresh fruit bowl handy for those who prefer it. If some of your guests are vegetarians, have an extra vegetable dish ready which they can eat instead of the meat course.

Many people today tend to offer red or white wine, spritzers (white wine with soda water) or Kir (white wine with cassis, which is black currant syrup) for before-dinner or brunch drinks. If you prefer to serve cocktails, make sure your guests don't linger more than an hour before the meal is served, or you might have restless or tipsy guests by the time you sit down to eat. It's generally a good idea for the host and hostess to go easy with alcohol — you're supposed to be relaxed, but not so much so that you can't move. Have lots of sparkling water, diet soft drinks, or (a nice touch) nonalcoholic fruit punches on hand for nondrinkers and fitness fans alike.

Establishing a budget for a party is wise — you won't be able to stick to it, but it makes a good starting point and keeps something of a rein on the spending. Consider whether you need your barman to stay on after midnight at double pay, whether the champagne need be top of the line or a good wine made by the champenoise method will fill the bill. Do you need or want a caterer? If so, there are hundreds of them in

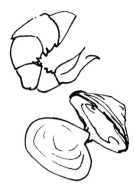

Canada, each with a slightly different approach. Ask friends whose parties you like for some leads. Never let a caterer dictate what you should serve — figure out what you want in advance, be flexible when discussing it, but be firm enough that the party will be an expression of you (and your spouse), not what the caterer thinks is fashionable. If you have a flower garden use your own flowers and greenery — it feels homier. Don't have flower arrangements that make it difficult for guests to talk across the table.

Budget restrictions should never be a reason for not having friends over for a meal. It's better to produce a carrot salad dressed with a sharp, homemade vinaigrette than to open an expensive tin of limp asparagus tips — and it's much better to search out the many wines that are sound and sensibly priced and be generous with them than to buy too little of an expensive, esoteric wine. Be lavish with garnishes such as parsley, watercress, lemon and lime wedges, and cherry tomatoes for color and interest, or garnish dishes with fresh herbs or even flowers from your garden.

The most important part of your entertainment is your guests. If they're happy, relaxed, and well fed, you've done your job as a hostess or host and can feel pleased with the results of your get-together.

SEASONAL MENUS

January

Spanakopita
Brisket and Cola
Potatoes Romanoff
Endive and Orange Salad
Apple and Raisin Crisp
A lager such as imported Grolsch, from
    Holland, or a pub beer of your choice

February

Prosciutto Breadsticks
Pork Fillets with Fig Purée
Scalloped Potatoes with Rosemary
Shaken Peas
Kiwi Sorbet
Wine: French Red Côtes du Rhône

March

Elaine McIntosh's Antipasto
Kulibyaka
Fresh Spinach, Orange, and Mango Salad
Banana Ginger Soufflé
Wine: French Chardonnay

April

Sun-Kissed Melon
Chicken with the King
Fennel and Broccoli Purée
Blueberry Mousse
Wine: Australian White Hardy's
    Fumét Blanc

May

Snow Peas Stuffed with Crab
Ruffled Cheese Torte
Red Lettuce Salad with Pecans
Rice Pudding Creole
Wine: French Red Bordeaux

June

Nibblers
Rosemary Lamb Chops
Charcoal Grilled Zucchini
Quilter's Potato Salad
Cinnamon Ice Cream with Raspberry Sauce
Wine: Spanish Red Rioja

September

Chicken Liver Pear Pâté
Kitty Pope's Orange and Ginger Pork Roast
Carrots with Lettuce and Cream
Silvia Wilson's Frozen Lemon Mousse with
 Sauce Cardinale
Wine: Spanish Marques de Casceres
  Rioja Rosado

October

Leeks Vinaigrette
Alsatian Onion Pie
Spinach Salad
Bread and Butter Pudding,
 the Dorchester Grill
Wine: French White Tokay Pinot Gris

November

Chicken Wings with Blue Cheese Dipping Sauce
Tomato-Crowned Cod
Braised Belgian Endives
Orange Charlotte
Wine: California Chardonnay Jekell Vineyards

July

Avocados with Rum
Jim's Cold Beef Summer Salad with
 Honey-Garlic Dressing
Dessert Crêpes filled with
 Chestnut Purée
Wine: Canadian Bright's Baco Noir or
Australian Hardy's Cabernet
 Sauvignon-Shiraz

August

Eggplant Siciliana
Grilled Chicken with Garlic Mayonnaise
Super Succotash
Cold Chocolate Soufflé
Wine: California Rosé or
  Carbernet Firestone

December

Cream Cheese and Cucumber Mousse
Festive Ham with Kiwi and Orange Glaze
Green Beans with Pecans and Yogurt
Parsnip Pie
Authentic English Trifle
Wine: Sparkling such as German Sekt

APPENDICES

METRIC COOKING MEASURES

The standard metric measures are described under Canadian General Standards Board National Standard CAN2-26.3-M77, available from:

Canadian Government Publishing Centre
Ottawa, Ont. K1A 0S9

The standards are:
1 Liquid measures:
   250 mL graduated in 25 mL increments
   500 mL graduated in 50 mL increments
   1000 mL (1L) graduated in 50 mL increments
2 Dry measuring set
   to include three measures:
   50 mL   125 mL   250 mL
3 Small liquid and dry measuring set to include five measures:
   1 mL   2 mL   5 mL   15 mL   25 mL

Measurements for adapting recipes

Volume:
1 mL replaces ¼ teaspoon
2 mL replaces ½ teaspoon
4 mL replaces ¾ teaspoon
5 mL replaces 1 teaspoon
15 mL replaces 1 tablespoons
25 mL replaces 2 tablespoons
50 mL replaces 3 tablespoons
50 mL replaces ¼ cup
75 mL replaces ⅓ cup
125 mL replaces ½ cup
150 mL replaces ⅔ cup
175 mL replaces ¾ cup
250 mL replaces replaces 1 cup

Weight:
7 grams replaces ¼ ounce
15 grams replaces ½ ounce
25 grams replaces 1 ounce
125 grams replaces ¼ pound
250 grams replaces ½ pound
350 grams replaces ¾ pound
500 grams replaces 1 pound 1⅔ ounces
1 kilogram replaces 2 pounds 3½ ounces

Temperature:
140°C replaces 275°F
150°C replaces 300°F
160°C replaces 325°F
180°C replaces 350°F
190°C replaces 375°F
200°C replaces 400°F
220°C replaces 425°F
230°C replaces 450°F
240°C replaces 475°F

EMERGENCY FOOD SUBSTITUTIONS

For	Substitute	For	Substitute
1 whole egg	2 egg yolks plus 1 tablespoon water (in cookies) or 2 egg yolks (in custards and similar mixtures)	1 cup sugar (in baking)	½ cup maple syrup plus ¼ cup corn syrup less 2 tablespoons liquid
			1 cup molasses, plus ¼-½ teaspoon baking soda omit baking powder
1 cup fresh whole milk	½ cup evaporated milk plus ½ cup water or 1 cup reconstituted nonfat dry milk plus 2 teaspoons margarine or butter	1 tablespoon maple sugar, grated and packed	1 tablespoon white granulated sugar
		1 cup honey	1¼ cups sugar plus ¼ cup liquid
1 cup sweet milk, to sour	Add 1 tablespoon vinegar or lemon juice to 1 cup minus 1 tablespoon lukewarm milk; let stand 5 minutes	1 ounce unsweetened chocolate	3 tablespoons cocoa plus 1 tablespoon fat
1 cup buttermilk	1 cup plain yogurt	1 cup sifted all-purpose flour	1 cup, plus 2 tablespoons cake flour
1 cup cream, coffee (at least 20%)	3 tablespoons butter, plus ¾ cup milk	1 cup sifted cake flour	⅞ cup sifted all-purpose flour (1 cup less 2 tablespoons)
1 cup cream, sour	3 tablespoons butter plus ⅞ cup sour milk	4 cups/1 pound white flour	3½ cups whole wheat flour
1 cup cream, sour, cultured	½ cup butter, plus ¾ cup sour milk	1½ teaspoons cornstarch	1 tablespoon flour
1 cup butter	1 cup margarine or ⅘ cup bacon fat, clarified or ¾ cup chicken fat, clarified or ⅞ cup cottonseed, corn, nut oil solid or liquid or ⅞ cup lard or ⅘-⅞ cup drippings	1 teaspoon baking powder	½ teaspoon baking soda plus ½ teaspoon cream of tartar or ¼ teaspoon baking soda plus ½ cup buttermilk or yogurt
		¾ cup cracker crumbs	1 cup bread crumbs
		⅛ teaspoon garlic powder	1 small clove garlic

WHAT'S AVAILABLE AND WHEN
Canadian Fresh Fruits and Vegetables

Legend:
- █ PEAK
- ▨ GOOD
- ✳ LOW
- ☐ NOT AVAILABLE

	J	F	M	A	M	J	J	A	S	O	N	D
APPLES	▨	▨	▨	▨	▨	✳	✳	✳	▨	▨	▨	▨
APRICOTS							█	█				
ASPARAGUS				█	█	█	✳					
BEANS							▨	█	▨	✳		
BEETS	▨	▨	▨	✳	✳	✳	▨	█	█	█	▨	▨
BLUEBERRIES							▨	█	█	✳		
BROCCOLI							▨	█	█	█	✳	
BRUSSELS SPROUTS							✳	▨	█	█	█	▨
CABBAGE	▨	▨	▨	✳	✳	▨	▨	▨	▨	▨	▨	▨
CANTALOUPES								█	█			
CARROTS	▨	▨	▨		✳	▨	✳	▨	█	▨	▨	▨
CAULIFLOWER						✳	▨	█	█	█	✳	
CELERY							▨	█	█	█	✳	
CHERRIES						✳	█	▨	✳			
CORN (SWEET)							▨	█	█	✳		
CRANBERRIES									█	✳	▨	
CUCUMBERS			✳	▨	▨	▨	█	▨	▨	✳	✳	
EGGPLANT							✳	▨	█	▨	✳	
ENDIVE	✳	✳	✳	✳		✳		█	█	▨	▨	✳
FIDDLEHEADS					█	▨						
GARLIC							✳	▨	█	✳		
GRAPES (TABLE)								✳	▨	█		
LEEKS	▨	✳	✳	✳	✳	✳	✳	▨	▨	█	█	▨
LETTUCE				✳	▨	█	█	▨	✳	✳		
MIXED MELONS								█	▨	✳		
MUSHROOMS	▨	▨	▨	▨	▨	▨	▨	▨	▨	▨	▨	▨
ONIONS	▨	▨	▨	✳	✳	✳	✳	█	█	▨	▨	▨
PARSLEY	✳	✳	✳	✳	✳	✳	▨	█	▨		✳	✳
PARSNIPS	▨	▨	▨	▨	✳	✳	▨	✳	▨	▨	▨	▨
PEACHES							✳	█	█	▨		
PEARS	▨	▨	✳	✳				▨	█	▨	▨	▨
PEPPERS							✳	█	█	▨		
PLUMS & PRUNES							✳	▨	█	✳		
POTATOES (IRISH)	▨	▨	▨	▨	▨	✳	✳	█	█	▨	▨	▨
PUMPKINS										█	✳	
RADISHES				✳	✳	█	█	▨		✳	✳	
RASPBERRIES							█	█	▨	✳	✳	
RHUBARB	✳	▨	▨	✳	▨	█	▨	✳	✳			
RUTABAGAS	▨	▨	▨	▨	▨	✳	✳	▨	█	▨	▨	▨
SPINACH					✳	▨	▨	█	▨	▨	✳	✳
SQUASH	✳	✳					✳	▨	█	█	▨	✳
STRAWBERRIES						█	█	▨				
TOMATOES				✳	▨	▨	▨	█	▨	▨	✳	

SEASONAL FOOD

SHORT-CUT COOKING

Recipes that take 30 minutes or less to prepare and cook

RECIPES THAT ARE ILLUSTRATED

ACKNOWLEDGMENTS AND PERMISSIONS

CUISINE '85 RECIPE CONTEST

Homemaker's wildly successful recipe contest: From 3349 recipe submissions, we proudly present the 20 semifinalists, winners, and the grand winner.

Cuisine '85 winners: Kitty Pope, Candace Anderson (front); Silvia Wilson, Joanne Ferrari (rear)

Appetizers

Winner   Candace Anderson, Vancouver, British Columbia
Lemon Thyme Pasta with Grilled Baby Artichokes

Paula Dillon, Markham, Ontario
Spinach Salad with Strawberries

Carole Rambharat, Downsview, Ontario
Chicken Crescents with Green Apple Chutney

Thanaa Soliman, Winnipeg, Manitoba
Stuffed Vine Leaves with Yogurt Sauce

Mary-Ann Symes, Winnipeg, Manitoba
Seafood Timbales with Red Pepper Sauce

Soups

Winner   Joanne Ferrari, Burnaby, British Columbia
Brandied Pumpkin Soup

Christina Edge, Winnipeg, Manitoba
Netley Marsh Wild Rice Soup

Aileen Lamont, Calgary, Alberta
Christmas Soup

Joy Stevens, Ottawa, Ontario
Tomato Soup Elana

Barbara Thompson, Ottawa, Ontario
Red Pepper Soup

Main entrées

Grand winner   Kitty Pope, Yellowknife, Northwest Territories
Orange and Ginger Pork Roast with Corn Bread Stuffing

Rose Fishman, Thornhill, Ontario
Stuffed Chicken Legs with Apricot Orange Sauce

Gene Emily Russel, Weston, Ontario
Fillet of Sole with Red Pepper Sauce and Walnuts

Jim Wies, Toronto, Ontario
Jim's Cold Beef Summer Salad with Honey Garlic Dressing

Jennifer Zuk, New Westminster, British Columbia
Pork Fillets with Fig Purée

Desserts

Winner   Silvia Wilson, Mississauga, Ontario
Frozen Lemon Mousse with Sauce Cardinale

Ian Alexander, Burnaby, British Columbia
Gingered Pear Mousse Pie

Kathy Briscoe, Vancouver, British Columbia
French Silk Chocolate Pie with Raspberries

Debbie Lexier, Winnipeg, Manitoba
Poppyseed Cake with Lemon Butter Filling and Coffee Whipped-Cream Icing

Melly Weisel, Toronto, Ontario
Three-Tiered Lemon Curd Cake

Acknowledgments

If by oversight or mischance we have not obtained a particular permission to reprint, or have not made acknowledgment where such is due, we hope that those affected will accept our most sincere apologies, and inform us of the oversight so that it may be corrected in future editions.

Alex Colville's Sole Florentine — a recipe by the Nova Scotia artist — is adapted from Joan Mackie's *A Culinary Palette* (Merritt Publishing, 1981)

Almond Soufflé is courtesy of Stephen Young, Toronto, Ontario

Al's Cinnamon Buns is courtesy of Al's Restaurant in Winnipeg, Manitoba

Alsatian Onion Pie is courtesy of chef Michel Jacob of Vancouver's Le Crocodile restaurant

Authentic English Trifle is from *The Best of Mme Jehane Benoit* (The Pagurian Press, 1972)

Autumn Harvest Salad is courtesy of Sidney Shadbolt, Vancouver, British Columbia

Avocado Bacon Club Sandwiches is from Joan Fielden's *The Great Canadian Sandwich Book* (The Bakery Council of Canada, 1982)

Baked Brie is courtesy of cheese expert and caterer Leona Chase of the Cheese Wheel Shop in Toronto

Baked Fennel is from Lopategui's *Cooking for Special Occasions* (Barron's Educational Series, 1985)

Baked Ham in Maple Syrup is adapted from the recipe by Marcel Kretz of La Sapinière restaurant in Val-David, Quebec

Baked Trout with Lemon is from *Cooking for Special Occasions* (Barron's Educational Series, Inc., 1984)

Barney's Rock 'n' Rye is from Irena Chalmers and Friends' *Gifts from the Christmas Kitchen* (Irena Chalmers Cookbooks Inc., 1983)

Beggars' Purses is courtesy of Jeraldene Ballon of Dr. Cheese and the Cake Lady bakery, Toronto, Ontario

Blueberry Chocolate Cheesecake Pie is courtesy of baker Sue Devor of Toronto's Sweet Sue Pastries

Blueberry Grunt is courtesy of Winnie Allen, Pleasant River, Nova Scotia

Bok Choy with Bacon is courtesy of the British Columbia Department of Agriculture

Boston Baked Beans is courtesy of Mrs. P.C. Kent, Toronto, Ontario

Bow-Tied Escargots in Pasta is courtesy of Barbara Gordon, owner-chef of Toronto's Beaujolais Restaurant

Brussels Sprouts is courtesy of Mrs. E. Watkinson, Scarborough, Ontario

Butter Tarts is from Cynthia Wine's *Across the Table: An Indulgent Look at Food in Canada* (Prentice-Hall, 1985)

Cabbage Salad is courtesy of Marshlands Inn, Sackville, New Brunswick

Camembert with Herbs is courtesy of Christine Mullen of Toronto's La Cuisine caterers

Cardamom Orange Olives is from Claire Clifton and Matina Nicolls's *Edible Gifts* (Bodley-Head, 1982)

Carrot and Orange Soup is from *Jane Grigson's Vegetable Book* (Penguin, 1981)

Cheese Crêpes is courtesy of Lily Schreyer

Chef Michel Clavelin's Blanquette de Veau Vermouth is courtesy of the Four Season's Hotel, Vancouver, British Columbia

Chestnut Bavarian Cream with Kiwi Fruit is courtesy of Perzow and Masson Fine Foods in Westmount, Quebec

Chicken Galantine is from Helen Gougeon's *Original Canadian Cookbook* (Tundra Books, 1975)

Chicken in Sour Cream is courtesy of Mrs. Carl Brewer

Chicken Stew with Dumplings is courtesy of Judith Comfort, Port Medway, Nova Scotia

Chicken with the King is courtesy of Vancouver's Gucheese restaurant

Chili Chicken is courtesy of Marlene Proctor, Winnipeg, Manitoba

Chilled Asparagus with Yogurt Sauce is from Jane Brody's *Good Food Book* (Penguin, 1985)

Chocolate Brownie Tart is courtesy of baker Sue Devor of Toronto's Sweet Sue Pastries

Cod Jigger's Dinner is courtesy of Mary Darcy, Conception Bay, Newfoundland

Cold Pasta with Asiago Cheese, Pine Nuts, and Sun-Dried Tomatoes is courtesy of Toronto's Fenton's restaurant

Cold Water Orange Cake is courtesy of Lorna Berringer, Halifax, Nova Scotia

Combo Special is adapted from the recipe in Joan Fielden's *The Great Canadian Sandwich Book* (The Bakery Council of Canada, 1982)

Crabmeat and Watercress Salad with Kiwi Vinaigrette is courtesy of chef Dante Rota, Toronto, Ontario

Cream of Parsnip Soup is courtesy of home economist Barb Holland, Toronto, Ontario

Creamed Broccoli is from Lopategui's *Cooking for Special Occasions* (Barron's Educational Series, 1985)

Créme Caramel à l'Orange is courtesy of Sheila Kierans, Ottawa, Ontario

Curds 'n' Sprouts Pita Bread Pockets is courtesy of Chantal Farand and Michel Viau of Toronto's La Crotterie

Curried Lentil Soup is courtesy of Jocelyn Shipley, Newmarket, Ontario

Dessert Crépes Filled with Chestnut Purée is courtesy of Marguerite Préfontaine, Aylmer, Quebec

Dinah Koo's Wild Rice Salad is courtesy of Dinah's Cupboard, Toronto, Ontario

Dingle Cake is courtesy of Danielle Foster

Dora's Apple Pie is courtesy of British Columbia Tree Fruits Limited

Double Chocolate Malt Brownies is adapted from the recipe in Virginia Rich's *The Cooking School Murders* (Ballantine Books, 1982)

Dropped Yorkshire Pudding with Fresh Fruit is courtesy of Ann Bartok

Duck with Blueberries La Belle Auberge is courtesy of Bruno Marti, owner of La Belle Auberge restaurant, Ladner, British Columbia

Elaine McIntosh's Antipasto is courtesy of Sheila Kierens, Ottawa, Ontario

Evan Jones's Gratin of Sliced Tomatoes is courtesy of American cookery writer Evan Jones

Fernand Point's Chicken Fricassee is from Point's *Ma Gastronomie*

Fettuccine Alfredo is from Jane Rodmell and Kate Bush's *The Getaway Chef* (Key Porter Books, 1983)

Fettuccine with Mushrooms is courtesy of Toronto's Bersani & Carlevale restaurant

Fettuccine with Smoked Salmon is courtesy of Bonnie Stern, director of Bonnie Stern Cooking Schools, Toronto, Ontario

Flapper Pie is from Cynthia Wine's *Across the Table: an Indulgent Look at Food in Canada* (Prentice-Hall, 1985)

French Silk Pie is courtesy of The Speakeasy, St. John's, Newfoundland

Fresh Salmon Scallops Georgia Straits is from Cynthia Wine's *Across the Table: An Indulgent Look at Food in Canada* (Prentice-Hall, 1985)

Frozen Grand Marnier Mousse is courtesy of home economist Barb Holland, Toronto, Ontario

Gaspé Seafood Casserole is from Cynthia Wine's *Across the Table: An Indulgent Look at Food in Canada* (Prentice-Hall, 1985)

Glorious Goldeye is courtesy of Mary Elizabeth Bayer

Great Wild Rice Casserole is courtesy of Linda King, Scarborough, Ontario

Hazelnut Cake is courtesy of John and Hazel Spencer, Aberthnau Nut Farm, Rosedale, British Columbia

Heavenly Pumpkin Pie is courtesy of Stephanie Cameron

Homestyle Beans is from Cynthia Wine's *Across the Table: An Indulgent Look at Food in Canada* (Prentice-Hall, 1985)

Iced Irish Coffee is from Zabar's *Deli Book*, New York, New York

Icy Borscht is courtesy of Diana Bennett, Toronto, Ontario

Italian Sandwich is courtesy of Monique Fernandes, Montreal, Quebec

Jalapeño Jelly is from Cynthia Wine's *Hot and Spicy Cooking* (Penguin, 1984)

Kulibyaka is courtesy of Barbara Sentis, Regina, Saskatchewan

Lamb Noisettes with Candied Lemon Peel is courtesy of the New Zealand Lamb Information Centre

Leftover Lamb with Onions is courtesy of Jean Gascon

Lemon Meringue Pie is from *Jane Grigson's Fruit Book* (Penguin, 1982)

Lentil Salad is from Michel Guérard's *Cuisine for Home Cooks* (William Morrow, 1984)

Lobster and Spinach Salad is courtesy of Barry Lee and Cate Simpson-Lee of Vancouver's Eight One Nine restaurant

Mandarin Sweet and Sour Pork is courtesy of Winnipeg's Mandarin Restaurant

Manly Apple Meringue Pie is from the Josephburg Men's Choral Society's fundraising cookbook *Country Church Cooking* (Centax, 1984)

Marilyn's Chili is from Jane Butel's *Chili Madness* (Workman Publishers, 1980)

Marinated Four-Pepper Salad is from *Elizabeth Baird's Favourites: 150 Classic Canadian Recipes* (James Lorimer, 1984)

Marinated Goat Cheese is from *Bonnie Stern's Cuisinart Cookbook* (Collins, 1984)

Marinated Shrimp in Lime Juice is courtesy of Toronto food consultant Barbara Pathy

Mary Pratt's Oatmeal Bread is courtesy of artist Mary Pratt of Newfoundland

Mexican Coffee is from Zabar's *Deli Book*, New York

Monte Cristo Sandwiches is from Arthur Schwartz's *Cooking in a Small Kitchen* (Little, Brown and Co., 1979)

Onion Jam is from Cynthia Wine's *Across the Table: An Indulgent Look at Food in Canada* (Prentice-Hall, 1985)

Pasta Salad Niçoise is adapted from the recipe in *The Harrowsmith Pasta Cookbook* (Firefly Books, 1984)

Penne Aglio E Olio is from Vancouver restaurateur Umberto Menghi's *Umberto's Pasta Book* (Whitecap Books, 1985)

Pheasant and Partridge Pie is courtesy of Toronto's Delta Chelsea Inn

Pierre Dubrulle's Chicken in Cointreau is courtesy of Pierre Dubrulle, Vancouver, British Columbia

Potatoes Romanoff is courtesy of Mrs. W.H. Carlton, Victoria, British Columbia

Prosciutto Breadsticks is courtesy of Toronto's Noodles restaurant

Quail with Black Peppercorns and Strawberries is courtesy of Le Manoir Mauvide-Genest inn, Île d'Orléans, Québèc

Quenelle of Scallops La Belle Auberge is courtesy of Bruno Marti, owner of La Belle Auberge restaurant, Ladner, British Columbia

Raspberry Cranberry Crumble Pie is courtesy of Carole Kreidstein, Willowdale, Ontario

Rhubarb and Strawberry Pie is from *Elizabeth Baird's Favourites: 150 Classic Canadian Recipes* (James Lorimer, 1984)

Rice Pudding Creole is courtesy of Morand Dare, Toronto, Ontario

Rich Dark Fruit Cake is courtesy of Eileen (Edith Adams) Norman

Roast Cornish Hens with Raspberry-Tarragon Sauce is courtesy of Louise Knowles, Hamilton, Ontario

Rosemary Lamb Chops is from Jeanne Voltz's *Barbecued Ribs and Other Great Feeds* (Alfred Knopf, 1985)

Ruffled Cheese Torte is from the Dino De Laurentiis Foodshow in New York

Rum Pie is courtesy of Barbara Gordon, owner-chef of Toronto's Beaujolais restaurant

Saffron Pasta with Veal Sauce is adapted from the recipe in Giuliano Bugialli's *Foods of Italy* (Stoddart Publishing, 1984)

Salmon in Sorrel Sauce is courtesy of executive chef Casari of Toronto

Salmon Loaf is courtesy of M. Machin, Regina, Saskatchewan

Sardine Butter is from Patricia White's *Food as Presents* (Penguin, 1983)

Sauté de Lotte aux Champignons Chinois et au Parfum de Gingembre was developed by Rollande DesBois for Les Marmitons gourmet club in Montreal

Scented Geranium Floating Islands is from the Vancouver Botanical Gardens Association's *The Van Dusen Cook Book: Flavours of the Gardens*

Scotch Eggs is from Sara Waxman's *Backroads and Country Cooking of Ontario* (McClelland and Stewart, 1985)

Scottish Beef and Kidney Pie is from *The Best of Mme Jehane Benoit* (The Pagurian Press, 1972)

Semiahmoo Salmon is courtesy of Vancouver's The Cannery restaurant

Sesame Dip is courtesy of Christine Mullen of Toronto's La Cuisine caterers

Shrimp in Pernod is from *Cooks* magazine

Smoked Salmon and Onion Cheesecake is from *Cooking with Craig Claiborne and Pierre Franey* (Times Books, 1983)

Snow Peas Stuffed with Crab is courtesy of Dinah Koo, Dinah's Cupboard, Toronto, Ontario

Sour Cream Cinnamon Loaf is from *Cooking with Style* (Meredith Publishing Services, 1984)

Spaghetti Alla Joso is from Cynthia Wine's *Across the Table: An Indulgent Look at Food in Canada* (Prentice-Hall, 1985)

Spaghetti Nuovi is courtesy of Toronto's Pronto Ristorante

Spanish Red Snapper is courtesy of Manuel Jarrin, La Vieille Gare, St. Boniface, Manitoba

Spinach Salad is courtesy of the Walper Hotel, Kitchener, Ontario

Spicy Steak is courtesy of American cook Barbara Tropp

Squid and Mussel Salad is courtesy of Helen Kates, Arowhon Pines, Algonquin Park, Ontario

Steak, Kidney, and Oyster Pie is courtesy of Toronto's Fenton's restaurant

Strawberry Tart with Marsala Crust is adapted from the recipe in Giuliano Bugialli's *Foods of Italy* (Stoddart Publishing, 1984)

Stuffed Sardines Il Posto is courtesy of Il Posto restaurant, Toronto, Ontario

Supreme of Duckling with Calvados and Apples is courtesy of Perzow and Masson Fine Foods, Westmount, Quebec

Sweet and Sour Prunes is from Irena Chalmers and Friends' *Gifts from the Christmas Kitchen* (Irena Chalmers Cookbooks Inc., 1983)

Sweet Red Pepper Tart is from Interim Place's *Fare for Friends*, a fund-raising cookbook for the women's emergency shelter in Mississauga, Ontario

Sweetbreads in Puff Pastry is courtesy of chef and author Jacques Pépin

Terrific Tomato Aspic is courtesy of Diana Wright, Saskatoon, Saskatchewan

The Britannia is from James Villas's *American Taste* (Fitzhenry & Whiteside, 1982)

Three-Fruit Marmalade is courtesy of Marshlands Inn, Sackville, New Brunswick

Toffee Berries is courtesy of Suzanne Demers of L'Atre restaurant on the Île d'Orléans, Québec

Tomato Apple Chutney is courtesy of Kathy Chute, Milton, Nova Scotia

Tomato Basil Soup with Salted Cognac Cream is courtesy of Faye Schmidt, Victoria, British Columbia

Tomato-Crowned Cod is from Jane Brody's *Good Food Book* (Penguin, 1985)

Tony Roldan's Vegetable Terrine is courtesy of the late Tony Roldan

Tortellini and Fontina Salad is courtesy of Toronto's Bersani & Carlevale restaurant

Tuna, Broccoli, and Mushroom Casserole is courtesy of Joyce Kossman, Downsview, Ontario

Umberto Menghi's Fettuccine with Prosciutto and Peas is from Cynthia Wine's *Across the Table: An Indulgent Look at Food in Canada* (Prentice-Hall, 1985)

Veal Scallops with Fresh Orange Sauce is courtesy of Au Tournant de la Rivière, Carignan, Quebec

Walper Goose is courtesy of the Walper Hotel, Kitchener, Ontario

White Chocolate Mousse with Raspberry Sauce is courtesy of Vancouver's William Tell Restaurant

Whole Wheat Raisin Bread is courtesy of Winnie Allen, Pleasant River, Nova Scotia

Wild Rice with Apples, Apricots, and Walnuts is courtesy of chef Terry Seed of Toronto's Hazelton Café

Wild Rice with Pine Nuts is from Jane Brody's *Good Food Book* (Penguin, 1985)

Zwicker Inn Seafood Chowder is from Cynthia Wine's *Across the Table: An Indulgent Look at Food in Canada* (Prentice-Hall, 1985)

Permissions

© **Jehane Benoit, 1968, 1969, 1970, 1971, 1972**

© **Carroll Allen, 1972, 1973, 1974, 1975, 1976, 1977, 1978, 1979**

© **Marilyn Linton, 1984, 1985**

© **Thelma Dickman, 1986**

INDEX

NOTES